Careers in Audio

Jeff Touzeau

D1400605

Course Technology PTR
A part of Cengage Learning

NEW HANOVER COUNTY
PUBLIC LIBRARY
201 CHESTNUT STREET
WILMINGTON, NC 28401

COURSE TECHNOLOGY
CENGAGE Learning˙

Australia • Brazil • Japan • Korea • Mexico • Singapore • Spain • United Kingdom • United States

COURSE TECHNOLOGY
CENGAGE Learning

Careers in Audio
Jeff Touzeau

Publisher and General Manager, Course Technology PTR: Stacy L. Hiquet

Associate Director of Marketing: Sarah Panella

Manager of Editorial Services: Heather Talbot

Marketing Manager: Mark Hughes

Acquisitions Editor: Orren Merton

Development Editor: Cathleen D. Small

Project Editor/Copy Editor: Cathleen D. Small

PTR Editorial Services Coordinator: Erin Johnson

Interior Layout Tech: ICC Macmillan Inc.

Cover Designer: Mike Tanamachi

Indexer: Broccoli Information Management

Proofreader: Gene Redding

© 2008 Course Technology, a part of Cengage Learning.

ALL RIGHTS RESERVED. No part of this work covered by the copyright herein may be reproduced, transmitted, stored, or used in any form or by any means graphic, electronic, or mechanical, including but not limited to photocopying, recording, scanning, digitizing, taping, Web distribution, information networks, or information storage and retrieval systems, except as permitted under Section 107 or 108 of the 1976 United States Copyright Act, without the prior written permission of the publisher.

For product information and technology assistance, contact us at **Cengage Learning Customer & Sales Support, 1-800-354-9706**

For permission to use material from this text or product, submit all requests online at **cengage.com/permissions**
Further permissions questions can be emailed to **permissionrequest@cengage.com**

All trademarks are the property of their respective owners.

Library of Congress Control Number: 2008923826

ISBN-13: 978-1-59863-460-0

ISBN-10: 1-59863-460-7

Course Technology
25 Thomson Place
Boston, MA 02210
USA

Cengage Learning is a leading provider of customized learning solutions with office locations around the globe, including Singapore, the United Kingdom, Australia, Mexico, Brazil, and Japan. Locate your local office at: **international.cengage.com/region**

Cengage Learning products are represented in Canada by Nelson Education, Ltd.

For your lifelong learning solutions, visit **courseptr.com**

Visit our corporate website at **cengage.com**

Printed in the United States of America
1 2 3 4 5 6 7 11 10 09 08

For Kim, with all my love—"Time has told me you're a rare, rare find."

Foreword

I'd like to thank Jeff Touzeau for inviting me to write the foreword to his book, but I'd like to come clean and tell him that I played hooky yesterday and went down to Asbury Park, New Jersey (I know we all know where Asbury Park is, thanks to Bruce, but I include the geographical reference of New Jersey for our international readers) to meet up with some old friends. I had spent some time the previous week writing some truly lame beginnings for this assignment: "Are you ready to join the club?" or "A life in audio—is it for you?" or "We few, we happy few, we band of brothers...." (When in doubt, reach for the classics.) You're lucky you won't have to endure any of those beginnings. And I spent some valuable time Googling concepts like audio, recording, community, audio community, recording audio community—the Internet can be a wonderful time-waster.

Photo by Jimmy Katz.

Jim Anderson.

But I started thinking, apart from the obvious reasons of procrastination, why would I rather go hang out with some friends than sit alone, thinking and typing? The reason is clear to me: These are friends that I made over 30 years ago, when I was starting my career in audio. We had all found our calling at National Public Radio (NPR) in the '70s, when we were all in our early 20s and, thankfully, the listening audience was small for this group's first explorations in broadcasting.

At that time, NPR gave us an important grounding in our lives: deadlines, discipline, structure, and, most importantly, a sense of community, a sense of shared purpose. These are qualities of an employer that I hope you seek at any point in your career.

Many of my contemporaries have moved on to other things—advertising, sales, et cetera. Some have stayed and continued working at NPR, and others have gone on to use their skills to work in related fields: film, television, recorded music, and education. But we still share this sense of community, even to this day. We've survived the audio wars and speak an audio vocabulary unique to our profession. Sometimes this language is spoken in shorthand that only the initiated know, like a secret handshake. Or sometimes it's in an even shorter shorthand, where nothing is said and only a telling glance is exchanged. (I recall the first time I heard—or should I say *didn't* hear—a digital error. I was producing my first session recorded in digital multitrack. I saw the engineer and the assistant give each other a knowing look. When I asked what they heard, they introduced me to the sound of a digital error. Someone had to take me by the ear and show me what to listen for. I'm forever grateful, I think.) We, the initiated, hear something and, instinctively, we know what each of us will think about what we've heard. You could say we have a collective form of "Golden Ears." Now, this "Golden Ear" experience is not uncommon to anyone who has spent time in the audio community, but for someone wanting to come into the circle, it takes work.

When I mentor students at Audio Engineering Society conventions or at New York University, a phrase comes to mind: "Do you want a job or a career?" Anyone can get a job in audio, but to get on the trajectory for a major career in audio, it's another direction. Both paths take work, education, and perseverance, but the longer road takes a dedication and commitment to bearing the standard of those who built the profession: Edison, Berliner, Blumlein, Armstrong, Neumann, Sennheiser, Pickering, Lansing, Lear, Dolby, Martin, and Ramone. All of these surnames should be familiar to you. If these names aren't, start cracking the books. Anyone who is truly a part of the audio community can rattle off a catalog of their achievements and then turn around and accuse me of leaving at least 20 other pioneers (if not more) off the list. (They can probably relate a fascinating firsthand story about them, as well.)

Now, how do you add your name to the record? (The pun is intended.) Well, I'm sorry to say that it takes time and more hard work, a lifetime of work. There are few overnight sensations in the audio world. The individuals who have been doing great work have been doing great work for a long time. For example, one of my favorite albums when I was growing up and listening to music was Henry Mancini's *The Music from Peter Gunn*, recorded by Al Schmitt in 1959. In 1959, I was in elementary school and hadn't begun learning to play an instrument, and there's Al in Hollywood, working in a world-class studio with world-class musicians, creating timeless music. He must have been 12 years old at the time. Let's fast-forward 35 years to a typical day at Avatar Studios in New York City. I'm mixing a project in Avatar's Studio B, and there's Al recording in Studio A. Al was an inspiration to me as a youngster, although I didn't know his name then, and he is still an inspiration to me now. We're both a part of the larger audio community, and, as you can see, that takes time. To complete the circle even more, in my time, I've gone on to record sessions with some of the musicians who were on the original *Peter Gunn* album that I listened to as a kid. It's a wonderful life.

Studio life and recording may not be for you. You may find yourself more inclined toward researching, publishing, or teaching, but still wanting to have some foothold in audio. I can understand. I know I just couldn't imagine myself being involved in a career that didn't have some relationship to audio, and I'm sure it's the same for you.

These days, I find myself in the studio on a daily basis. When I'm not recording and mixing my own projects, I'm working in the studio with my students at the Clive Davis Department of Recorded Music at NYU. It's been a logical progression for me from NPR to NYU. (I didn't mention that I have a degree in music education from Duquesne University, did I? I couldn't have made it without that.) I'm helping students find their way into the world of audio. Some will be artists, some engineers, some executives, but all of them will play some part in the audio community of the future. And so will you. Keep searching, and you'll find your place in the audio world.

Jim Anderson, January 2008
Chair, Clive Davis Department of Recorded Music, New York University
President-elect, Audio Engineering Society

Acknowledgments

Thanks to Kim, Caroline, and Ashton—none of this would be possible without any of you, and I'm forever grateful for all your support. Also thanks to Mom, Dad, Mark, Lynda, Bing, and Marcy. Thank you to Cathleen Small and Orren Merton for providing invaluable editing and moral support for this book.

There are so many other people I would like to thank—some of whom were very important in the development of my own career, and all of whom are my friends. Here are some of them in no particular order: John Storyk, Duncan Potter, Janice Brown, Frank Wells, William Hornbeck, Michael Wax, Matt Harper, Michael Filer, Brian Chipman, Ian Catt, Stephanie Susnjara, Mark McKenna, Richard Burke, Thomas Allen, Lily Bornstein, Robert Kessler, Howard Sherman, David Miles Huber, Larry Crane, Carlos Delgado, Ken Weinstein, and Catharine Steers. Special thanks to each and every one of the people I interviewed for this book—your time and insight was incredibly valuable, and your collective knowledge immeasurable.

About the Author

Jeff Touzeau is a writer and musician living in New York. His last book, *Making Tracks: Unique Recording Studio Environments* (Schiffer, 2006), was released to critical acclaim. As a journalist, Touzeau's work has appeared in *EQ, Pro Sound News, Tape Op, Performing Songwriter, Professional Sound,* and many other magazines. When he isn't writing, he enjoys composing and recording music at his studio, Hummingbird Sound.

Contents

Chapter 3
The Audio Book Market   49

Chapter 4
The Sound for Picture Market   71

Chapter 5
The Audio Publishing/Audio Trade Media Market   93

Chapter 6
The Live Sound Market   115

Chapter 7
The Broadcast Market   141

Chapter 8
The Manufacturing/Distribution/Retail Market   161

Chapter 9
Services to Professional Audio

Chapter 10
Careers in Academia

Chapter 11
Bioacoustics and Audiology   235

Chapter 12
A Career in Freelancing   265

Appendix
Additional Resources   283

Index 293

Introduction

This book was written with the understanding that everyone's career path is unique. Although we may share common interests, passions, and experiences, it is up to each of us alone to decide where to spend our time and efforts, and ultimately what is important in the course of individual careers. This book is meant to leave you with more questions than answers, and will hopefully inspire you to become more knowledgeable in whatever area(s) you choose to pursue.

In creating this book, I not only tried to illustrate what career tracks are out there for audio enthusiasts, but I also tried to bring individual human experiences to light. In the interviews that appear throughout these pages, people of all backgrounds provide a treasure trove of knowledge, talking about their struggles, their fears, their passions, and their successes.

On speaking to these people and looking back on my own career, I realize there are unchanging principles that can help us as we strive to reach our individual goals and, in turn, increase the strength of our community as a whole. Although these principles might appear simple at first glance, some may actually take a lifetime to master. Some of this is my own advice, so please take it with a big grain of salt:

- **Trust your intuition and listen to your heart.** As tempting as it is, don't go for the money first. If you do, you will never be completely satisfied and will likely spend the rest of your life chasing what you *really* want. Your intuition can be the most valuable asset in your career; learning to listen to it and trust it are two critical steps toward moving a career forward.

- **Get the skills you need.** Ironically, this is one of the easy ones. Learning a DAW platform, for example, is just the beginning. You need to identify early on what skills your field requires and start to fill up your toolbox with skills employers will find valuable both today and tomorrow.

- **Put yourself in an environment where you can succeed.** You must surround yourself with people and experiences that will nurture your growth. A good teacher, mentor, or manager can make all the difference in helping you get to the next level, even if the job itself isn't very sexy. Put yourself in a position where you will have the ability to do what you love while increasing your skill set, knowledge, and value to the market.

- **Don't let anyone else define you.** Throughout your career, people will try to create ceilings for you. Maybe they'll even tell you that you're not good enough. However tempting it may be, don't listen to them. Most of the time, when people try to impose this kind of opinion, they are revealing an insecurity in themselves. You and you alone can decide what you are capable of, and nobody has the right to impose boundaries on your dream.

- **Learn to leverage serendipitous events.** I learned from one of my mentors fairly well into my own career that you can learn to spot the patterns of serendipitous events around you. By looking out for things that could create forward momentum for you, you sharpen your awareness and create a sort of unconscious sonar that can help you leverage new opportunities.

- **Appreciate the mystery of what you don't know.** Curiosity is the best driver for any career—try to be a student of your field and remain inquisitive. If you don't know something, strive to understand it and try to develop a love of learning.

1 Why Should You Pursue a Career You Are Passionate About?

Many of us have become attracted to the audio industry—mostly through music, but also through other avenues and interests, such as electronics, performance, and even physics. Whatever sparked your interest initially, there is no real cure once you have been bitten by the audio bug. Most of us have a story about our first experience in a recording studio or our first encounter with an audio gizmo of some sort. As wonderful as these experiences were, however, nothing compares to listening to a satisfactory end result—whether it is a recording of the human voice, an electric guitar, or an ambient synth pad.

People tend to gravitate toward the audio world because they want to help create the conditions so that this kind of listening experience—dare I say magic?—is possible. There are so many ways people contribute to this: Acoustic designers, live sound engineers, sound designers, mix engineers, component manufacturers, audio retailers, and even health practitioners help create these conditions for us to experience audio in our lives every day.

Needless to say, there is a ton of opportunities to become gainfully employed—and even have a career—doing any number of these things. The only real limit is your own imagination and perseverance. If you think for a minute that it has all been done before, think again. We are at the crossroads of a monumental period of redefinition in the industry, which introduces very exciting and potentially rewarding possibilities for those who are passionate about audio and who are prepared to immerse themselves in it.

Hopefully, this book will challenge your imagination and help you identify a way forward into an audio world that is becoming less and less traditional. It will inform you in your career choice not only by making you aware of key trends in the marketplace, but also by laying out the various developments and career options available to you in the field. Throughout this book, I call on the personal experience of many people and examine what has and hasn't worked for them during the course of their own careers—past human experience is the very best guide for future success. By assimilating all of these aspects, you can chart out your own path with greater confidence and conviction.

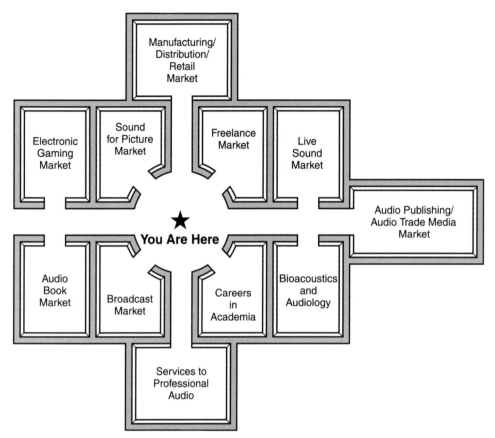

Take charge of your destination.

If this book does what it is supposed to do, it will help you begin to think about where you can apply your energies and talents both now and well into the future, helping you pave a course on which you can grow and be a part of something much larger than yourself: the audio community.

What This Book Covers and What It Doesn't

This book is meant to be used as a guide that can serve as a useful reference to you when you are making real-life career choices. Just as in recording music, there are no hard-and-fast rules to planning a career in audio—only guiding principles. There is no single way to record music, just as there is no single path toward a successful career—there are many, many different variables that you need to consider, and in making your career decisions, you should use every resource you have available. This book will help you identify solutions and raise the correct questions.

Obviously, the career paths and ideas outlined here will not apply universally—there will always be unique situations specific to individuals and organizations, as well as pockets of the industry that are different and even undeveloped. For example, employers might regard compensation, job titles, and desirable backgrounds differently. Some areas within audio, such as gaming, are still in their infancy, and future job titles and roles are being defined as we speak. The intention of this book is to highlight elements that might help you in your decision-making process—and these decisions must be your own.

As you begin to read through the book, you might notice a fairly obvious omission from the chapter sequence in this book: commercial recording studios. This is not an oversight and has been done intentionally for a couple of reasons:

1.   Commercial recording studios account for a significantly diminishing number of audio jobs per year in comparison to other areas. Although it is clear that commercial recording studios still provide an extremely valuable service to the industry (they do appear in this book, but are couched within different categories), it has proven difficult for many recording studios with a traditional rent-based model to remain viable. This unfortunate trend has been well documented throughout the course of the last two decades.

2.   The purpose of this book is to present careers in audio—thus the title! Although there will always be notable exceptions, for most people it isn't realistic to present commercial studios that rely on this traditional rent-based model as a viable career alternative. For those who choose to pursue this path, the successful commercial facilities are easy to spot, and of course, many of the principles outlined in this book can be applied.

Do What You Love

Each of us is invariably shaped by our own knowledge, interests, and experiences. Our interests usually take hold at a very early age, and our environment can function either as a catalyst or as an obstacle in developing our interests.

The underlying force at work for the vast majority of careers is the need for financial security—all of us face this need, since financial security directly correlates to our ability to survive as human beings and provide for our loved ones. Therefore, at the most basic level, the need for financial security is the primary driver for any career—interest or passion very logically falls into second place.

For this reason, unless you are a trust-fund baby or you have another source of life-sustaining wealth, most of us are forced at one point or another to develop a career that will pay the bills. For some, such a realization can occur during the formative high school years or as a midlife crisis sets in. Obviously, there is a greater benefit to knowing what you want to achieve sooner, but each person develops on his own timetable according to his own personality. The trick—and an elusive one at that—is finding a job that will pay the bills and also bring intrinsic satisfaction.

A Career versus a Vocation

There is a very significant difference between a career and a vocation. To understand this difference, we should take a basic look at the meanings of each word. Career, by definition, means "an occupation or profession, especially one requiring special training," while vocation means "a strong impulse or inclination to follow a particular activity or career."

Many of us eat, drink, and sleep audio.

The word "vocation" implies that there is some greater force at work—a "calling" or other navigational force that guides an individual through his or her career. Interestingly, people who have a vocation typically don't consider their career work at all, and their love for what they do often makes them an endless well of productivity.

These days, almost anyone with any degree of initiative can get a career. It isn't difficult to develop the skills and knowledge the market requires, and adequate compensation can often accompany this. The concept of a vocation, however, puts the principle of a "sensible" career on its head, placing the interest and passion in front of the need for financial security. Paradoxically, by putting your interests first and the need for a traditional career in the backseat, people tend to be more successful financially—and they are generally happier as well. So why doesn't everyone get a vocation instead of a career and become happier and wealthier?

Cultivate Your Passion

Carefully managing your interests over the years can lead to the development of lifelong skills—however, these interests need to be kept on track and cultivated. This can be especially challenging in a world that is relentlessly attacking us with information every second. You need to retain focus and keep your original goal in sight while constantly striving to improve yourself. For many people, identifying what they are passionate about can be difficult—sometimes it is not so obvious. Having the courage to follow that passion can be even more difficult and requires many degrees of virtues: most importantly, perseverance.

Don't let financial security drive your career.

Sound Impressions

What attracts us to the audio field? The answer may lie in the fact that music and audio have a profound influence on our very existence and correlate directly to our deepest emotions as human beings. Although many are people are drawn into the visual arts, others are intrigued by auditory perceptions and are thereby drawn to careers involving sound.

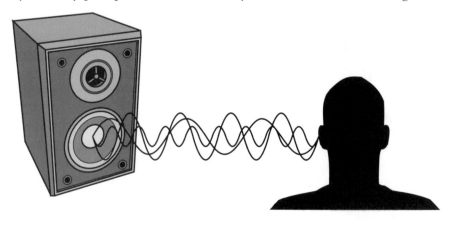

Sound can obviously have an enormous impact on emotion. It can also have a profound influence on our physical bodies. Has music ever made your hair stand on end or made you cry? Sound is connected to our deepest emotions from our earliest days in the womb. For each of us, our mother's beating heart was the very first thing we could sense in the world.

Music can dramatically influence the mood of a scene.

Sound directly correlates to the visual landscape and can help us interpret its meaning. For example, suppose you have some video footage of someone driving down a narrow road

Audio connects us all.

from the driver's perspective. The flavor of the music tells the viewer whether it is a foreboding scene, a tranquil scene, or almost any other conceivable emotion in between. Sound helps us define our world and connects us all as human beings. Music crosses all cultures, ethnicities, ages, and backgrounds. It helps define who we are as individuals and as a world community. It is difficult to imagine any of the other arts having the ability to affect our hearts the way music can—music is an art of passion and intellect, but mostly passion.

The Pale View

It makes sense to come right out with the bad news. If you've always dreamed of working in a humungous studio producing your favorite band, you are not alone—and, to be honest, you face almost insurmountable obstacles. Not to be discouraging, but many commercial recording studios are having difficulty sustaining a profitable business model and certainly no longer employ dozens of recording engineers and techs. To be clear, the commercial studio is no longer the gravitational force of the audio business, and this isn't expected to change anytime soon.

In case you haven't noticed, the recording industry is currently undergoing a major upheaval and redefinition. Contrary to the opinion of many, this upheaval hasn't resulted in the death of the industry—far from it. It has, however, resulted in a major reorientation of how we look at audio products and services. As consumers seek music through new distribution channels and alter their buying behaviors, these changes invariably affect the traditional model of how recordings are made and financed while impacting the very core of the recording industry.

Although the recording industry experienced phenomenal growth during the '60s and '70s, things began to slow down in the '80s. The compact disc arrived just in time to provide a false sense of security to the recording industry as everyone replaced their record collections with CDs—until relentless high prices forced the consumer to seek still other playback media, such as MP3s. CDs are still enormously overpriced, and the major labels still show no signs of coming to their senses.

For a pessimist, it would be very easy to look at the culmination of these things and come to the conclusion that the glass is indeed half empty. On the surface, things would appear to be crumbling from the inside out. The paltry earnings of brick-and-mortar record companies have been well documented, and all the gloomy predictions have been cast. The future of the major recording labels seems increasingly gloomy, and a standard music distribution model has yet to emerge. The recording studio market itself is a bleak shadow of what it once was; indeed, relatively few of the recording studios from the '60s, '70s, and '80s still exist, and those that do had to reinvent themselves from the bottom up. Like other companies that have faced challenges, they have found ways to become more efficient—both in how they run their businesses and in how they manage human capital.

Other issues come into play—digital rights, the advent of the DAW, and dwindling recording budgets. Although there is no denying that the Internet has fostered distribution, collaboration, and communication, it has also been responsible for the piracy of recordings—to the tune of more than a billion dollars worldwide. The DAW, while bringing unprecedented production power to the home- and project-studio user, is a wolf in sheep's clothing and has served as the wrecking ball for many commercial studios. Major-label recording budgets, which at one time could support massive equipment purchases, hefty producer fees, and the occasional smashed hotel room (usually at the expense of the artist) are now almost nonexistent. This adds up to a pretty pale view indeed.

But not so fast....

The glass really is half full. If you twist your perspective a little bit, even rationally, it would appear that this is still a relatively immature industry going through a healthy, if radical, transformation. Each of the items just mentioned is not only displacing but also helping germinate the new seeds for what will become a more exciting field to work in than ever before. Our entire society is discovering revolutionary new ways to produce goods and services, and audio is no exception. For example, it is very clear that audio plays an integral role in multimedia—and quite frankly, that's where the whole train is headed.

Before you get on the train, find out where it is heading.

New channels for content delivery are being created every day. In the last 10 years, satellite radio, wireless devices, iPods, and gaming consoles have all emerged as important dimensions in delivering music and other audio content to the masses. These additional channels to consumers have generated greater demand for content.

Just the Facts, Ma'am

U.S.-based research firm eMarketer estimates that the worldwide market for recorded music, live music, and music licensing will reach $67.6 billion by 2011, growing at an average annual rate of 2.19 percent. Juniper predicts that the mobile entertainment industry could reach $76 billion by 2011. That is a lot of content, and of course, audio plays a major role in these statistics.

The U.S. Department of Labor—one source of information on national jobs—defines audio/video technicians as people who "set up or set up and operate audio and video equipment including microphones, sound speakers, video screens, projectors, video monitors, recording equipment, connecting wires and cables, sound and mixing boards, and related electronic equipment for concerts, sports events, meetings and conventions, presentations, and news conferences." They say that 95,000 people fall into this category and that jobs rose by 2.9 percent on a national basis last year. These are relatively encouraging statistics and certainly do not take into account the entire audio field—it is safe to assume that the real total is likely much, much higher.

Not for the Timid

With all this said, the audio industry is not for the weak of heart. It carries some degree of risk—possibly more than many other career choices. Competition may be fierce, and there is no guaranteed path to success. You can offset the risk with the right measure of skills and perseverance, though, making the path less risky overall. Calculated risks aren't a bad thing and are often met with great reward. (Remember your first kiss?) By taking these kinds of risks early in your career, you stand a greater chance of being more successful later.

Some of the most successful people I interviewed for this book had a high tolerance for risk early in their careers—say between the ages of 18 and 30. Younger people can often afford to take such risks, since they may not have dependents or other responsibilities, such as a mortgage. Also, the younger you are, the more time you presumably have to recover should things take a turn for the worse. As people age, they become less risk-tolerant and are usually burdened with greater financial responsibility; therefore, they often are less willing to experiment.

There are a few principles you can leverage to maximize the effectiveness of your approach, no matter what stage you are at in your career. Read on...

You Are Only as Good as Your Network

The world's most advanced cell phone or wireless device is only as strong as the network with which it is associated. The same is true for your talent—you must be connected to a broader network of people so your skills and talents can be realized. Your ability to socialize, create acquaintances, and develop long-term relationships with people is absolutely required for you to be successful. Careers are built on relationships with human beings, and you leave an impression with everyone you meet—no matter what point you are at in your career.

Developing a solid network can give you an insider's lead to where the opportunities are and increase your chances of getting hired just because you are a known entity. If you are a likable person, you show a strong interest to learn, and you have marketable skills, chances are people will want to open doors for you. Skills and talent are very important, but people who can vouch for your integrity and determination are invaluable.

Work Multiple Revenue Streams Where Possible

Another interesting, developing trend is that people in audio are creating more revenue streams. Many full-timers put their skills to work at night in a related field. This not only develops their network, but also provides additional security for income. You can compare maintaining multiple revenue streams to keeping a balanced investment portfolio. You put more effort into the areas of the portfolio that grow, and you pull back in the areas that are stagnant or fully matured. By having diverse revenue streams, you lower your overall risk.

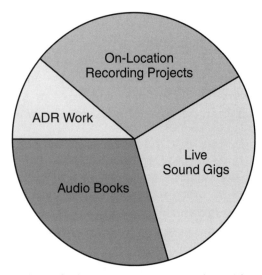

A diversified income stream can reduce risk.

For some, relying on a single employer for 100 percent of their income can be risky on a number of fronts. For one thing, it makes you much more vulnerable if you are ever asked to leave. It also limits you to a single source of knowledge and growth. There are increasingly few employers that can possibly deliver all the skills you need to stay on the cutting edge, ahead of the market, and it is advised—nay, expected—for you to seek out and master the skills you need to succeed in your chosen career path—regardless of whether these are provided by your primary employer.

Have a Vision and Build Your Confidence

The old saying goes, "If you don't know where you are going, any road will take you there." If you don't have a clear direction in your career, you can easily wind up somewhere you really didn't want to be in the first place. You should be able to visualize your success as concisely as possible so you can influence the outcome. If you have a concise idea of where you are going, your intelligence and perseverance should be able to help you get there.

"If you don't know where you are going, any road will take you there."

Remember: Nobody else can define who you are. Align yourself with good people who support you and who will open doors for you. As soon as you realize that you are in charge of your own destiny, your confidence will soar, and you will begin to feel more empowered and in control. There is nothing worse than feeling as if someone else holds the key to your success. Put yourself in a position where you can strongly influence and shape the evolution of your own vision.

Finally—and this is a less empirical suggestion—learn to spot patterns in your career and to be aware of your surroundings. Opportunities come into our lives every day, and we choose to act on only a few of these opportunities while letting many others slip by. Be aware—learn to spot the opportunities in everything you do and ask yourself, "How can I make this into something that will help me move my career forward?" Learning to remain optimistic is one of the keys to finding the way forward.

Now Is the Time

Make no mistake—a new day is finally dawning on the audio industry, and the dust is finally settling. New business models have taken hold that embrace web technology, multimedia, and collaboration. For enterprising individuals, there has never been a better time to succeed in this field. However, more often than not, opportunities are emerging from hidden places and non-traditional settings.

On the whole, the audio community is a very tight-knit group of individuals who share a common love of sound and audio. Whether you are an audiologist, a front-of-house engineer, a game audio composer, an audio book specialist, or an acoustic designer, the overarching goal for most people in this field is to improve the human listening experience. This common goal creates unity—the audio industry shares a common passion and consists of professionals who are perhaps more familiar and friendly to one another than in other fields. The members of the audio community share a certain affinity that is understood.

A Closer Look: Peter Spellman and the State of the Audio Industry

Peter Spellman is the Director of Career Development at Berklee College of Music. When I spoke with Peter, he was decidedly upbeat about where things are headed, while highlighting the industry's mistakes of the past. He has had provided guidance and insight to countless students at Berklee College of Music and has personally witnessed how Berklee's curriculum has effectively adapted to changing times.

Peter Spellman.

Peter, there is no denying the doom and gloom that has been cast on the music business over the last couple of decades. Are there any areas of audio that appear to be promising?

Probably the area where there has been the greatest expansion of opportunities in audio is in multimedia. The entire business world has gone multimedia, and one of the legitimate mediums is audio. This has created a lot of opportunities for people who have been able to target companies that are sort of outside of the traditional music business, but that still have audio requirements.

Can you elaborate on this? What kinds of trends have you seen?

One of the trends I've seen is with the so-called miniaturization of music technology. It has given companies a chance to create in-house audio production facilities on the desktop as opposed to going and leasing out a studio for a lockout per day and paying in excess of $100 an hour to do it. Of course I'm talking about desktop recording technologies as well as mixing and mastering technologies as opposed to using the big studios. This is obviously not good news for the larger recording studios, but in effect, their lunch has already been eaten. They are strapped with tremendous overhead and equipment.

So it sounds like the opportunities are out there, but you have to look at the market in an unconventional way.

Yes. You have to think about what the companies need in terms of audio. It's important to think of it broadly, such as in terms of audio production, instead of narrowly, in terms of music production. You have to think of audio production in all its manifestations; this includes the creation, manipulation, and editing of sound. If you look at it this way, the opportunities are there—you just have to sniff them out. Look at the book publishing industry and how they have created audio formats, for example. I just heard of a big ad agency here in Boston that is going to be developing their own record label and music production house, all in house. This is the kind of stuff that's going on. Why are these kinds of businesses doing this? Because they can. The tools and technologies have come down in price so people can do these kinds of things in house without outsourcing.

So where are the opportunities and how do you go about uncovering them?

They are in the corners of the margins. It takes a bit more of a search strategy to find them, but they are certainly there. Berklee graduates who have come out of the music and engineering production program, or the contemporary writing and production program, or the music synthesis program—all of those folks are finding work. Wherever there is multimedia development, they are finding work. There are positions in TV, film, and all the different corporations that are doing corporate video development. These are full-time audio production positions with benefits.

Are they simply finding jobs or are they really able to build careers? Can you actually build a career in this environment?

I think so. As with any career choice, you have to find your niche and determine where your skills and passion are. Ultimately, you have to become a master of it, and then you have longevity. But I still think there is a lot of contract work as well that is going to present itself to musicians, especially in the early stages. They have to try on different hats and cobble together a number of different gigs and contracts before they find the real niche that is going to support them for their lives.

How does one identify what skills are most desirable in such confusing times?

It's funny, technology changes. When I interview graduates, I ask them the question, "Of all the things you learned at Berklee, what skill has benefited you the most?" Usually what comes back to me, strangely enough, is that it's their arranging skills—in all its manifestations. The skill they say is valuable is their ability to synthesize disparate pieces into a whole.

This is an almost unconscious trait or skill that musicians manifest, but they learn it over time. The other aspects our grads say are important are people skills and team building. People learn this at Berklee with our ensemble requirements. These are the traits that seem to bode well for careers.

Which areas of audio aren't doing so well, and what should be avoided?

When I think of music industry, I usually think of it in four pieces: the recording industry, the music publishing industry, the music products industry, and the live performance industry. The music industry is generally healthy, and the recording industry segment is really the one that is suffering. We are going through a whole redefinition of what recorded music is and can be, and its perceived value is changing. That bodes badly for the large record companies, which have built all their systems on the full-length CD in a physical format—they are in trouble. They've been in trouble for a long, long time. They were declining in the late '70s, then they received an artificial shot in the arm with the CD format when everyone had to re-buy what they had on vinyl. They really got fat on this, and now there is sort of a karmic debt that the music industrial complex is starting to pay for because of all that greed.

The peripheral segments, including the indie world, have been able to respond much better to the market. They provide niche music to segments of the market where they don't have to sell 200,000 units to break even. They can sell 10,000 and uncork the champagne. Still, the physical format is in trouble. The new emphasis on singles is a good trend for music. There is incredible songwriting going on now, and all the dynamics are out there for consumers to find exactly the music they are looking for.

What has this done for overall demand?

There is no lack of appetite for music, and the demand is only increasing. The question becomes: How can the business model shift to meet that need? How can we provide *access* to music as opposed to distributing music? It's an important shift that will take several years before we can really create some new forms that will be viable in this shifting marketplace.

Peter, what level of sacrifice and commitment is required in this day and age? Is it more or less as substantial as before?

You're in the arts—it has always been tough, and there's nothing new there. The industry is still very much relationship-driven. It's still about who you know and who knows you. This is and has always been important for getting jobs, getting contracts, and getting gigs. There is definitely a dues-paying phase that everyone has to go through, but the key is, how do you not overpay your dues? How do you rise above the noise with your own good signal? How do you use the network of contacts that you have developed in higher education along with those who have gone before you to help open up doors?

There are some key constants I am always emphasizing here that never change: punctuality, people skills, even spelling your words right. It's all so basic in the end. But if you do these things consistently, you stand out from the crowd. Berklee has 50,000 alumni, so wherever you go in the industry, you're going to run into someone somewhere who will be able to help you. That makes us pretty unique in influencing student outcomes.

Has your online program been a good impetus toward helping students achieve their goals?

It has become a very profitable sector of the college. Its mandate is different from the .edu college, but it's thriving. Our online offerings are increasing, and the online operation eventually becomes a feeder for the regular school. Demand is outstripping supply.

Do you find that geographic location is still an important consideration among your graduates in finding work in the audio world?

Once you've established yourself, you can go where you want geographically now. I really do see people all over the map doing their work. That said, it's good to set yourself up first in a more metropolitan area. New York, LA, and Nashville are all still strong, but you have other available now, such as Austin, Denver, Miami, and Charlotte—people are doing fine in those regions, too. Regardless of where you are, networking is still the key—you need to get out there and get involved in organizations and events. I know a guy who lives on this little bluff in Marblehead, Massachussetts, and he does all his film scoring there. He had to pay his dues in Hollywood first, but now he is able to go and do that.

One common theme I'm finding is that many folks need to rely on multiple income sources now, versus some time ago, when perhaps income from a single job was sufficient.

This ties to another important concept—I see more entrepreneurial types of people succeeding. All the tools and resources are in place for these kinds of people to create their own success. Many have multiple income streams, but they love it. It's all music and audio to them. Other individuals who are perhaps less entrepreneurial and more focused on the security of a steady paycheck and benefits gravitate toward education or corporate jobs that integrate audio production—game companies, film studios, that kind of thing. To each his own, but in general I see an entrepreneurial swelling that isn't going to abate anytime soon—just look at the tools that are available out there.

A Closer Look: Doree Rice on Preparing for an Audio-Based Career

Doree Rice is a career counselor at Full Sail. Full Sail prepares students for a variety of careers, providing them with skills that will help them identify opportunities well beyond the traditional recording studio. In speaking with Rice, I also realized the strength of Full Sail's alumni network of more than 27,000 people who all share a common passion in audio.

Doree Rice.

Doree, what do you see in the audio market at the moment?

Well first, the opportunities in the big studios are less that what they were previously. I see more graduates looking to get involved in personal project studios or other areas of audio. Obviously, there is audio everywhere you turn—there are opportunities in the audio-visual world, the corporate convention industry, and many other areas. There are also private producer studios that are starting to open up as well.

So would you say that the jobs are popping up in areas where we're not exactly used to seeing them?

Exactly. The outlook isn't dismal at all—it is better than ever. It's just that you have to open your mind and look in less traditional places. The indie-music arena is also very encouraging—artists are taking their destinies into their own hands.

What is your philosophy at Full Sail and what do you expect students to walk away with?

It's a given that they walk away from here with the technical basics and the foundations that are going to be used in the marketplace. What we are really trying to focus on teaching as well are the intangibles: the people skills, the critical thinking—the types of things that both studio owners and corporate audio environments are screening for. They are looking for that level of professionalism that is a cut above. We teach these types of skills, and it is often more challenging teaching these types of things versus the hands-on technical expertise.

Which areas seem particularly hot for you in terms of job opportunities?

Installation is huge. Home theater and commercial environments constantly need audio upgrades, installations, and A/V work. A lot of corporations that put on conventions have their own A/V departments to set up for meetings and things like that—providing that tech experience can be invaluable. Somebody who can work on gear rather than just run it is huge.

What areas are going to command the highest salaries?

Highly technical avenues, such as installation, offer the most income as well.

Where do you have to be geographically these days?

We tell our students that there is audio everywhere in the world; it just depends on what you want to do. Atlanta and Miami we see as big markets, particularly around hip-hop and R&B. Chicago is fairly strong with post. L.A. is strong for both post and music. North Carolina is building also in terms of post and audio for video. These are areas where you can also do location sound for film and video—this is one area where I feel like there will be greater demand.

What is an ideal educational background that would complement a Full Sail education?

Probably communications, so students can get a touch of video—or some kind of business application. Programming and computers are also very important—another area that is growing exponentially is the gaming world. If you have the ability to do sound design and audio post and also can do a little bit of programming, you are golden. Not just from a job-opportunity standpoint, but from income potential as well.

How important is the brand like Full Sail when you are looking for a job? How can this reassure an employer?

Well, we have been around almost 30 years now, and we have over 27,000 grads. They are out there working in the industry, building reputations and forging their path. So chances are extremely strong that a company in the industry has had one of our grads and knows that our students will come in more prepared and with a better skill set than someone from another school—they know what they are getting. The world moves at such a fast pace now that there is no longer a long mentoring apprenticeship type of situation. You need to be able to come in here and run this stuff and know your way around the gear.

Any other thoughts?

I am just very excited at the potential and the directions I see the audio industry headed. I am extremely encouraged.

2 The Electronic Gaming Market

Since its inception in the '70s, the electronic gaming industry has been arguably the most promising and fastest growing sector in audio. The industry's explosive growth has exceeded the expectations of computer and entertainment industry analysts alike. Electronic gamers have had a ravenous appetite for product, supporting a wide range of audio roles in the field from all imaginable devices, including consoles, handheld devices, casino machines, and many other types.

Market Viability

The growth of the electronic gaming industry has not been limited by geography—in fact, some analysts predict that the gaming market in China alone will triple by 2010. New business models and delivery mechanisms for games continue to emerge worldwide, leveraging wireless technology and new, more sophisticated mobile devices.

The Industry Shatters Records

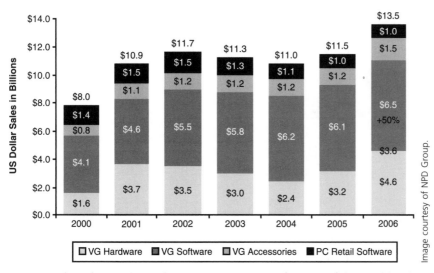

U.S. growth in the gaming industry represents just a fraction of the worldwide gaming industry as a whole.

Michael Cai is the Director of Broadband and Gaming for Parks Associates, a top electronic gaming analyst based in the U.S. He says the market is still poised for growth: "It's definitely very healthy. In 2006 alone, in the U.S., we were probably looking at 11 to 12 billion dollars, combining retail, console, PCs, mobile, and portable sectors. This half a year was phenomenal—the reported market growth for retail hardware sales has completely exceeded everyone's expectations." Cai notes that the largest revenue stream is still console gaming and that the three big console manufacturers—Microsoft, Nintendo, and Sony—have already released their next-generation consoles. He also spots other large companies getting in on the action: "From a corporate perspective, now you see companies like IBM and Sun Microsystems moving into the gaming space—both of whom have executives who are directly responsible for this area."

Microsoft Xbox 360.

The gaming market is still relatively young and has proven to be more than a fad. It has survived the ebb and flow of a tumultuous technology market, including the dot-com boom and bust of the 1990s, and has delivered year over year growth in an unpredictable economy. What has made it so successful? The answer generally centers on relentless innovation and fairly predictable demographic developments. Here are some of the reasons why the market has expanded and why we can expect even greater growth and innovation in the future:

- **Continued buying habits of Generation X and the iPod generation.** The term "Generation X" was not coined after the Microsoft Xbox, but this group of consumers has represented the primary cornerstone of the industry's growth. Generation Xers, who now have more money than they did a few years ago, are buying consoles and games for their own kids. Meanwhile, the newer iPod generation has responded favorably to innovative portable devices on which many of the newer games are based.

Scott Gershin of Soundelux composing a score for a video game.

- **Alignment with evolving technology platforms and content delivery mechanisms.** Gaming technology has constantly evolved with the latest technology platforms and will continue to do so. Examples include utilization of consoles with embedded chips, software discs, DVDs, high-speed Internet, and wireless and portable devices. Sony's PlayStation 3 and Microsoft's Xbox 360 have already proven immensely popular.

- **Widespread consumer demand on nearly every continent.** Many gaming titles were introduced internationally as titles that were simply translated and dubbed to meet language requirements of local regions. Overwhelming consumer response has led to many new markets opening well beyond the U.S. and Western Europe, sparking more manufacturing and development worldwide. This has caused a chain reaction, leading to increased consumer demand.

■ **Increased availability of high-quality content.** There are simply more titles, increased competition among content producers, and more talent emerging from the gaming workforce. Electronic games are not unlike Hollywood movies or a top-10 pop record—in fact, *Billboard* magazine, the U.S.-based authority on tracking performance of entertainment content, charts the performance of gaming titles, just as it does music and DVD titles.

Shannon Loftis, who is Director of European Production for Microsoft Game Studios and responsible for Microsoft's European-developed gaming titles, comments on Microsoft's own expansion in gaming: "Demand is increasing, and we're hitting all kinds of emerging markets that we've never played in before. We're doing new launches in Eastern Europe and many countries in South America. We'll have around 10 million consoles in the marketplace this Christmas, and we're only one year into the lifecycle of our current product." As far as a possible career path, Loftis is enthusiastic: "This would be a very promising industry for someone coming in from the audio world."

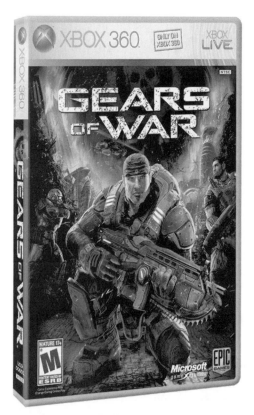

One of Microsoft's recent hit titles, *Gears of War.*

An interesting dimension that is occurring in gaming is the ability of a title to develop into its own brand identity. This has helped the manufacturer bring the experience to places such as movie theaters, concert tours, and all kinds of other media. Cai explains, "There is a feature film called *Beowulf* that features Anthony Hopkins and Angelina Jolie—the movie is based on a video game and uses video game technology. The stuff we see on screen is not actually the actors—rather, it's a digital engine. For *Warcraft*, the most popular online game ever, there was a concert tour featuring the original music soundtrack." More and more big-name movie producers, including Steven Spielberg, John Woo, Peter Jackson, and others, have been involved in or are currently involved in films that relate to gaming.

When you add it all up, there are enormous opportunities to enter and develop a career within the electronic gaming industry, including from an audio perspective. Cai continues, "The hard-core gamers are very demanding when it comes to audio—gamers are all early adopters with technology. 'Power gamers' want the graphics and the gaming environment to be as realistic as possible."

Job Profiles and Career Opportunities

Because dialogue, sound effects, and music are such integral parts of the video game experience, companies producing computer games rely on a wide range of audio experts. The most commonly known of these positions is a composer; however, there are many other positions, and with the right combination of audio and programming background (most audio games are written in C++), you can literally write your own ticket. One very important distinction of game audio versus the audio in most other visual media is that games are nonlinear in nature. Games are interactive and influenced to a great degree by the gamer; therefore, audio in this medium is not linear. This is a difficult concept for many aspiring composers to grasp.

The available job descriptions vary according to how large the operation is and how it is set up—indeed, many of these roles are evolving or haven't even been properly identified because the field is so young. At a smaller production house that handles perhaps a single title a year, there is often a single audio expert (an "Audio Guy") who is expected to handle every task from field recording, to composition, to mixing, to editing. At medium-sized manufacturers, such as Midway or Take 2, some detailed audio work may be outsourced. At larger corporations, such as Microsoft, Nintendo, Sony, Sierra Entertainment, and Electronic Arts, roles are much more specific to the task and usually fall within project teams or in central operations.

In the gaming industry, roles are still evolving and job titles extremely volatile. Even at the very large companies, it is often a less structured environment. Each area within the project teams is becoming more and more specialized as games become more complex and more complicated to produce.

Overall Team Composition

In electronic gaming, there are usually project teams that have audio directors (often referred to as *audio leads*). Audio directors have enormous responsibility and contribute substantially to the overall consumer gaming experience. Shannon Loftis illustrates: "Most of our games ship with some form of interactive music that responds to the action on the screen. Our audio people also handle sound effects, voice casting, and technical programming to support the game."

Having the right creative toolset is critical in creating compelling gaming soundtracks.

The project teams at companies such as Microsoft and Electronic Arts usually remain intact throughout the development of a title. Once the title ships, team members are given a chance to remain on the franchise or move on to another one. "At Microsoft, we have some teams that have been together for quite a long time, but we also have teams that shift around a lot," says Loftis.

Audio directors create the vision for what the broad audio experience will be like in the game. Audio directors work with many people inside and outside the company to pull the audio portion of a project together, including junior and senior audio specialists. Independent contractors are also hired by the audio directors, and they are often held responsible for rounding up a variety of resources that might be necessary for the game's audio content, whether that be speech, music, or sound effects. These are the folks who manage voiceover recording sessions and orchestral sessions, as well as the creation of sound effects.

Let's take a look at some of the audio positions available in gaming from the top down.

Director of Audio ($70,000 to $140,000)
The director of audio's time is often split between a few projects at once. This individual is at the top of the hierarchy and is primarily responsible for ensuring that his direct reports, including audio specialists, sound editors, recording/mix engineers, and operational staff, have all the

resources they need to keep departments running efficiently and according to the company's business plan.

It is also the director of audio's responsibility to manage relationships with outside personnel, which may include other audio contractors, content providers, musical instrument manufacturers, acoustic architects, and many audio types. Ultimately, the director of audio is responsible for the quality and performance of the audio that appears in every title.

This position typically reports to a project director or managing director at the larger organizations, and the individual can choose to be either very hands-on or remain at a very high level. This depends on his working style and the nature of the company. A significant portion of the director of audio's time is spent interacting with corporate officers in other departments and possibly corporate board members; therefore, this person must be able to present and communicate ideas clearly and have excellent leadership skills.

Career Path in Gaming

Director of Audio

↑

Senior Audio Specialist/Tool Developer

↑

Sound Effects/Music/Speech Specialist

↑

Junior Specialist/Assistant Engineer

↑

Tester

This illustration represents what a career ladder might look like in gaming.

When not producing audio in-house, it is the director of audio's responsibility to decide whether to engage well-connected contractors for source material. Directors of audio can also license material instead of creating it from scratch if required—budgets typically drive this decision. If a title is on its third episode, there is likely more budgeting flexibility to create new content because it has a proven successful track record.

Shannon Loftis says good directors of audio are hard to come by: "It's a specific market that requires very specific talent—there's an element of 'you have it or you don't.' Good judgment isn't necessarily something that you can learn, so getting someone with the right combination of talent and experience, who is looking to move, is very unusual. We have had director of audio positions open for quite a long time simply because we have not been able to find the right person."

Audio Lead ($60,000 to $95,000)

As indicated previously, most of the positions in electronic gaming fall within project teams or in central operations. Audio leads are responsible for meeting the day-to-day deadlines of the project delivery cycle, which can last anywhere from one to three years. In a project's early stages, Audio leads are expected to deliver rough audio segments, or "comps," to the project lead or producer to help him get funding for the title—they also help the director of audio formulate the creative vision for the sounds that will accompany the visuals. This might include mocking up sound effects and having broad ideas on voice talent.

On a project team, the audio lead supports the producer, and at the end of the day, it is the producer who must deliver the product that meets the requirements of the business plan or the funding party. In larger organizations, audio leads have junior-level specialists and assistants who help create and pull together required assets.

Audio leads fall within three broad categories: sound effects, music, and speech. These roles are fairly well defined, and each role has an enormous impact on the overall outcome of the product.

"One of the biggest jobs of the audio lead is ensuring that all the audio assets fire correctly in the game," says Ed Dolinski, former Director of Audio at Electronic Arts. "Did the sample fire twice and is it layered? Is there phasing going on and are my stereo tracks coming out in mono? Are my fades right? These kinds of things are interactive nuances that have to be addressed." Following are some of the specific audio lead roles.

Sound Effects Specialists

These folks are responsible for creating all the user-triggered sounds, as well as all the other non-triggered effects that one experiences throughout a game. On a game console, when pulling a trigger, rotating a steering wheel, or moving a joystick, cannons may fire, tires may screech, or dogs may bark. When driving through a tunnel, a special reverberant effect may be required, accenting the sound of tires hitting the pavement. If there is a crash, sounds of glass and crunching metal would likely dominate the soundscape. All of these effects need to be perfectly timed—otherwise, the consumer's perception of reality will be shattered, and the experience will be diminished.

Depending on the time and budget available in the development cycle, sound effects specialists create their own effects from scratch in folio studios or source effects from sound libraries or field recordings. The larger the title, the greater the budget is to creatively source effects.

Speech Specialists

It is the speech specialists who work with the scriptwriter to add the voice dimension to characters. They help identify and develop the attributes, personality, and other required qualities that a script calls for. As with sound effects specialists, the decision to engage well-known actors or high-end recording studios corresponds to the available budget and the overall profile of the title. The work of speech specialists must also be convincing to the consumer—if a local translation is required for a title, it must be authentic. For example, a French ex-patriot who has been living in San Francisco for 20 years might not lend a credible enough accent to the French consumer. Speech specialists understand that these details have a dramatic impact on the consumer's overall perception.

Speech specialists also engage junior-level associates and assistants to assist with the timing and labeling of audio assets. This kind of work requires a great deal of discipline, accuracy, and accountability and is not unlike the exercise of cataloging takes, labeling edits, and filing master tapes in a recording studio. Entry-level assistants are paid to get it right and manage the details so the specialists can be confident in the accuracy of the material they are working with.

Music Specialists

Music specialists are the composers who create the music landscape or overall soundtrack for the title. Creating a soundtrack for electronic games is vastly different from creating a soundtrack for film or television. In gaming, the score consists of dozens of short segments, usually depending on the action of the character or direction of the game. It is important to remember that music specialists aren't working in a bubble—they are working on a team alongside a producer, a scriptwriter, a speech editor, and many other team members. All the pieces of the music specialist's efforts must complement and converge with the other aspects of the game and other contributions from the team.

Typically, music soundtracks for games are completed in MIDI-based DAW programs, such as Digital Performer, Logic Studio, Nuendo, and many others. Although these soundtracks are often built and composed with convincing samples and virtual instruments, if budget allows, sounds are often replaced with authentic orchestral instruments recorded in professional studios.

Junior-Level Specialists ($25,000 to $38,000)

Junior-level specialists are responsible for managing all the audio assets that come into play during the project cycle. They function as the "tape librarians" who maintain and track the audio files. A core requirement of this position is to tag assets as they are created so they can be identified and retrieved at a moment's notice. For example, in a game title that utilizes multiple languages, each asset or segment must have an individual filename that can be cross-referenced to an English script.

Larger companies have "localization teams" consisting of junior audio specialists. Their job function is 100-percent audio and entails tracking and managing speech translations for different release territories. Smaller companies and production houses typically have more junior positions—these people often have job descriptions that contain a variety of tasks, unlike the job descriptions of their more vertically focused counterparts at larger companies.

Recording/Mix Engineer ($35,000 to $75,000)

Large gaming companies often have on-staff recording personnel who aren't necessarily tied to individual project teams—they are part of the operational staff. Electronic Arts has a

20,000-square-foot complex in Vancouver, British Columbia, featuring three dedicated control rooms, complete with live rooms and iso booths. Project teams often utilize these company-owned facilities, which function much like real client-based studios. A recording/mix engineer might work on three different projects for his "clients" in a day: vocal overdubs in Control Room A, tracking a string quartet in Control Room B, and mixing 48 tracks of audio in Control Room C.

For the recording/mix engineer, the team leader or producer is his client—he must ensure that the technical outcome of the recording aligns with the requirements of the project. The mix engineer is also one of the final stops for quality control—any major changes or technical enhancements to the master recording will usually occur at this stage. Recording/mix engineers must bring not only a working recording knowledge to each project, but also a positive, team-oriented attitude.

Maintenance Engineer ($25,000 to $50,000)
Similar to the recording/mix engineer, this is an operational, non-team-based position. As within a traditional recording studio, the maintenance engineer needs to ensure that all the equipment is running properly so there is no equipment failure—this could ultimately result in a missed session or a blown deadline. It is also the maintenance engineer's responsibility to identify any shortcomings in the equipment setup, as well as acquisition opportunities to improve the overall quality. Maintenance engineer positions often lead to recording/mix engineer positions, very similar to traditional studios—in fact, a common recruiting ground for this job is the traditional recording studio.

Assistant Engineer ($18,000 to $28,000)
The assistant engineer is once again an operational-based position that fully supports the recording/mix engineer. Tasks in this role mirror those of the recording studio assistant—warming up the recording console, handling patching, setting up mics, performing some editing tasks, labeling audio files, and getting the studio ready for a session. Although all these tasks might appear to be tedious, they build a foundation of understanding and attention to detail that is required for any recording/mix engineer. Assistant engineers may also help with fades, edits, and tape transfers.

Audio Tool Developer ($45,000 to $150,000+)
Audio tool developers are the audio gurus within the programming team, or the people who write the code that allows the games to work. These folks spend most of their time coding, with the end goal of maximizing the CPU cycles that are allocated for the audio segments. Although audio tool developers fall within the "computer geek" category, they need to be able to understand and communicate basic audio principles, such as phasing, compression, and frequency modulation. It is their job to take the master audio files and turn them into

bits and bytes. They can also build and code customized tools that may be required in a program specification, such as an equalizer or an onscreen volume control.

These folks likely have the most secure jobs in the electronic gaming industry, and their talent and contributions are coveted. They usually have programming or mathematical backgrounds and have the ability to design custom tools for a title. Audio specialists need to be able to communicate basic audio and user requirements to the tool developers so they can turn ideas into reality. Audio tool developers have highly transferable skills, because nearly every pro audio manufacturer is investing in (or has considered investing in) electronic renditions or improvements of their products.

Entering and Succeeding in the Gaming Market

Those who succeed on the audio side of the gaming market generally have any combination of computer science, programming, mathematical, or audio background. At a minimum they are high school graduates, but most have a bachelor's degree from a university. If you have a strong programming background coupled with good audio sensibilities—specifically voice work and sound design—you will excel. "The things I would emphasize in your skill set would be sound design, voice work, and speech editing," says Ed Dolinksi. "These are the principal areas where most of the work lies. The whole bit about writing music for games is a bit of a crapshoot."

The best college-level audio programs have dedicated coursework on electronic gaming—these programs can go a long way toward landing a job in this area, depending on the pedigree and reputation of the institution. Most audio staff positions require a very solid background in audio engineering. A traditional understanding of consoles, digital signal processing, signal flow, and microphone techniques is mandatory.

There are many paths to getting an audio job within the gaming market, although the industry does tend to promote from within. Following are some common avenues of entry.

Through an Internship

Internships are still a tried-and-true method of getting in almost *any* area in the professional audio industry, including electronic gaming. Although you cannot expect much more than minimum wage from most internships, you *can* expect to learn the overall mechanics of how project teams work, as well as gain an opportunity to network with other people who could be instrumental in helping you land a job.

The obvious benefit of internships is that they apply to college credits as well, and there is a good chance that a recognized educational program will count your internship as coursework toward a degree. Also, interns typically start at the bottom and therefore can have a good lateral view of how the organization works. This can be used to their advantage later, when it comes time to obtain a "real" position.

Through an Educational Placement Program

Audio for gaming now has dedicated tracks at many audio universities around the world. Institutions such as the Institute of Audio Recording Technology, Expression Center for New Media, Full Sail Real World Education, and SAE all have placement programs that can assist students wanting to enter the gaming market, as do many of the top audio-oriented institutions. Graduates of these kinds of specialized programs are often looked on more favorably than other students with perhaps less of a concentration. "Candidates coming from specialized audio-oriented schools are harder to come by and more desirable on the whole," says Shannon Loftis.

As a Tester

The gaming industry requires testers, and lots of them. Testers come from all kinds of backgrounds, and their sole mission is to play the games until they crash or until an error is exposed. These folks work directly with the project teams, albeit on the outside—they are often highly paid. If you are a tester for long enough, you will likely have the chance to help a project team member with editing or some other audio-related task. Many audio-oriented individuals began their career in gaming as testers.

"Testers are a very necessary part of the whole chain. They put in long hours and beat up on the games, which can be very buggy before public release," says Ed Dolinski. Testers are hired dozens at a time from a variety of sources. If you prove your skills as a tester working alongside the project team, it is very likely that you'll eventually get asked to do something. "The first thing you'll get asked to do is the grunt work—put the 10,000 speech files into the game. You're also going to be the guy that chops the head and the tail and puts the name on every file that came out of the voiceover session," he adds.

Shannon Loftis agrees that this is a solid entry path toward the project team: "It's a great idea to start as a tester. In fact, one of our current directors of audio came from testing. We don't have an audio track in our test group, but it was his passion so he really focused on that, and eventually he made the team."

As an Outside Supplier

Gaming companies utilize outside recording studios all the time—especially smaller gaming companies and production houses. If you have a chance to work on a game project (either on a score or on the dialogue), you can likely apply your skills on the inside of a firm and help them save money. In fact, many small gaming companies have very primitive audio setups, and writers often compose and mix on headphones. Typically, gaming companies tend to work with the same recording studios on a regular basis—if you are looking to break into the gaming industry, you should research which recording studios have the gaming companies as major clients.

As a Freelancer

There are a great number of freelancing opportunities in gaming. If you have a professional studio set up at home with a DAW, you can deliver audio files over the Internet. You can do much of the editing and cleaning up prior to send-off. Typically, freelancers end up with the less glamorous work, such as labeling and parsing through the thousands of speech samples. If you do good work as a freelancer, you can build solid contacts from outside the organization and make your way in through a relationship.

Through Networking

Put your interest and skills to work and network with the people who can help you. As in nearly every industry, all you need are passion and a desire to learn to break in and find your strength. People all across the audio industry are inclined to be helpful, and many are genuinely interested in what you hope to achieve.

Ed Dolinski feels that the audio part of the gaming industry isn't very competitive to break into for those who are focused: "Most of the competitive jobs in this industry consist of artists and programmers—these jobs are at the core." At a minimum, before the conversation for a position in audio can begin, you must have a solid background in audio, as well as a reel or examples of your work that you are prepared to share. Resumes are important, but it is always the experience and personality that shine through in an in-person job interview.

There are dozens of video game companies to go after, including many upstarts. "It's easier to get a job at the upstarts," says Dolinski. "However, at these facilities, you might not even have a soundproof room—it could just be headphones." This should not discourage job seekers, though, since the opportunity for growth is fantastic—if not within the small company, then outside of it. Importantly, job security at a startup—where you are only as good as your last hit—would be much more volatile than at an established gaming company.

Not surprisingly, geography has a lot to do with your ability to find employment in this industry, at least at the development level, where many of the jobs exist. There are many electronic gaming hubs around which most of the work is generated, including Vancouver (Electronic Arts), the San Francisco corridor, Seattle (Nintendo, Microsoft), Austin, New York, and Los Angeles. You can still succeed in gaming if you live outside these cities, but your chances of success are likely improved if you are in close proximity to these areas.

Traits Valued in the Gaming Industry

As in any other industry, certain traits are valued in the gaming industry. The following sections discuss these traits.

Creativity and Drive

As a predominant entertainment medium for the next generation, the electronic gaming industry first and foremost rewards creativity and innovation. "Creativity and problem-solving abilities are very important—you need to have ideas and be able to run with them," says Shannon Loftis. The ability to creatively confront and solve problems is also key, because often the path forward may not be clear, and other team members may not be able to provide guidance.

Flexibility   Organization

Creativity

Communications Skills   Innovation

Drive   Collaboration

Leadership

Technical Skills

Some of the basic traits the gaming industry values.

Collaborative Thinking and Flexibility

The way project teams are composed demands teamwork—if you do not work well with people, you will not succeed. "It's really different from independent audio contracting, where you get your instructions, then go into your rabbit hole and pop up with a CD at the end," says Ed Dolinski. "The people who are really self-absorbed and introverted really won't do as well in this industry—it requires such a team effort."

On project teams, you need to be open minded and be able to bend toward other people's ideas. "Perfectionists fail," Loftis says. "It's harsh, but true—game development is all about compromise, and sometimes you have to flex in everything you do for the better of the team."

Good Communication and Leadership Abilities

It pays to have good presentation and leadership abilities. Because the audio aspect is only one facet of a game, the director of audio on a project team needs to be able to present and communicate ideas in a clear and compelling way to other team members who may have conflicting interests. For instance, toward the beginning of the development stage, CPU cycles are allocated for a title. "Right up front, you're up against people who want to use the CPU cycles for visuals," says Loftis. "You need to make the case for processor time and memory space. There are many battles you have to fight up front and make a strong case for your audio—otherwise, you can find yourself in a crippled position at the end of the game because there's not enough cycle time to add a live reverb if you need it."

Knowledge and Skills

It goes without saying that one must have a solid understanding of audio concepts and applications. These can be derived from an audio school or even in the industry—but this is an industry in which you are expected to take the ball and run with it. There is no time to learn on the job, given the intense deliverable deadlines and schedules. A programming background is less important, but certainly desirable as an additional skill, especially if that programming background involves audio. "If you're an audio programmer, you're like gold in this industry—you can go work anywhere. You can write the actual code, scripts, even invent the tools to implement sounds into the games," says Dolinski.

Composing for video games obviously requires a strong visual sensibility. Producers expect that the audio specialist will have sensitivity and skill with regard to applying appropriate music for different characters and scenes. In this respect, composing for games is not unlike film composing, albeit in short segments. To evoke the emotions of characters, you must know sounds in your arsenal like the back of your hand—from reverbs, to effects, to frequency modulators. An audio specialist is creating a reality for the player—that reality needs to support the visual aspect of the game and be credible throughout the duration.

Benefits and Drawbacks of Working in the Gaming Industry

If you decide to pursue a career in the gaming industry, you'd better be passionate about it. Although there is definitely an upside to the equation, long hours, intense deadlines, and a work environment that can be highly unstructured are just some of the obstacles that await you.

Stress and Work/Life Balance

The timing of the project cycle can generally help point to how much personal time and/or job stress an employee will have. For example, at the beginning of a title, the schedule and requirements can be very loose, and audio specialists simply might need to look busy while researching and mocking up sounds. However, as deadlines and delivery dates approach, longer hours, more intense effort, and harder deliverables are typically required—it is not uncommon to find audio specialists pulling all-nighters or 60-hour workweeks toward the end of the cycle. This is commonly referred to as *crunch time* and is a difficult aspect the entire industry has to deal with.

"Toward the end of the game cycle, you find that people are doing insane hours because there is simply no other way to fine-tune the game," says Dolinksi. "The timing can't slip because there are so many things that are cued up. Time is already scheduled for the manufacturing plants, the printing presses, and corresponding ad campaigns. Many, many elements hinge on that launch date, and it just isn't flexible." Dolinski says titles can slip, but if they slip past Christmas, 50 percent of the potential sales may be lost. Once crunch time is over and the title ships, the cycle begins all over again.

As far as achieving a work/life balance, Dolinski reminds us what is really at stake: "Your producer has already put his life on the line to say, 'I'm going to spend $10 million of the company's money, and we expect to sell *x* amount.' In so doing, they also make a time commitment of when it will ship." The deadlines are real and have enormous impact on workloads and personal time.

If there is a bright side to the cyclical nature of the product, small firms doing, say, one title per year often have paid time off for six to eight weeks before a new title begins. This contrasts with the process in larger firms that do multiple titles, where team members will likely be thrown on the next project without delay.

Work Environment

One of the most attractive benefits to working in the gaming industry is that it is composed of a very stimulating environment that constantly changes with the consumer audience. If a particular title is successful, it can turn into a long-running series, and the whole team can benefit financially through bonuses in addition to regular salaries. Titles can be vastly different from year to year, reflecting the overall interests and trends of the entertainment industry and the buying public. If a title you work on is successful, it can mean access to other teams producing more commercially popular work. If the audio portion of a title you worked on is particularly noteworthy, it can lead to a more influential position on a project team.

As you would expect, most gaming companies allow casual dress (such as jeans, T-shirts, and so on), and workdays are fairly flexible, similar to ad agencies. The start of a business day is about 10:00 a.m. and can typically extend beyond 6:00 p.m.

Benefits and Drawbacks of
Working in Gaming

Long Periods of Time Off	Can Be Very High Stress
Stimulating Environment	Long Hours/Crunch Time
Can Be Lucrative/Bonuses	Smaller Companies Risky
Low-Key Environment	Inflexible Deadlines
Flexible Hours	Lots of Competition
Often Good Job Security	Rapidly Changing Hardware

Career Stability

The gaming industry is somewhat insular, and this can mean more job security than in other audio jobs. The gaming industry is also large and can offer lateral career movement along with relative stability—and the tight-knit audio group looks out for its own. This aspect often contrasts with the traditional recording studio market, which can be notoriously cut-throat in this regard. On the other hand, smaller gaming companies are not immune to poor business results and failed product launches. If a title goes south or underperforms in the consumer market, this can spell layoffs, and folks from every discipline may suffer. If this occurs at a small company, depending on people's investments, it can mean the end of their business.

Compensation

As noted earlier, compensation is generally very good. In addition to base salaries, bonuses and profit sharing are possible. The more technically challenging your position is, chances are the higher the pay will be. When you are looking at potential companies to work for, one very important consideration is whether they share royalties with members of the creative team. Although this used to be considered rare, it is becoming increasingly more common to compensate team members this way at some of the more progressive studios.

The gaming industry is not unlike Hollywood or the recording industry in the sense that it rewards industry achievers. Ever major award body in the gaming industry features audio work, and if you are recognized in this way, it can lead to almost limitless opportunities as your work may become sought after by the field's top studios.

Geography

If you are not engaged with a project team on a day-to-day basis, you might be able to live anywhere your means allow. "Audio is one of the leading disciplines in globalization," says Shannon Loftis. "The audio guys were the first ones to take advantage of European resources and started producing assets for much lower fees. You can live wherever you want—just make sure you are available when you're needed."

This doesn't necessarily hold true for audio operational staff or those tied closer to the project team, however. These folks will need to be near the facility and the rest of the project team—in the case of Microsoft, they need to be near Redmond, Washington. "It's such a give and take in terms of memory budgets and CPU bandwidth for audio that many of the audio specialists need to be located with the rest of the project team. However, if you're on the content production side, sourcing the orchestras or whatever, you can live anywhere."

Smaller, independent firms have production facilities all over the country and would provide more flexibility as far as geography is concerned. However, this might be a tradeoff and should be considered carefully because such firms may not offer as much attractive career growth.

Is the Electronic Gaming Industry Right for You?

The electronic gaming industry can be a lucrative, rewarding choice for the right person. Creativity, passion, team spirit, and knowledge are all critical cornerstones to the kind of person who will succeed. Loftis paints a picture of what it looks like when it goes right: "Ideally, your audio 'vision' is integrated seamlessly with the rest of the vision of the game. The person who excels will be able to bring that vision to the table and articulate it, raising the common denominator for everyone."

Audio folks in the gaming industry are very passionate about what they bring to the table, and at times they have to remind visually oriented people about the indelible contribution to the music, voiceovers, and sound effects they make, says Loftis: "In many cases our audio guys are super talents, and they are actually raising the standard and advocating the audio. When it comes to debugging the game and making it run faster, a lot of the times audio is the first thing on the chopping block—our audio leads are really good about communicating what you lose if you take away that component."

A Closer Look: Guy Whitmore and the Gaming Industry

Guy Whitmore is Director of Audio at Microsoft Game Studios. He is renowned in gaming circles for his success in creating adaptive music techniques, which take advantage of the nonlinear nature of the medium. When I spoke to Guy, I realized that the way he looks at the theater—"you have to get it right the first time"—is one of the very reasons why he has been so successful in his own career.

Where did you get your feet wet in this industry?

I wanted to go into music during high school, so I went to Northwestern University outside of Chicago and got a music performance degree in classical guitar. I kind of got a dual education: one of them formal, the other ad hoc in the studio recording and electronics world. While in college I played in rock bands and helped produce some records on campus—so this occurred while I was studying guitar. After that, I took a year off, then I went to grad school at Southern Methodist University in Dallas.

Why did you choose to go to grad school?

I was still on the classical guitar track, and my teacher's teacher taught at Southern Methodist University. I participated in some master classes with her teacher and liked him so much that I wanted to study with him. Plus, I had the idea that I wanted to get a composition degree as well—that was the key there and kind of changed the direction of my career. I had some composition classes in undergrad, but when I got to grad school, I decided to do a double major.

Most grad programs are two years, but I spent three years and got two master's degrees because the composition program at SMU was great. They had a great electronic music studio and electronic music program, and I had already been playing around with samplers and stuff. This really gave me a formal background in digital signal processing, mixing, sampling—these kinds of things.

The other great thing about that program was that the instructors at SMU were very open minded. The music I was doing wasn't strictly academic—it had flavors of that but was also very avante-pop, reminiscent of Laurie Anderson and Frank Zappa to some degree. Then I started composing music for theater production at SMU, where there is also a great theater program—and that's what started getting me my first professional gigs. I wrote a whole score for Chekhov's *The Three Sisters* and literally started getting professional work right after that.

Was this a hard gig to get on your campus?

No. The director and I really hit it off—it was a fun collaboration. He was also involved in the Dallas theater community. So right after that gig, I stared getting both sound design and composition work at the Dallas Theater Center, the Dallas Children's Theater, and other places.

But at this point, the fundamentals are in place, right?

That's right. By that point, people were telling me, "Wow, you can do this for a living." So the gigs just started coming in. It was an interesting place to cut my teeth professionally before moving to games because there were a lot of similarities. There is a context of a story; there is a team where you have a visual director, costume director, a technical director, and sound director—there were all these parallels. It is very much a team atmosphere, and this translates well to games.

This was traditional art theater, and the director wanted a lot of music context and underscoring, so they would hire somebody like me. The other thing is that theater is entirely different every night—just like games are different every time you play. Half the art is preparing the cueing for the different elements in the performance. A lot of this I did by triggering samples with a keyboard and cues with a DAT player—prerecorded segments. Everything would then be assembled for real time in the theater. The team atmosphere and the nonlinear nature of the theater made it very similar to gaming.

When did you get your first professional gig beyond the theater?

The shift to gaming was all of a sudden. I eventually got a call from someone I had gone to school with at SMU. He was a composer and was from the Seattle area. He had a job in gaming and asked if I wanted to apply for an open staff composer job where he worked at Sierra Online, one of the early game developers in the '80s.

So you ultimately got this opportunity from a community that you were in, SMU.

Yes, the lesson there is to treat every gig as if it is the last and as if your life depended on it. This guy Jonathan and I would always help each other out, and we gained a lot of respect for each other. When the time came, he knew that the quality of my work would be good and that I would put in the necessary effort.

People sometimes treat a project like, "This isn't the real one; I'm waiting for the real one." But you have to take the one that's at hand, do really good at it—even if it is a school assignment. I used to treat those assignments like they were professional gigs. That enhanced my portfolio and made an impression for me even before I left school. I had a little network that really helped me get my foot in the door and gave me a shot.

But obviously you had to have the talent to back it up—they must have been impressed by that.

As you can imagine, I was not the only person they looked at, and there were a whole series of demos that I had to do. In addition to the work that I had already done, they gave me a game scenario challenging me to arrange this music for this game. The position was in children's music, which was a great place to start, and it worked out really well. For the audition, it was literally, "We're going to send you a package, and send back a demo." I had to write, record, and send a DAT back to them in a week. I got the gig, and the first gig I got there was to arrange 16 *Mother Goose* rhymes to various pop and rock styles of different eras.

What was the acclimation period like? How long before you felt in command of what you were doing?

It was interesting because at that point in time, October of '94, I didn't feel really over my head. In fact, I felt that the theater world really helped me because in the theater world, there's no bullshit—you get your stuff done on time. It's like clockwork, and the show does go on. Game productions slip, but theater productions don't slip their deadlines. I think that discipline really got me ready, and in some ways I was taken aback by how schedules were handled. The gaming industry at that time was still grappling with the whole process of how to make a game. So there were all kinds of experimentation going on with team structure and what goes first—the whole process of putting a game together creatively and technically.

In the early gaming industry, there weren't a lot of producers or managers who really knew what was supposed to be happening in music or sound in a game. We were writing our own rules, so I was pretty much set to do it the way I felt was best.

I bet there was a certain satisfaction in having a product to show. Was there a certain pride of ownership?

Yeah, there definitely was that. There's almost nothing I like more than seeing a live audience react to what you've done, so that's why I like live theater. But you're right; at the end, when the first CD-ROM comes out and it sells a couple hundred thousand, that's pretty cool. I still have it and can pull it out for my daughter!

At what point did you really feel like you had a career rather than just your first gig?

I think I was in gaming to stay probably by the second game, which probably took two years. I thought, "This is great." Writing for games has changed the way I think about music. There isn't a formal beginning, middle, and end. Some games are more linear than others, but you have to allow it so your cues can ebb and flow with the different styles of gameplay. You don't know how long someone is going to be sitting down listening to a particular cue, so it makes you think about how time passes or how many times you get to hear something.

How different is it from a film in terms of sequence?

It is hugely different. In a game, you can be approaching these monsters—you hear this tension music, but you don't know when the music needs to pop up and do a crescendo as the monster jumps. So you go, "Okay, I'll just make this loop that just kind of goes until it crosses a certain threshold, and then pop up that other cue." How you spot cues in a game has less to do with exact timing and more what to do with events and the data that the game is giving you about what the player is doing. So there is a push and a pull there between what the player is doing and what the music needs to do. We are still only scratching the surface in terms of figuring out what the music can do.

So how are you writing it to the events?

Interestingly, when you are writing a film, sometimes you are just looking at picture and saying, "Okay, I need to mark that point, and I have about 10 seconds to this point." When you are scoring a game, the first thing you need to ask is, "What does this game need?" Does it need action music or ambient music? Once you've identified that, you get to specifics like, "Do different characters need themes? Do different areas of the world need themes?" And then from there, "How do I transition from one to another?" So you kind of start looking at it as a whole, and then breaking it down into components. "Now I need to write some ambient music for this level."

What happened with your career after Sierra?

After Sierra, I jumped to a company named Monolith Productions. It was a small developer at the time. Sierra had been very, very slow to give raises, and I felt like I was doing a ton more for the games than I was being compensated for, so that got me looking around. I also knew that if I wanted to get established in this, I had to get a wider range of genres under my belt. At the time, Monolith was doing a combination of action arcade, side-scrolling cartoony ones, but also first-person shooters. That is still what they are best known for.

So it was a great way for you to diversify.

Yes, but it also turned out to be a good move for growth because I came in as a staff composer reporting to the audio director. After he moved on, I moved up to be audio director at a team at Monolith. This is where I established a lot of industry credibility among my peers.

What kind of managerial capacities are you building at this point, beyond the technical and compositional skills?

A lot—you're managing a team that is working on a particular game and also managing within a corporate structure. That was different, but felt easy for me. It is not outside of my personality to manage people. I was still honing my composition skills and learning more and more there, too. Monolith was doing about two games per year.

What happened after Monolith?

I did freelance work after that because I kind of felt like I topped out what I could do at Monolith. I don't like to stand still. I did about three years there—it was an okay situation, but I definitely made enough contacts that I felt I could go freelance. I wanted more credibility and wanted to get involved in some other work. The transition to freelancing was great. It was in the middle of a game or two I was working on for Monolith, and I presented it to them. I said, "I'll make this totally painless for you guys—here's what I am offering to finish up these two games as a freelancer." They were my first client, and there wasn't a lull in work for me at all. They actually wound up saving money, too, because they had less overhead.

Surely your recognition in the industry was increasing at that point I would imagine.

Yes. Among my peers, at places like the Game Developers Conference, I was really getting known as one of the premier experts in not just creating music for video games, but interactivity of music within video games. When I was at Monolith, I pioneered a couple of techniques that had people scratching their heads. Up to that point, other than a few MIDI scores, music cues were typically cross-faded. If you needed to go from an ambient cue to a battle cue, you just cross-faded between two themes. In a movie, you don't usually do cross-fade cues—it's more like a crescendo. You move into it smoothly without breaking the composition. How do you do that in a game when you don't know when the players are actually going to move into a place where there is action?

So I created a system of matrix of transitions that could move between the various emotional intensities so it would sound like the game was completely seamless even though every time you heard it, it was a different set of variations and transition points. That got me further work—just having that expertise. Even more than my compositional chops, which were at a good standard. It gave me another edge.

How long did your freelance career last?

Interestingly, freelance didn't go on as long as I thought it would because I jumped onto a company founded by Robert Fripp of King Crimson. He started this company called Bootleg TV around 1998. Robert had a side interest in nonlinear music that could be different every time you hear it. So he hired me and another guy [Tobin Buttram] to head up their interactive music wing, which was a handful of people. I lived the dot-com bomb to a T, and that went down. Ultimately I went freelance again, eventually leading to my gig with Microsoft.

What was the position?

The title was Audio Lead. When I read the description, it looked on paper like a real step down. You're working on one or two games, not even over a division. But when I looked into the gig more and talked to them, it was clear that I was going to be the audio director for one of their publishing divisions and that there was room for growth, so I took it. Since I've been at Microsoft, things have moved pretty quickly.

How big was the adaptation?

It was totally huge but also totally familiar. The biggest change was being on a development team and the fact that I was responsible for several titles. I was used to diving in deep on one title and not coming up for air for months and months—a hyper focus. The same was true for freelancing, even if it was week to week. When I first started at Microsoft, I was overseeing four or five titles, then I'd move to six or seven titles. So I had to change my vision from myopic narrow scope to this broad, light-touch approach. Setting direction and letting that ball spin— all delegation. The most important thing I have done since then is to hire really key people. I now oversee eight audio folks right here in Redmond, then there are all the teams at the developers.

Tell me about the development team.

The development team is typically a group of 100 to 200 people. They are on the ground making the game, writing all the code, making all the content. The publisher is the one funding it, providing direction, getting it into stores, marketing it, and all that. Microsoft's approach is to have discipline leads. For every single project there is an art lead, a design lead, an audio lead, a development lead, a test lead, as well as text, script, usability, and localization. For example, I have an audio lead whose responsibility is to make sure that the audio for *Gears of War* is coming along well in terms of production schedule, quality, and features they are trying to push.

We are shepherding these games along, and sometimes we get neck deep in production ourselves. We evaluate whether the development teams need extra resources or require more expertise— maybe they fall short in a certain area, like sound design or music. Those are the kinds of assessments we make. Quality is always the biggest benchmark, and we are setting the bar for what other developers and publishers will do. So if *Gears of War* comes out with cool new sound tech and it makes the game sound better, it prompts other developers to raise the bar.

It seems like this system encourages creativity.

Absolutely. My first role in engaging a new development team is to ask them what their vision is and what they would like to bring forward. It is almost like being a music producer. The best music producers get out of the way and only get involved when something is off track. So we have a production studio, and we do varying degrees of production support as needed. The best thing about this job is working with some of the most brilliant audio directors in the industry.

What skill do you have right now that is getting the most mileage for you in your current position?

Personality is a good friend of mine. Particularly where I am now—we don't have a dominant position, and we don't tell people what to do. It has to be a collaborative thing if you are going to get the best work. It really is about just helping them see their vision through. I try to hire people with not only sound design and music skills, but also personal skills to be able to engage and talk intelligently about this stuff. Communication is so vital. There is a lot of diplomacy and nurturing.

How do you manage stress and work life?

I still work a good amount and have a decent commute—my hours are far less than, say, when I was at Monolith, but those were also years when I was cutting my teeth and had something to prove. We lose a lot of folks, and there is a lot of talk about GDC about the work/life balance issue. There is still a lot of balance being sought in gaming, quite frankly. I will speak strongly about Microsoft Game Studios, though—they have been awesome about work/life balance. Maybe it's because Microsoft is a good place to work in general, but it's also about the team you work with. I don't go in many weekends at all anymore and only occasionally stay late.

What moment stands out in your career?

The reach for perfection is kind of a continuous thing. That first soundtrack I wrote at Sierra, the *Mother Goose* thing, was hugely eye-opening and extremely satisfying creatively and professionally. I thought, "I'm in the right place." Also, when I began to realize the potential of this medium. There is a game called *Shogo* that I did at Monolith, which was the first game that really highlighted a lot of my interactive concepts. This really kind of broke me through among my peers, and that was highly satisfying.

A Closer Look: Scott Gershin of Soundelux

Scott Gershin, Executive Creative Director/Founder of Soundelux Design Music Group, has worked extensively in gaming, film, and television. No matter what discipline he is working in, Scott remains especially passionate about one thing: The audio must tell a story. His career has been built with a no-compromise approach to his craft, from his early days of programming at MIT to his current role at Soundelux.

How did you become involved in the audio world?

After being in a ton of bands and touring with Up with People, I went to Berklee College of Music, where I studied audio engineering as well as synthesis; guitar was my main instrument. I think it was in those days that the worlds of synthesis and mixing began to converge for me. While I was at Berklee, they introduced the personal computer, so I decided to take some night classes in computer programming at MIT. This was around the time of the "Lisa," which turned into the Macintosh—as well as the Commodore 64.

Scott Gershin.

Did you have a concise idea of where you were headed?

I had no initial interest in using computers, but I thought, "Boy, wouldn't it be cool to use them with synthesizers?" I was mostly doing music at that point, but the writing was on the wall because I was always interested in non-musical sounds that had an emotional impact. When I moved to Los Angeles and was working at Cherokee and a lot of the other studios around LA as a recording engineer, I started programming synthesizers such as the Jupiter 8, DX7, basically the latest and greatest at the time—I was also being hired by a lot of studio players in town to come up with libraries.

That led me into doing weird sounds on synths—strange tones, exotic weapons, and so on. When I did do music sounds, it was more fun adding clavinets and trumpets together. I liked using instruments as elements to create sounds that didn't exist in nature. When I started my transition from music to sound effects, I got a gig paying my dues doing cartoons in LA. It was sweatshop-type stuff, and it was all about speed.

Where did things go after your first gig doing cartoons?

I went into television for about a year and then into the world of film. I met a guy named Wylie Stateman, who became kind of a mentor to me—and later my partner when I founded Sounde-lux Design Music Group with him and Lon [Bender]. He and Lon had started a brand-new company called Soundelux.

While doing TV I used a workstation called the Synclavier, a four-meg sampler that cost around 300k, and then used a workstation called the Waveframe. I became one of the first designers at

Soundelux and an early user of computer technology in sound editing and design. In addition to doing the post for films in those days, we were doing all kinds of projects, such as theme parks and music videos for Michael Jackson. We had been approached by companies to do sound for video games, but most of the time, the sound for a game was all FM-based. Programming in FM made it very, very time consuming and just didn't make sense for us at that time. Then Sega and Nintendo started coming out with devices on which I could play back audio—especially Nintendo.

I talked to some people I knew at a company called Activision, and we talked about trying to bring some of the creative film techniques to gaming. To give you perspective, at that time, a new format was coming out called the World Wide Web. I thought this was incredibly intriguing, and I realized that all the things I had been learning were accumulating and applicable to this. All the theory and the issues that I dealt with on some of the earlier gear were converging. Also, the fact that I had a background in programming really helped me open up some interesting conversations with early developers around tool sets. I started coming up with ideas they hadn't even really thought of at that time. Can I delay the start of the sound while still triggering it so I can do some interesting layers, random start points? Can I randomize the pitch? Can I assign controllers, such as filtering, to correspond with the Z-axis? I just saw the game hardware and software tools as another synth at that time.

For you it was just an extension of the computing capability and the ability to create these synthesized sounds, right?

Exactly. That's the technical side. The creative side was about audio storytelling: How do you use audio to tell a story or bring out certain emotions from your audience? At the end of the day, I'm definitely a geek. I love technology and have lots of toys, but it comes down to the output or the product that is created by those toys. Everything else is just a tool to be able to get to that place.

A lot of gaming people were interested more in the technology of the game rather than the game play itself. Sometimes the technology was amazing, but it wasn't an interesting game. At the end of the day, you have to answer the following questions: Was it fun, was I entertained, was I challenged? If it is a simulator, did we accomplish the realism and excitement we needed to? If it was an adventure, did we capture the energy? Did we get the juices going? It's the same as what I try to do in my movies.

How did your position grow at Soundelux?

While at Soundelux, I started a brand-new division, which today is called Soundelux Design Music Group—it used to be known as Soundelux Media Labs. This group is focused on audio production: VO, which includes casting directing; recording and editing; sound design; and music composition for gaming, theme parks, and commercials. We are now 17 years old. We try to provide our clients with an audio solution, and they can use as much or as little of our services as they want. Much of our client base consists of publishers and developers.

How has gaming changed over the years?

It's changed a lot—it started off with dozens of groups of individuals who wanted to create a game, and they just did it. There used to be all these little gaming companies you'd see at the conventions, but they eventually became gobbled up by the publishers. Everything was done by the seat of your pants: guerilla audio. We'd get everyone in the office to do a character voice, for example. Now a lot more is at stake: bigger budgets, more risk, bigger deals and agents—Wall Street. It doesn't means it's bad now; it's just different.

Where was the industry when you entered it?

For me, the thing that I have enjoyed the most out of all of this has been being lucky enough to be active during an evolutionary time in two industries. When film went to electronic sound editing, I was one of the first people using samplers and computer technology. In gaming, I was one of the early sound designers. This meant that there were no rules in solving the problems; you needed to get the jobs done. You really had to use all of your brainpower to solve these problems. In some ways, creating a game became a game in itself, and overall it has been incredibly satisfying.

What are the key traits you bring to your field?

It's mostly left-brain—it's creativity. I do have a business and logic sense, but it is the creative side that gets you the most mileage. I am known for coming up with cool sounds. Being a musician, I don't look at music as music and sound design as sound design. I look at it as a soundtrack: a total landscape that has to work together. I see sound as colors, and they need to blend—if they don't, they turn kind of brown and muddy.

For example, when mixing music, if I need a solo piano, it should be harmonically rich and full bodied—the best sound you can capture. But if it's going to be in a band, the piano has a really wide bandwidth. Therefore, you have to carve out those frequencies that are going to clash with the other instruments. I may go in automatically carving up a piano knowing that the bass, guitar, synth, and strings are going to have to cut through. The same applies to gaming; if all you are concerned about is each sound sounding big and lush, it may not fit when all the other audio components are added.

What kind of advice would you give to someone just entering the field now?

The big thing is to start listening. Because we are surrounded by so much noise and sound in our lives, out of survival we learn how to stop listening because the world can be overbearing. We have to re-learn how to start listening again and listen to the specific sounds of life; you need to listen to music, TV, movies, and games and get an audio vocabulary. For example, a punch should sound like this and a laser like that—even though they are totally fictitious. We are like audio photographers and have to start listening and learning. Once you do that, then you must think, "How I can manipulate those sounds to create hyper realities and fictitious creatures?" Your audio life experiences are the things that are going to be in your head as you start creating.

When I was in high school, the first *Star Wars* came out, and it exposed me to other worlds and opened up my imagination. I didn't know what I was going to do with my life, but I knew it should be something like that—it gave me goose bumps.

What can someone focus on? There are almost too many tools out there now and too much information.

There are two things you have to learn, and it's kind of like music. You have to learn the techniques of your instrument, the "how to." Once you learn how to do that, you've got to figure out what you want to say with it. The same applies to any kind of technology and creativity. But remember: If you are in college, by the time you are out in the working world, the technology will have progressed and changed. It's best to learn the theory behind it so you can adapt that theory to the latest technology. Especially in the technological world of gaming—technology changes every six months, but the fundamentals are exactly the same. Right now I am learning several Middleware tools and other publishers' proprietary tools sets. But the questions will always be the same: How can I combine samples, filter them, pitch them, randomize them, pan them, prioritize them, and to which DSPs can I apply them? You need to experiment. There is nothing better than just playing with the toys.

You also need to network with other people who are trying to get into the business because as you finally break into the industry, it is those same people who will be your "class." You will have shared similar experiences and sweated together trying to break in. In my career, I have a peer group of great people with whom I started my career, and to this day we remain friends because we all shared moments in time. Those people are going to be the people who hire you, or you'll hire them. This network is crucial since they will help define your career. I look at so many threads of my own career, and it's all about that.

What basic personality traits are important in what you do?

What you really need is passion. You also have to be persistent. The harsh reality of our business is that nobody cares when you come, and you are quickly replaced when you leave. You've got to push, and you've got to have staying power. You've got to look at it, interestingly enough, as a video game. When you're trying to get in, sometimes the front door is not open. Those people who keep working at it until something budges get in. You've got to make the best of your own raw materials—there are no rules, and that's what I think is so great about the creative industries.

What are some of the best things you like about being in gaming?

I love storytelling with sound. I love making people feel emotions. I also love the technical challenges that gaming gives me—I am fortunate to have a successful career in both industries. I consider myself very lucky.

Where are things going in gaming? Is this an exciting time?

When I started, gaming was a baby; now it's a young adult. There were similar changes in the film industry when it was young. As game budgets have been increasing, games will have to attract a larger audience to support those budgets. At the end of the day, it's about how many games we are selling and whether we are making product that will attract a lot of players. We will have our *Star Wars* and our *Matrix* that will propel the industry to keep raising the creative bar. I think a lot of gaming is going to go online; casual games are becoming huge. It has gone from games being made for gamers to games being made for the masses. You look at *Guitar Hero* or the Wii. Of course, I 'm hoping for my own *Halo* suite.

A Closer Look: Ed Dolinski and the Gaming Industry

Edwin Dolinski is the former Audio Director for Electronic Arts. Dolinski joined Electronic Arts back in 1992, just before the gaming boom of the mid-'90s. By 1999, Electronic Arts had built a massive 20,000-square-foot facility near Vancouver, British Columbia. When he started, the company had around 100 employees in its North American operation—now the company employs more than 1,000 people all around the world. Dolinski describes his first position with Electronic Arts: "I started as a composer. We were writing MIDI music for PCs and the early cartridges, such as Sega Genesis."

Ed, how did you break into the electronic gaming industry?

I was really good at MIDI and computer music. I was in a two-piece band, and we had this guy design our album cover who I happened to stay in touch with. He ended up moving to Electronic Arts, and when they needed another composer, he gave me a call. There was a job opening, so I threw my hat in the ring with about 30 other people who applied at the time. Ultimately, they picked me because of my MIDI-based background.

Was there any kind of technical aspect that especially captured your interest?

It seemed like electronic gaming was poised to start incorporating CDs as delivery systems for their games. What this implied for audio folk like me was that you weren't going to be limited by some crippled FM chip with no reverb on a soundcard—you could stream audio. Companies like Electronic Arts were on the cutting edge. Back then, the people with audio jobs had predominantly a code-writing background but were recording hobbyists on the side.

I was able to position myself as the audio "expert" since I came from a professional recording studio. At Electronic Arts, I could apply my knowledge of acoustics, microphones, monitoring systems, and everything else I had learned at the studio, while leveraging my network of professional audio colleagues I knew in the Vancouver area.

Tell me about the timing of your move—did the transition feel right for you?

I got into the industry at the perfect time. They were just building a new facility in Vancouver that was going to be their biggest development studio in the world when it was completed. Everything was state of the art, and the place was going to be at the center of their developmental universe. I rode the wave perfectly and eventually became director of audio there.

Tell me what the culture was like.

We had such a good vibe going on in our audio department. There was a tremendous amount of sharing and learning that was going on, and it was incredibly exciting. The closest comparison I can think of might be a post-house with six or seven editors, all sharing talents and unique perspectives for the broader good. There wasn't any of the "Hey, if I know how to do something cool, I'm not going to show you!" kind of attitude—we were the antithesis of that. It was very collaborative and socialist with a flat hierarchy. I was at the top of it and directing the whole operation.

Can you recall some of the early experiences at Electronic Arts that ultimately led to the need for dedicated audio rooms?

Sure. When we started, there would be three composers in a 30-foot room, all writing MIDI music through headphones. I thought, "This is crazy—we need a room to evaluate mixes and work in a real room." So I built two recording studios for them and a bunch of soundproof offices. We had to get out of listening through headphones, and I saw this as an opportunity.

Ultimately, I oversaw the construction of three professional recording studios that were designed by Walters-Storyk Design Group. We needed real control rooms because we were doing real post work. There are a lot of different components when you make a game, but one of them is that you have the title sequence, which is a canned movie. This is like typical post-production—you've got to be able to see it on a good screen and synchronize your multitrack. I convinced them of the need to improve the rooms for this reason.

What was the composing routine like for games back then, and how structured was it?

We had this really cool culture going on in the '90s, where the guys who were working on the games were also writing the tunes that went in it. We had these monster musicians on staff, along with a Yamaha Birch kit and a Marshall amp that was always set up in the studio. If you wanted a wicked guitar part, you just called someone from upstairs. He would take an hour, lay it down, then go back to work!

The funny thing was how that aspect kept growing in the culture. At one point we had 10 writers on staff who, in addition to their duties of designing and building the sounds for the games, wrote at least one song for the games. There wouldn't be any royalties associated with these, but everyone would get paid a good, steady salary with all the benefits.

What kind of success was Electronic Arts enjoying when it undertook this massive construction project?

At the time we built our state-of-the-art recording studios, we were selling about $400 million of software per year. The results were so good that it simply didn't make sense *not* to invest in the studios. No economic model was required for the improvements since the need and the benefits were obvious to everyone.

3 | The Audio Book Market

A udio books are at the root of America's storytelling tradition, and opportunities in this field continue to grow, attracting candidates from both the audio and literary arts. The development of the MP3 format and the unleashing of online storefronts (most notably iTunes) have resulted in a new generation of consumers who appreciate the convenience and selection that online distribution affords.

Market Viability

Last year, the Audio Publishers Association estimated the audio books market to be $871 million, reflecting a 4.7 percent increase from the previous year. The market shows no signs of slowing, either, as people of all ages—both male and female—continue to download many titles across all genres. According to the Audio Publishers Association, 25 percent of the entire U.S. population listens to audio books. Although CDs are the most popular format, MP3 and other digital formats have slowly taken hold as consumers become more familiar with online retail environments, such as iTunes and Simply Audiobooks.

Audio books are here to stay. For generations, people have enjoyed titles such as Dylan Thomas's *A Child's Christmas in Wales*, H.G. Wells's *The War of the Worlds*, and Sergei Prokofiev's *Peter and the Wolf*. More recently, listeners enjoy everything from current events, to biographies on sports figures, to classic fiction by modern authors such as Cormac McCarthy. Audio books are a perfect example of the power of content—they continue to find a path to consumers despite changes in music formats and technology. Here are some reasons why the audio book industry continues to thrive:

- **Increased online retail outlets.** Online outlets, such as iTunes and Audible, have created seamless storefront environments where users can quickly download almost any selection to suit their interest—and at a reasonable cost. Additionally, traditional online outlets, such as Amazon.com and BarnesandNoble.com, have made finding and buying audio book CDs easier than ever before.

- **An abundance of content delivery mechanisms.** The days of the audio cassette are nearly over, and content is now channeled via CDs, MP3s, satellite radio, iPods, and the Internet.

RSS feeds, blogs, and other social media have made it very easy for consumers to identify and purchase exactly what they are looking for.

- **Development of an increasingly global market.** Although the appetite for audio books predominantly originated from the United States, high-quality compression of audio files and the Internet have torn down geographic barriers to consumers—this will likely result in higher sales trends and greater demand.

- **More facilities capable of producing content.** Although some might argue that MP3s and other audio files have deteriorated the quality of audio books overall, it is clear that more studios and production houses have become involved in producing audio books. Through new technology advances and a greater pool of talent, there are more high-quality releases being produced and delivered to the market than ever before.

Audio Book Formats, 2003–2006

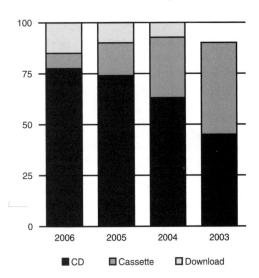

Courtesy Audio Publishers Association

Robert Kessler, owner of Katonah, New York–based Kessler Media, is a pioneer in the audio book industry and handles dozens of titles a year for many of the major publishing houses. Although the world of audio books has been immensely satisfying for Kessler, he is the first to point out that the field is undergoing a dynamic shift: "Many more audio publishers seem to be entering the field as more and more product is being offered." He says that online distribution has had both a positive and a negative impact on the market. "Online retail outlets such as iTunes have been very helpful to the industry in terms of making audio books available to the masses. In fact, many more people have gotten into audio books as a result, and the market has gotten bigger."

He says that he has seen changes, though, in terms of attention to detail and production values—additionally, production budgets have been shrinking. "The publishers still care about quality, of course, but in some cases the audio quality is suffering."

Photo by Jeff Touzeau

An interior shot of Kessler Media, a prolific audio book producer.

Overall, the market for audio books is very healthy, with many interesting content dimensions. For the right person, it is an excellent opportunity to combine technical, production, and musical skills in a single working environment.

Job Profiles and Career Opportunities

Companies that produce audio books have use for a wide array of talent, both technical and non-technical. Because a staff can consist of as few as two people, up to, say, five people, employees are usually able to gain exposure to all the areas that comprise production.

The smaller the production house, the more you will have a chance to understand and master different roles. At larger audio book production houses, people fit into roles more concisely and tend to have their roles carved out more explicitly. An audio book production house can be a fulfilling environment, both from a content perspective and as a production environment, because there is the opportunity to combine the literary arts with high-quality audio production.

Overall Team Composition

Audio book houses have room for both junior- and senior-level people. Some of the common roles include audio editors, engineers, and music composers. Increasingly, many "one-stop shop" audio book houses also include voice talent on staff.

Director/producers work with the publisher to define the overall vision for the audio book. They pull together the required resources on staff to get the job done on schedule, while ensuring the quality of the final product. They are also the glue for the project, responsible for choosing and interfacing with the appropriate voice talent, specifying the music, and seeing that the project passes through the entire lifecycle without a hitch.

Career Path in Audio Books

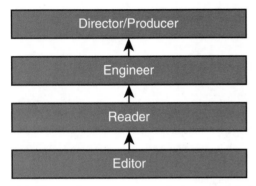

This illustration represents what a career ladder might look like in publishing for audio books.

Audio book production houses typically rely on their own staff and a host of freelancers who can help provide the necessary resources as impending deadlines loom. Because this business is based around publishing calendars and deadlines, there can often be an intense push toward the end of a project—this may entail long hours.

Next, we'll take a look at some of the audio positions available in audio books from the top down.

Director/Producer ($65,000 to $175,000+)

The director/producer is often the owner of the facility. In addition to his other duties, he is responsible for hiring and maintaining staff, managing payroll and expenses, as well as seeking out new business. The director's main responsibility is to gain an understanding of the clients' intentions and provide artistic direction and guidance on how to best execute the project. This can include specifying and sourcing the appropriate talent and music, providing direction to the talent (especially during narration), and providing relevant guidance to engineers and editors.

It is not uncommon for the director/producer to juggle several projects at once. During the morning, there might be a tracking session with a voiceover artist, and during the afternoon, the director/producer might supervise a music composition. Ultimately, the director/producer is at the top of the hierarchy and is responsible for whether the artistic vision has been carried out successfully.

Because he is ultimately responsible for the quality of the finished product, the director/producer often has a very intimate understanding of the roles that come into play with respect to editing and engineering the audio book. He usually works with a stable of editors who know how things should be presented sonically, since the art of editing speech can be very intricate indeed.

Robert Kessler describes dialogue as "music" and says that people who have a natural aptitude for music tend to really understand the product and process. "In terms of the audio book world, those people that are musical are often the best editors," he says. "People without the musical sensitivity generally do not understand that narration and voice recording is singing without melody. It's all about phrasing, delivery, art. It's music, but without pitch. I've trained hundreds of editors, and either they get it or they don't. When they're musical, they generally get it. Being technically proficient with digital editing is simply not enough."

Engineer ($25,000 to $100,000)

The engineer functions as a kind of co-pilot to the director/producer. Not only is he responsible for things such as the quality of the signal chain, microphone selection, and mixdown, he also is an important sounding board for the director/producer for the duration of the project. The engineer is intimately aware of not only the technical and scheduling goals of the project, but the artistic ones—he can often sit in the director/producer's chair when necessary.

If an engineer is working independently alongside the director/producer, his role will typically entail opening up the studio and setting up for the session. He will set up microphones, make sure all the equipment is working properly, and basically ensure that once the director/producer is working, everything is running smoothly from a technical perspective. The pressure to get things right in an audio book session is exactly the same as in a music session—the engineer must ensure that performances are captured accurately and without technical glitches, because the narrative performance of a voiceover artist might be impossible to replicate.

The engineer must document all the technical conditions for each performance. This means keeping immaculate records of how far the artist is speaking from the microphone, the microphone(s) used, the input gain levels on the preamplifier, and any outboard settings on EQs or compressors. It is common for audio book houses to use a clean signal chain, meaning that any effects, compression, or EQ are usually applied during the mix phase rather than the tracking phase to ensure that they are starting from a known position during the mix.

Because the engineer is essentially second in command, in most shops he is aware of all the required roles in audio book production. He can handle any of these roles if required, and he is usually an expert editor with deep knowledge of DAW systems, as well as other hardware and software. The audio book engineer's role often entails tasks such as re-routing cables, dialing in DSP settings, and sourcing the correct microphones or other outboard gear for a project. It can also involve archiving and filing previous audio projects, as well as maintaining the sound library—a very important component of an audio book environment.

One of the most important roles of the engineer is to help keep the producer focused on the talent's performance. The engineer needs to be sensitive to tone, inflection, and phrasing, as well as be able to catch any mistakes or misreadings, since the audio book must exactly mirror the manuscript. This is a very important job indeed—if a mistake isn't caught and the final work is submitted to the publisher, the publisher might reject the recording or demand a retake.

An example of what a DAW environment might look like in an audio book facility.

Editor ($18,000 to $35,000+)

Editors are the last stop before the final project gets mixed and mastered. Their role is very important as well, because they have a strong influence over the flow of the narration. They have the ability to make pauses between words longer or shorter, and this can have a direct effect on how convincing the flow of the storyline is. They are also responsible for ensuring that level mismatches or EQ anomalies are taken care of before the final mixdown stage.

The editing process involves cutting together the correct takes, as well as eliminating any coughs, breaths, lip smacking, or other noises in the recording that might be distracting for the listener. This job can be long and tedious, but it definitely requires a certain skill. Robert Kessler describes the "zone-like" condition editors can often find themselves in: "You enter a zone where you are no longer thinking—you're just doing. It's such minutia type of work. You're going after little mouth noises that you know just have to be clean, and there are often hours and hours of this stuff. You can ask an editor, 'What do you think about the book?' But they have no idea because they are totally focused on the flow—this can be a *good* thing."

Diplomacy   Technical Skills
Client Skills
Musical Ear Attention to Detail
Literary Background   Patience
Empathy

Some of the traits that the audio book industry might find valuable.

Entering and Succeeding in the Audio Book Market

To enter the audio book market, a background or interest in the literary arts is especially useful because producing a successful audio book requires an understanding of what the author was trying to accomplish with words. The translation of these words into recorded audio is entirely in the hands of the production staff; therefore, a decent command of the English language, as well as an appreciation of good literature, is always a benefit. This can make a liberal arts education especially desirable.

Many people in the audio book industry emerge from liberal arts colleges and music schools, but this isn't necessarily required if you are able to gain a technical understanding of the required gear from another source. Having full competency of DAWs is a prerequisite for any applicant, as is true in many other career fields in audio. Another key competency many audio book employers require is previous experience with voice work, which can come from commercials, ADR, or other voiceover work.

Two common ways people gain entry into the field are by interning and through freelance work. Because audio book studios are typically small shops, this gives the owners a chance to screen the abilities of prospective employees without making a long-term commitment. Bringing someone on board as a full-time staff member can be a big decision for an audio book employer, and a wrong choice can disrupt plenty of business activities.

This arrangement works well for both parties. Clearly, there are benefits to having an internship or a freelance arrangement. This gives the intern or freelancer the ability to feel out the employer before making a commitment, as well as the ability to cherry-pick skills or roles that appear to be interesting or lucrative.

Good audio book freelancers can develop an eco-system of audio book employers. If they gain a good reputation through their reliability and high-quality work, they can gain the loyalty of several employers while commanding a good hourly or project-based wage. Loyal relationships can lead to full-time employment—an audio book employer is far more likely to employ a known entity than to hire an audio-school grad.

Another way folks can gain entry into the world of audio books is as a supplier or a client. Often, audio book shops work with outside music library companies, equipment rental facilities, voice talent, literary agents, publishers, freelance maintenance engineers, and a host of other parties. As pointed out earlier in this book, your audio career is really all about connections, networking, and developing relationships over a career.

Many audio grads have the required skill sets, but having the right personality and temperament can make all the difference. Kessler describes this temperament: "People who want to get into this business should have a tolerance for ambiguity," he says. "I keep jumping from project to project, and I just love the mosaic jigsaw puzzle of managing multiple projects." He says that it is important for someone to be able to shift gears on a moment's notice.

Benefits and Drawbacks of Working in the Audio Book Industry

Working in the audio book industry can bring great intellectual satisfaction, but as in any other field, it has its stressful and boring moments. There is no getting around publishers' deadlines and no escaping the occasional droll manuscript, which can take a seemingly endless amount of time to record and edit.

Stress and Work/Life Balance

Audio books tend to work on a project cycle, and most audio book houses can have several titles due during a common timeframe, coinciding with book publishers' release dates. Because manufacturing, book reviews, advertising, and so many other business requirements correspond to these dates, deadlines are not flexible. This can mean long hours toward the end of a book project

Benefits and Drawbacks of
Working in Audio Books

Reliable Clients	Intense Deadlines
Reasonable Hours	Must Juggle Many Projects
Good Job Security	At Mercy of Publisher
Increased Distribution Options	Uncertain Future Technologies
Intellectually Stimulating	Increasing Competition
Can Work Anywhere	Can Be Monotonous

because the entire staff (and often freelancers) have to do what it takes to get the title completed. "Deadlines are usually based around seasons, which hit at the same time," says Kessler. "At any given time, I might have 15 audio books going on at a single time—that's a lot of work. You spread it between four publishers, but suddenly all the due dates can occur around the same time."

Audio book houses can be different from traditional recording studios in that many owners and clients maintain regular business hours, except when facing the abyss of deadlines. This can be a very welcome industry trait to the seasoned engineer, who might be used to 14-hour days and working the occasional all-nighter. "I have the advantage of having my own studio," says Kessler. "In the beginning, though, I was working 14- or 15-hour days. I would enjoy the feeling of just pushing. Eventually I wanted regular hours, though. So now we try to work Monday through Friday, 10 a.m. to 6 p.m. Of course things come up, but we really try to maintain normal hours."

Another dynamic is that audio book facilities are to some degree at the mercy of the book publisher. For example, the book publisher might have a very light catalog of books coming out in the spring, but might have a load of books scheduled in the fall. The owner of the audio book operation has to plan for these discrepancies the best he can, and the staff must pick up any unexpected slack.

Overall, this is a highly desirable field for someone interested in the technical and artistic side of audio who is also intent on having a life outside of audio.

Work Environment

The work environment of the audio book industry is, as Kessler describes, a mosaic. Often, many recording projects are going on simultaneously, and the entire staff needs to be able to shift gears seamlessly to a completely new project. One day they might be working on a music score for a children's project, and another day they might be recording a high-profile politician, author, or celebrity actor.

The beauty of audio books is that the environment can be intellectually stimulating and can shift genres or cultures at a moment's notice. In this kind of environment, employees need to stay on their toes and be aware of emerging recording technologies.

Job Security

The world of audio books can offer some degree of job security. Just as death and taxes are certainties, books will likely always be published, and the onset of the electronic revolution won't change that anytime soon. Many of the big publishing houses have been in business for more than a century and rely on modern-day talent to help get their content across to the widest possible channel of audience. This means that as long as publishers stay in business, the income stream for talented audio book houses can remain relatively uninterrupted.

Compensation

As noted earlier in this chapter, compensation is reasonable, even for entry-level workers. Many audio book production houses include health benefits for employees, something one can never take for granted or ignore in this day and age of rising healthcare costs. For freelancers, there is a huge opportunity for overtime work—especially during deadlines—because, as mentioned earlier, audio book houses must do what it takes to hit the publisher's deadline.

Geography

Geography has become less and less important with the advent of the Internet age, but the key publishing houses remain in New York City, London, and other international cities. This isn't going to change anytime soon, and developing an in-person rapport with the client team is always important. Therefore, for people seeking employment in the audio world—particularly freelancers—it is highly recommended that you are located where there is a geographic concentration of publishing houses.

Is the Audio Book Market Right for You?

The audio book industry, though definitely a niche part of the overall audio business, offers a secure, intellectually rewarding environment for audio professionals. In the world of audio books, you can apply your musical sensitivity, interest in literature and culture, and technical acumen in a single project. Multiple projects over a long period of time can make for a rewarding career.

Most audio books are recorded in voice booths such as this. Proper acoustic isolation is absolutely critical.

Kessler concludes, "Audio books is a wonderful field that has kept me current. Publishing is everything. Not just books—it's media, it's news, everything. It's a means of delivering current thought. As a result, you get to work with the thought leaders of the day." Working in the audio book world has given Kessler and other audio book professionals a window to the changing world's stage: "It's a close look at ideas and trends that are affecting cultural expression. You see the formation of ideas, you see how they grow, what media starts to glom onto it. Just the way public opinion develops."

A Closer Look: Robert Kessler and the Audio Book Industry

Robert Kessler is one of the audio book industry's pioneers. He arrived in the audio book industry by way of his love for music and the arts. Though he didn't specifically target being an audio book producer, he developed a myriad of skills that would ultimately prove to be invaluable to his role as an audio book producer. One of the skills he picked up along the way was public relations, a skill that comes in handy every day with his clients. In speaking with Kessler, I realized how good he is with people. I also realized that he considers achieving a high-quality end result to be of paramount importance.

Robert Kessler.

When did you first feel the urge to spread your wings and leave Carnegie Hall?

Carnegie Hall was going through a major renovation in the mid-'80s. I had been almost 10 years in the business and had really worked with the best. Meeting legends like Segovia, pianists like Vladimir Horowitz, and violinists like Isaac Stern and Itzhak Perlman was fantastic, but after a while I was feeling the need to become an artist again. At the same time, equipment costs were coming down so that you could just get into home studio recording. I decided to pursue my own thing and went after music composition. At the time, audio books was an area that was just getting off the ground, and I was working in all different styles getting jobs freelance composing. Many of the gigs I would get in those days were writing music for audio books.

How did you get interested in the audio side of things?

I got very interested in the Carnegie Hall studio when I was working there. They had just moved in and built it. There was a wonderful engineer there named Ceszek Wojcek, and I got very interested in the recording side of it. The studio was being hired out to do audio book recordings and some post-production with Simon and Schuster, so that's how I was connected. I started writing music for Simon and Schuster. This was the mid-'80s, and the entire industry was still new. There were obviously some early audio recordings, like Cadmon's recordings of Dylan Thomas readings and such, but these had never really hit the mass market as far as I know.

Did you know that this could lead to a full-time gig?

I started writing music, going after other publishers, and I started getting a lot of work writing music. It was very creative and truly a balancing act. When the Hall was shut down for the renovation, it was oddly serendipitous. There were these weird, circumstantial things hinting at me to just quit and go do it. So I finally did. I quit my job and started doing a lot of documentary films—a lot of short films. I networked. I would do things like look up alumni at my college, Vassar College. I would look for people doing what I wanted to do and network. I also did lots of short industrial films, including films for Ronald Reagan. One of their clients was a defense contractor, and it was right during Star Wars. I would create these seven- or eight-minute scores about components of SDI. It was definitely a weird gig.

How did you manage such high levels of expectation? Did you have a lot of confidence in your ability to deliver?

What was odd about it is that I have a music partner that I write with, Ethan Neuburg, who has now been arranging for Warner Bros. and Alfred Music for more than 20 years. We would get these gigs, and after a while, we knew we could write. We had all our bases covered and had the training. The only thing I doubted was how to charge for it. I remember after doing several films telling the client, "This is too much work for what we're getting paid." So I doubled our rates, and they said, "Fine." The thing you learn is that the more you charge, the more people respect what you are doing. I also felt competent in the recording, even though my initial setup was pretty basic. The first piece of gear I owned semi-pro was the Tascam 388 with 7-1/2" reels and built-in DBX, a Juno 60, and a Yamaha RX15 drum machine.

Was there an important moment that served as a catalyst to move things forward?

The one gig that turned a lot of things around was the time we wrote a music library for Harper Audio. We had to write 300 pieces of music, 32 styles. We wrote an entire library. At the time, everyone was using music libraries, but you'd hear the same pieces and you immediately knew the music wasn't terribly original—so we created a custom library for them. After that project, we knew there was nothing we couldn't write.

You seem to have taken a few risks early on to get into this line of work. Would you consider taking similar risks now?

I definitely wouldn't have even considered quitting my job if I had a family. I was focused on doing documentaries, audio and industrial stuff. Random House was just getting their audio book business off the ground, and they were looking for producers. I originally pitched them as a composer, but when they saw my resume, they assumed I knew my stuff so they gave me a shot at producing. In the beginning I had so little work that I created systems to keep me busy. The phone would rarely ring. But as nature calls, you wander in the smallest room in the house and always, it would ring at that moment!

So ultimately, there was a shift for you from writing music to producing/directing. When and how did that occur?

I started producing and directing, and that just turned into more producing and directing! Once I started doing that, not many people knew what audio book production was all about. At that point there were about five or six of us scattered around New York. At that point, most of the work was divided among us—we're friends today. There was always so much work that nobody was feeling really competitive. Looking back, it's too bad we didn't unionize—but that's another story.

After a while, I'd be doing these productions and hiring all these freelancers to do the edits and the mixes. When there were appropriate budgets, they would hire me to write the music on top of producing and directing. I got to record with extraordinary talent and then, after recording a book, I would know exactly what kind of music would be appropriate. There is a tone to every book, and your musical queue might be based on a certain geography or a particular time period.

Obviously inter-client skills must be important in your role. What are some of the first things that become important?

You learn very quickly how to work with talent and not to get in the way. You align your directorial patterns to the artists' performance patterns to find out where the hole is to come in. I've worked with many difficult artists—high-profile, difficult kinds of characters. The press work in my past was invaluable in preparing me for this.

What about the technical side? How did that evolve? You weren't an engineer by trade, so you had to pick up this side. Was it rough going?

After a while I realized I didn't need to pay another engineer to record, and I got into it. Before Pro Tools entered the system, mixes were really fun. We would have an edited voice track on one two-track machine with Dolby SR, which was just beautiful. We would then re-record and have two DAT machines with mine and Ethan's music and mix on the fly. It was like a performance, and we did it live. We became accustomed to doing it really well.

Digital editing took away this spontaneity, but it opened up enormous capabilities for the audio book producer. However, to this day, I still love the sound of tape. For me, the sound of tape compression and the SR noise reduction on the human lends a very natural, rich, full-bodied sound that plays well both soft and loud. But we had to make the jump into the audio world; we have five Pro Tools systems now, and I love it. I still have a couple old Otaris in the studio, though.

Is the attention to audio quality deteriorating in some ways?

Now that technology is so accessible to everybody, including the talent, it's spreading the quality thinner. There are audio companies that are telling narrators, "Go out and find public-domain material. You record it, edit, send it to us. If we use it, we'll pay you." The end result is that narrators are recording themselves and editing themselves. Everyone in the business starts to wear a lot of hats at once.

So people are becoming a jack of all trades and master of none.

Right. The last thing I want to end up being in life is doing a lot of things poorly. I'd rather do a couple of things really well. It's a little bit of a changing field right now. There are many more publishers and published books than there were before.

Robert, what are some of the most important things to you in approaching your business?

Quite honestly, one of the most important things to me is becoming a mentor to younger people. I always like to work with folks who are just getting going in their career. These could be recent audio school grads or even high school kids who just don't know what to do next. That piece is almost unrelated to the business, but I have an interest in helping them succeed in their audio careers.

Does the size of an audio book house correlate to the kind of work they get? If you are a bigger audio book house, do you get higher-profile jobs?

We're a little cottage operation here, but just the other day, President Clinton was here. We do very high-end work. Geographically, it turns out we are kind of in a hot spot, Hollywood East if you will. There is a lot film talent that works out here, and we are involved in recording for film and television as well.

So did you put a lot of effort into navigating your career to where it is now?

No. I would say that my getting into this field was very uncalculated. At times I envy those who do know what they want to pursue with a clear path. Mine has always been one of, "I like this; let me see where it's taking me." You're following streams, but you're being honest with yourself, and that gives you satisfaction.

I've always enjoyed different people—learning what makes them tick. I work with people whose politics I don't agree with, and I find that interesting. You have to understand how they work and help them understand immediately that you are not in an adversarial position. You say, "The only reason I am interrupting is to make you sound better."

What would you say future prospects are for someone in this career field and what is the best way to prepare?

Anyone who has an interest in the audio book business, it's here to stay. We're doing much more work for children's books, which I find enormously satisfying. It's material with a message that is trying to communicate directly, emotionally.

On the whole, if you can help the end product be voiced in a more clear way technically, there will always be work for you. It helps to have an interest in literature. As far as audio books, you're really in the publishing business, so you see young writers who develop into major writers. You work with them book after book after book. This can be fascinating if you have an interest in the literary arts, and if you have an interest in the recording arts, it's an obvious place to be.

The interesting thing about spoken-word recording is that there is nowhere to hide. I would go to great studios wherever the author or actor was, and there would be so much signal processing in the chain. It would all just interfere; it was a joke! When we were building our place, we spent a lot of extra time and money on air returns—we had to run more duct to slow down the air volume so as to minimize the noise. Ventilation can be the bane of a studio's effectiveness to record audio books.

What was one of your most rewarding moments during your career as an audio book director/ producer?

I would say when I was co-composer on a 16-part PBS documentary, *Freedom: A History of US*. Christopher Reeve was the creative consultant for the series and brought many celebrities in to voice historical figures. I used to do a lot of work with Christopher Reeve before and after his accident. In fact, we won a Grammy together for his book *Still Me*, which I produced and directed. The same year, I was working as the sound designer with Chris Wedge on "Bunny," an animated short that won an Academy Award. That was a pretty cool year.

A Closer Look: Susan Mackewich

Susan Mackewich is responsible for audio book production at Gizmo Enterprises in New York City. Coming from a television background originally, Mackewich has had the benefit of working with talent for many years. For her, each audio book she records is a performance—one that will hopefully withstand the test of time. Susan loves interacting with voice actors and feels a deep sense of responsibility to her art to ensure that whatever is committed to tape is both accurate and representative of the author's intention.

When did you first become involved in audio?

We go back to 1992, and we built a studio in my home that was actually designed by Russ Berger. I am principally a television producer. As a television producer I was injured, and I couldn't really travel like I had been doing at one point. My husband wanted to start an audio-for-video business where we were doing mixing and layback. He wanted to set up a studio where we could do those things from our home because we were spending all hours out of the house. So we contacted Russ Berger, and he designed a studio for us, and we put it in our home.

Susan Mackewich.

Then we were asked by one of the people that came to us locally to record an audio book. He said, "Could you record one audio book?" He had a library of books that he hadn't done previously. So we agreed to do this recording. I come from television as a producer, and my husband was training me as an audio engineer and producer, and we were training engineers in our business at home. We were also beta testing for Pro Tools at that time. We wanted to record the book in a non-linear digital format. Of course, Pro Tools is much different today—it is much more arduous, and we didn't have a lot of memory. For audio books, though, it seemed like just about enough. So we started recording onto Pro Tools and started to get more requests to do audio books. We landed some work with Thorndike, and they were up in New Hampshire. They heard about us and asked us to take on some audio titles for them. So I began casting in the area and bringing in people to read to see who we could get for audio book narrators.

Quite frankly, there are a lot of gifted actors, but not everyone can do audio work. It is a very different medium for actors, and it uses a different part of their brain. We were doing narration where the actors were all of the characters and the narrator, so we needed to find people who were good character actors who had a good narrative voice and could find the voice of the characters. Not many people can do that—most people can only play a different version of themselves in different venues. You need to find gifted people who are diverse—they may not be famous, but they are excellent actors. These were the types of people we were looking for. So we started to get a stable of actors and began turning out these audio books.

I imagine this was appealing to the actors as well, since you were helping them break into a new area.

Right. We found that people with a good stage background were very good for audio books because they were well-trained and they loved language. They had good diction. If they were repertory, they would have explored many characters in their work. We would put ads in *Backstage* and *Variety*. People would come down by train and audition here. I would pick different sections from different books for them to read to push them vocally and see what they could do—to see how fast they would be with dialects and to see if they could understand and interpret the narrator, or the author's voice. That is essential to it. We were starting to find some very talented people. Some of them were actors, but we had a couple of cases where people came to us with non-acting backgrounds. We had one high school English teacher who was excellent but had never acted—she was quite good, and it came to her very naturally. Then we had excellent actors, but who didn't quite have the knack for audio books. It is a difficult skill that takes both sides of your brain.

Once we had built a stable of actors, we approached Shivers, who had bought some of the Thorndike library. I asked them, "Are you going to be doing audio books? Because we would like to produce some of these titles for you." They said, "If we get into production, we'll call you." And they did—and we started to take on more and more work for them. Then Shivers was acquired by the BBC eventually, and this resulted in an increasing amount of work for us. We've been working with them for about six years, then with Shivers about five years before that. The BBC is the principal publisher that we work for, but we do work for all the major publishers.

There is quite a list of people who are trying to get into audio books, and of course lots of celebrities who like to read audio books. Not all of them are good at it, but some of them are quite good. It is a new employment opportunity for actors.

What kinds of things have stayed the same and what kinds of things have changed in terms of your approach to recording audio books?

The technology has changed drastically. There are certain things about the audio book, though, that doesn't change. For instance, the record method: You are still recording in a very controlled environment—it is a very close-miked situation for the single-voice narration. Then there are simulcast recordings that require a larger space, but people must still be close to the mic. In this scenario we have an ensemble or a full cast. But most of the books are done with single-voice narration where there is just one person doing the title, and they are interpreting everything. The technology has gotten better and better. Pro Tools is our choice and has developed along the lines we had hoped it would for speed and accuracy.

The delivery mediums are different because we are doing an awful lot of MP3 delivery. There is also a lot of digital downloading going on—more so than the hard copies that you would see. The cassette eventually became the CD, and now the CD is becoming less significant as MP3 players become more popular with the digital download opportunities. Those things are changing.

Among the publishers, they have found that once a person listens to an audio book, they are an audio member from then on. They are hooked, and they like audio books. Publishers are therefore offering a diverse amount of titles. As far as genres, mysteries are a big favorite. But there is politics, religious books, all sorts of fiction, historical. The government, through the national library system, is recording everything for audio. So pretty much everything you see out there, the government wants recorded.

What personality traits have gotten you the most mileage in this career?

Having a technical knowledge of recording has helped me quite a bit. It has helped me to run down problem-solving in capturing the voice. Directing has been very helpful to me because it has trained me to work with actors and to be able to talk to them and get from them what they may not know they have. Also vocal coaching: I am also a vocalist. I talk to people about how they are using their voice, how to preserve it and treat it. We often do unabridged versions, so we may be recording a week at a time. During that time, the talent is talking constantly—so it is a lot of work on the voice and on the brain. I am constantly talking with actors about how to take care of their voices, how to hydrate in the winter season, even what things we can eat before we record—we can have problems with the sound capture otherwise.

Directing in television has helped me, but the great thing about working in audio books is that I don't have to worry about whether a person wears glasses or what their physical appearance is at all. I just need to worry about what kind of actor they are and what kind of depth they have. I have been able to direct and experience some of the greatest acting, beyond what I was doing in video. Some of the performances have been just spellbinding and wonderful. I do feel at times that I have participated in creating the history of this art form. Audio books aren't as popular as television yet, but they do have a very passionate audience. The reviewership has changed over the years I have been in it and is much more sophisticated now. The reviewer is highly aware of the process and really able to give us good criticism of what we are doing.

All of the classics, all of the public domain work that is out there, is being done because you don't have audio book rights for that. You don't have to get licensing, and you can record public domain titles. So all those are done. The trend now is on the new writers, and that has become a little more of a challenge because we have to wait for them to create these books. If they've recorded two in a series, and it has become very popular, we may wait for the author to finish the next one. It may not be ready when the publisher is ready to release it because it is a creative medium.

More and more, some of the authors are thinking about how their work is going to sound as an audio book as they are writing them. I know Stephen King does—he considers who the narrators will be and how it will sound when it goes out to the audience.

What are some of the common pressures that you face on a regular basis?

One of the pressures is getting a recordable manuscript before the record session and turning around the product before the publisher needs it to release. They are doing a simultaneous release now, where the print version and the audio version are published at the same time. The recordable manuscript is very often just getting done as the last print version is getting approved for release. So we are always up against that in terms of time. But Pro Tools has been a great help for us because it has allowed us to edit, turn around, and finish the masters pretty quickly. Now we have that lead time between record and mastering so that they can get it in time to duplicate and release to the general market. All the audio book producers will tell you that this is one of the pressures we face.

What kind of infrastructure do you need to get this accomplished?

The prep of the book has to be done quite extensively by the actor. Depending on what is going on with the book, the director and the actor will talk about the book beforehand and figure out what needs to be addressed. As the producer of the work, I need to know that all of the words will be said with the right intention as well as be pronounced correctly, because we cannot allow people to listen to words that are not pronounced correctly or in good English. Of course now, the authors also have a choice about actors. They are approving actors and wanting to know who is going to be recording the book. That has become more prevalent. So a lot of research goes into pre-production.

Then, when we get in the studio, we have to time the manuscript and see how many studio days we will need. That is always a bit of a gamble because the actor may not be able to do it in the time we allocate. They may have a higher pickup ratio of mistakes, et cetera, so that is always a little bit of a gamble. We have to manage that scrupulously because you are also paying the actor—sometimes by the studio hour, sometimes by the finished hour. Finished hour would be how long it would be in total to listen to the whole book. For example, to listen to an entire book, it might be nine hours. If the actor has a 3:1 ratio, it may take us 27 hours to record that book. If the actor lays it down faster, it can be a 2:1 ratio. That is always something we are trying to gauge, and it is always a consideration in the actors we use. We want to make sure we use the actors who can accomplish the work in the time that we have.

What is your typical staff on a project?

There is me, an engineer, and very often someone else who has some background in the English language. Sometimes we have terrific engineers who do a great job with the sound capture, but who may not have as much knowledge about the language or literature. Then the books have to be proofed—usually, that is on the publisher's end, where they have someone who will listen to it, and they send us corrections. We will then incorporate that into a master.

Pretty much because of the way the publishers acquire the titles, we need to deliver the master verbatim. So we can't interpret or allow something to be said another way because of how the actor wants to perform it. The actor can impart their influence, but they cannot go off the script, and all the words need to be right. If we have done our job, there should be no discernable difference between the text and the recording.

We use a universal script-noting technique, so if an engineer who is the recordist also becomes the editor, then they are following the same script. They will have the notes to do things like taking out breaths, doing volume changes in case someone is coming in hot on a pickup. Also, we will be recording the tone of the room. We have developed many techniques for recording and editing over time, and the technology has become our aid.

How do you find your editors?

We train them in-house mostly. All of our engineers have college in their background, although this is not mandatory. You have to be quite talented and understand the process and what we are doing. They need Pro Tools knowledge, although there are other platforms that are used, like Vegas. We use Pro Tools because we need to interchange files. We could be working on dialogue editing one day, then doing an audio book the next. Because we do post and audio files, we have to be able to create OMF files that can be laid against audio. So it has to be a complementary audio path for us. Our editors and recordists do lots of other things besides audio books. They do short-form commercials, dialogue editing for documentaries, any kind of audio.

How do you stay current with the industry? Is there a trade magazine that helps with this?

AudioFile started as a newsletter; now it is the foremost critical and technical review magazine for the audio book industry. Everything that is being covered—every author, every actor—is covered in depth. That is a standard over the years and is an amazing source for everything audio books. They talk about all the new technology, what everything is going to look like in the future. They talk to the publishers, they talk about the technical side, and they talk about the actors—so they really cover all their bases. *AudioFile* provides a forum for how the industry really works—kind of like *EQ*.

How does someone in college break into this field?

If they are taking literature or have had an opportunity to listen to what is out there, that is a plus. You can, of course, work on Pro Tools at home now, so there are many people doing editing at home, getting studio files, then turning them around. The home environment for capturing audio isn't really where it needs to be—you really need very isolated record spaces. You don't need Pro Tools|HD to get started.

What basic skills do you need to make it as an editor?

It is a very subtle ear that you have to develop; it is a very intense environment with lots of editing. You have to be very quick; you have to be able to evaluate, troubleshoot, and record.

It may take a week to record and complete one project. If you are doing commercials, it may take you two hours.

What are some of the subtleties of recording voice?

It is very difficult to record to make it palatable. People have to breathe, and they have to belch; sometimes we feel like we are gastrointestinal specialists. Sometimes a person will be healthy but come in with a cold the next day—we have to be sensitive to this. We may have to come back so we can match the voice, so the engineering ears have to be very good for what we do.

Tell me about a moment when you felt really aligned with your passions doing this work.

One was while we were doing a first-person account of a person who was imprisoned in Iran. We recorded a first-person account of what happened to her. I feel a great responsibility as a producer because I know that this work is going to be out there for several hundred years at least. So we really need to get it right and need to be scrupulous about it so that it will be around for future generations. We have to do right by the author today so that the audiences can enjoy it for a long time to come—long after we're gone. I did a book with Vernon Jordan, who was the chief consultant to Bill Clinton during his presidency. We did his book, and he narrated it. I never knew what tremendous work he did in civil rights. He is a tremendous hero who is unsung, and no one really knows much about him.

We were doing corrections on the book, and I was asking him for retakes. He is a little bit senior now, and he said, "Do we have to do all this?" And I said to him, "Mr. Jordan, my name will not be on this, but I am thinking of your great-great-grandson, who will want to hear this and will be listening to your voice. It is my responsibility today to make you sound the best you can sound. I can't allow anything but the best to go out." He then got a big grin on his face and said, "Let's do it!" We have a real responsibility to make sure we are getting the best that day. There is a lot of detail to it—it doesn't seem like it would be much; it would seem to be very straight-forward. But there is a great deal to consider, and that's why there is a lot of pressure—because you want to make sure you get it right.

4 The Sound for Picture Market

The sound for picture market is composed of two areas that can be relatively simply defined—location audio (in other words, audio done during a shoot) and audio post-production. The resulting work can appear in various forms, which may include advertising, films and DVDs, animated cartoons, sound effects (or Foley work), or even gaming (which, as one of the fastest growing areas of the sound for picture market, thus finds its own section in Chapter 2 of this book).

Location audio can include capturing dialogue from actors on a set or recording on-location sound effects. Audio post-production involves setting all things audio to picture after the footage is shot. This can include sound effects or Foley, music composition, ADR (*automated dialogue replacement*), and obviously mixing. Audio post-production has been an integral part of the television and film business since a musical score was first synchronized to a moving picture in 1926, with the movie *Don Juan*.

Sound continues to be an essential part of visual media today and can dramatically influence human perception of a TV ad, a major motion picture, or Saturday morning cartoons. And within the sound for picture market, there are dozens of roles—many of them requiring widely diverse skill sets.

Market Viability

Video as a technology medium has blossomed over the last decade due to relentless technical innovation. HDTV, high-quality mobile devices, DVDs (including HD DVDs under development), and the Internet have all contributed to our culture becoming more dependent on video as a communication vehicle. Audio has been moving in parallel with these developments, with 5.1 surround becoming more and more dominant as the consumer's preferred playback format and with 7.1 not too far off in the wings.

At first glance, you might think the market has become fragmented. Indeed, it has—but as a result, many submarkets have matured and can support a host of audio professionals. These distinct but interrelated markets include advertising, feature films and animation, television, and corporate communications—all of which are still experiencing reasonable growth. This provides a skilled audio professional with many options, says Ryan Collison, Foley engineer at New York's Sound One: "Stations like EFX and USA are all making shows, so there is a lot more work being generated. There are all these poker shows and reality shows—they all need post work. The most important thing to decide in this business is what your niche is."

Job Profiles and Career Opportunities

There are many job profiles in sound for picture, both creative and technical. The more creative roles include composer, sound designer, Foley artist, and music supervisor. More technical roles include recording engineer, mixer, and editor. Not surprisingly, creative and technical roles often intersect and interplay; therefore, it is certainly desirable (and often required) to have knowledge bridging both areas. For example, a composer should have enough technical knowledge to work in a DAW environment, and a mixer must have an understanding of how music affects the context of the moving picture.

Certain roles in sound for picture can be very lucrative, depending on how ambitious you are. The worth of composers and mixers on a project can directly correlate to their track record and past performance. Often, in-demand composers and mixers work for management companies and are hired on fee-based projects, similar to the way many high-profile record producers work (see Chapter 12, "A Career in Freelancing"). That said, there are many staff positions available in the business. Well-known audio post houses, such as Howard Schwartz in New York City, rely on seasoned employees to keep clients coming back. The key in any client-based environment is to develop a track record and loyal clientele who are willing to come back again and again.

Photo by Jeff Touzeau.

This poster greets you when you enter Vagabond Audio, a facility in Chicago that specializes in audio for video.

There are many, many roles in audio for video. Some large post houses employ dozens of staff, including specialists in ADR, Foley, mixing, and other disciplines. At smaller companies, the job titles tend to overlap more—therefore, you can be exposed more quickly to new skill sets.

Location Sound Recordist ($35,000 to $75,000+)

The location sound recordist must capture the dialogue and other required audio on location in real time, working directly alongside the film crew. He or she usually works against a script and with a supervising sound editor during the actual filming of television or movie sequences. The location sound recordist must have an excellent understanding of audio file types, microphone placement principles, signal chain, and remote audio capture practices. Typically, shotgun microphones are used because dialog often needs to be captured at far distances. When capturing on-location audio, the location sound recordist must take meticulous notes on settings and microphones used, in case these conditions need to be re-created later in ADR.

For the location sound recordist, a solid operational understanding of the gear is an absolute must—there is no time to reference operational manuals and usually only a single chance to get it right. The location recordist usually works alongside a boom operator, who specializes in ensuring that the microphone is positioned advantageously and as close as possible to the actors who are speaking—operating the boom is an art in itself and a highly desirable skill when on location. While ADR and effects are also sometimes captured on location following a shoot, location sound typically consists of sound deriving from the shoot itself—which is most always imperfect and incomplete due to less than perfect circumstances.

Supervising Sound Editor ($80,000 to $140,000+)

The supervising sound editor's role is to manage the mixers, ADR and Foley teams, editors, composers, and sound designers and pull together a comprehensive soundtrack. His role is to leverage the talents of everyone involved and deliver excellent results to the producer or post-production supervisor. This very often involves identifying the right talent for the individual roles, identifying and booking the studios, managing budgets and timetables, and signing off on final work in all areas before the final soundtrack mix is laid down.

Very often, the supervising sound editor works for the company producing the film or television show, rather than for the post house or other creative sound facility where the soundtrack is being created (unless the companies are one and the same, as in the case of Lucasfilm). Although this is not an overly technical role, the supervising sound editor must have a clear understanding of the parameters of each role and how they interplay. Very often, a supervising sound editor will have achieved technical mastery from his or her own experience as a composer, mixer, or location sound recordist.

Composer ($55,000 to $100,000+)

Composers can be either on staff or freelance, depending on the demand a particular production may experience. In many cases, composers have a salaried position with a bonus structure or another commission-based structure as an incentive toward bringing in clients. One very clear benefit to being a composer is that titles are often copyrighted under the artist's name, and song titles can kick off royalties—which can certainly increase overall take-home pay. For a composer who has been in the business a while, this can be a significant source of income over and above a base salary.

The composer's job is very difficult, however. He or she must understand the vision of the video piece and capture the emotional direction—very often removing his or her own creative views or preferences. A good composer does not necessarily have to be musically trained, as the Peter Fish profile later in this chapter illustrates, but he should be able to write music very quickly across a wide range of musical genres—from classical, to rock, to jazz and beyond—and capture the spirit of the picture, and not just his own creative vision. This role is also difficult because writing music often requires inspiration—it does not happen automatically, like turning on a water faucet.

Sample Career Path in Music for Picture

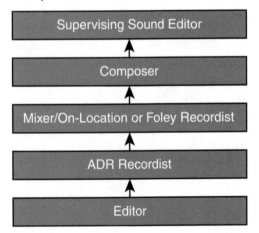

This illustration represents what a career ladder might look like in audio for picture.

Mixer ($40,000 to $120,000+)

When mixing sound for picture, the key thing to remember is that the audio must support the overall vision for the production. This makes sound for picture very different from, say, record production, where the only sensory perception is sound. Also, in sound for picture, there are often many more elements to mix, such as ADR, on-location dialogue, sound effects, and music. When you add up all these elements, a mix can easily exceed 96 tracks—considering tracks that are comped. (*Comped* is when a single track is a "composite" of several other edited tracks.) For this reason, a couple of the mixer's best friends must be organization and automation.

At many larger post houses, mixers' roles may be broken out to specific disciplines. For example, distinct job roles might exist for sound effects mixers, who ensure that the effects map seamlessly to the visual image and the rest of the soundtrack with no interruption or audible imperfection.

This includes how the sound effects are treated sonically—the perceived volume, reverb, processing, and other aspects must be perfectly aligned.

Foley Artist ($35,000 to $75,000+)

Foley artists have one of the more unique jobs in the business—creating sound effects that are otherwise not able to be sourced via samples or through sound design. This is a very demanding job that requires creative use of everyday objects and surfaces to create extraordinary sounds. A watermelon may be sliced to simulate a guillotine beheading, while celery may be broken to simulate the impact of a body blow. Foley artists give a motion picture or television show the added dimension to make it seem real.

Two of the key considerations for Foley work are sound quality and timing. First, the sound quality must match as closely as possible the sound environment of the on-location recording. For example, if dialogue is captured in a certain manner (such as in a quiet room with condenser mics), the Foley artist might want to capture his sound effects in a similar manner. And to ensure that the timing is just right, the Foley artist might work in front of a visual monitor on which the picture is playing; effects are performed in real time, and any minor adjustments to timing can be fine tuned later.

ADR Recordist ($25,000 to $50,000+)

While recording sound for picture, it is very common for much of the dialogue and other location audio to be rendered unusable due to unwanted noise or required changes in the production or script. Therefore, ADR recordists capture dialogue after the fact, usually with the same actors who appeared on the set location, but in more controlled conditions, such as in an acoustically controlled voiceover booth. This can be particularly tricky because the audio must match as closely as possible that which was captured on the set by the boom operators. ADR recordists take great care to ensure that common recording distances, EQ settings, processing, and microphone choices are similar to what was done during the live setting. Once again, ADR relies on video monitoring to ensure that timing is accurate.

Editor ($35,000 to $60,000)

Despite the revolutionary changes in audio technology, the editor's role has remained relatively unchanged. One of the key responsibilities of the editor is to document, organize, and archive footage so it is easily accessible and identifiable. The editor may be dedicated to working on ADR or Foley or may work alongside the mixer. No matter where he is working, the editor's role typically involves carving up the audio into pieces that are easily retrieved and usable for others to integrate into their work. The editor's work is also to remove undesirable artifacts in the audio, such as blips, breaths, buzzing, or other anomalies the mixer will not want to deal with.

Entering and Succeeding in the Sound for Picture Market

Success in the sound for picture market largely revolves around—what a surprise!—hard work and determination. Many of the traits that are valued in other aspects of the audio industry are important in sound for picture as well: client savvy, focus, a can-do attitude, and the ability to get along with others and work in a team environment. The operative word here is "team" because, unlike many other audio fields, sound for picture requires such an approach, especially when you consider the players and various components: Foley, mixing, location audio, ADR, and so on. These elements are all part of a machine that needs to work seamlessly toward a common creative goal.

It is relatively easy to get a foot in the door of the sound for picture market. However, decent pay comes after a dues-paying phase that nearly everyone must go through. It is not uncommon to have a mail clerk work his or her way up to become the lead Foley recordist or engineer; therefore, patience and perseverance are key.

In terms of technical preparation, by far the most important skill set to have is an understanding of Pro Tools. Whereas this may be required to a lesser degree in other fields, in video Pro Tools is used as the standard recording/editing platform to interface with video. Other formal education isn't required, but it is obviously considered desirable. Employers aren't just looking for individuals with skill sets, they are seeking well-rounded individuals who can grow, see the big picture, and help their business expand.

The most valuable training you can receive will be on the job. A key thing here is to align yourself with the right group of people who will support you, train you, and help you grow. In the initial stages of a sound for picture career, this often-overlooked fact can be far more important than the salary. In sound for picture, the people working alongside you will have very diverse backgrounds and connections, so establishing a strong network early and carefully selecting your peers can pay dividends later.

Post-production is one of the last steps in the film and TV production processes; therefore, there can be strict deadlines, often accompanied by stress. When a program is up against a deadline, long hours can ensue, though this isn't the norm.

Also, with the exception of location recording, sound for picture work usually occurs at the studio, so working remotely usually isn't a viable option unless you own a studio that is well equipped and you have an established reputation. And where you live and who you know can have a direct impact on your success: Vancouver, Toronto, New York, Chicago, and Los Angeles are all hot spots, with the overwhelming majority of work being located in Los Angeles.

An interesting aspect of the sound for picture world is that its ecosystem contains many different roles; therefore, it is entirely possible to transfer into a different role to extend your capabilities or further your career in a different direction if you so choose. Composing, mixing, sound effects, and voice dialogue all surround one another and are all within reach.

Traits Valued in the Sound for Picture Field

I've already covered the most common traits that will get you mileage in the sound for picture field: hard work, determination, and your ability to be a team player. These are common and enduring traits throughout many of the fields this book covers. Frankly, there is no replacement for these, and you should strive to learn and attain them if they don't come naturally. Obviously, the field values a strong creative sense—especially visual. If you are someone who has a keen eye for good photography or design or who has appreciation for a cinematic storyline, you might find yourself at a creative advantage.

Networking   Technical Skills
Client Skills
Collaborative Attention to Detail
Hard Work
Perseverance Determination

Here are some basic traits that may be valued in the sound for picture industry.

Another trait this field values is the ability to be happy in a supporting role. When working in sound for picture, 99 percent of the time you are working toward the success of someone else's vision—it is rarely your own vision. However, this does not minimize how rewarding the experience can be—film, television, and video tend to attract the most creative minds in the business, so if you are lucky enough to do Foley on a film such as *Ice Age*, you will be happy to go along for the ride. There is no shortcut to success in sound for picture, and it can take a very long time to reap the financial rewards that can be attained more easily in other fields—but persistence eventually pays off.

Benefits and Drawbacks of Working in the Sound for Picture Market

The sound for picture market is definitely growing as video continues to permeate our society. This means folks who develop a career in this area will have a relatively stable growth trajectory, which is surely a benefit. Also, skills learned in this field can often lead to a lucrative freelance career, depending on your resourcefulness. One of the more appealing aspects for many working in sound for picture may be the people: Many are drawn to the creativity and idealism of being part of the filmmaking process, all striving to achieve a common goal.

Because films and television shows follow a relatively linear production process, work is affected by seasonality. Although there might be periods of intensity toward the end of the production—when most of the audio is laid down—once the film is released, there is often a sense of gratification and relief. There is also more time to catch your breath and perhaps take a vacation before the next production starts.

One of the drawbacks to working in the sound for picture market is the possibility of being stuck on a boring film or television show where the creative vision is lackluster. In cases such as this, mixing or Foley work can seem to go on forever, and the project can seem never-ending. Also, long hours and high stress can pull you away from your outside interests and loved ones for extended periods of time. These effects can be all the more magnified if you have children or are planning to have them.

Benefits and Drawbacks of
Working in Sound for Picture

Growing Field	Mediums Constantly Changing
Many Applications	Erratic Hours/Schedules
Skills in Great Demand	Someone Else's Vision
Widely Varying Projects	Long Ladder Up
Web 2.0 Compatible	Very Competitive Market
Hours Can Be Erratic	Promotion Can Take Years

One of the advantages of working in sound for picture is that video is still considered a cutting edge medium. Internet technologies have only enhanced this view.

Drew Weir of Vagabond Audio adding a sound effects track to a film.

Is the Sound for Picture Market Right for You?

The sound for picture market provides perhaps the most flexibility of all the available fields in audio. There is a tremendous variety of content and potential visual media: cinema, television, DVD, and now even mobile devices. This is a challenging industry to keep up with from a technology perspective alone—but for people with the right kind of drive, it can offer nearly unlimited possibilities.

If you've ever appreciated the emotional value a musical score can bring to a movie, the dimension sound effects can add to a scene, or the vocal quality an actor can bring to an animated character, remember that these were originally just ideas that required development before they came to fruition. Your skills and natural abilities could play an equally important role.

A Closer Look: Drew Weir and the Audio for Video Industry

Drew Weir is owner of Chicago, IL–based Vagabond Audio. I have the greatest respect for Drew because he took on a lot of risk to build his business—there were no guarantees, but his self-assurance proved to prevail. One of the things I noticed about Drew in interviewing him was that he always had a strong compass on where he needed to be, and if things weren't lining up the way he wanted, he sprang into action.

Photo by Jeff Touzeau.

Drew Weir.

Drew, can you tell me the route that ultimately led you to do music for video?

Sure. I became interested in engineering music in college. I went to music school, where they had a recording studio, so I started recording a lot of musicians. Eventually, I was being asked to engineer more sessions than I was being asked to play on, so I assumed my skills were better in engineering. I made a decision pretty early on that I wanted to do recording in college, and I eventually went to Full Sail after completing my four-year degree.

In hindsight, what do you make of your liberal arts educational experience?

It was a wonderful experience to have. Full Sail and other audio colleges can have such a consolidated program—you're in labs or in classes every hour of the day. A liberal arts college is a completely different kind of experience from a trade school.

What did your coursework entail at Full Sail and how did it benefit you?

At the time, their only offerings were in post-engineering, live sound, and music. I took a bunch of courses in post because I liked the creativity in sound design, and it was becoming apparent that a lot of career opportunities were emerging in that area. In fact, many opportunities were emerging near Full Sail in Orlando as well as on the East Coast in general. New York was all post work at the time. After Full Sail, I went and did an internship at WSDG, and it was there that I got the bug to be an owner of a studio someday.

When did post and audio for video enter the picture?

Post hadn't really opened up to me at this point. I still wanted to be a rock star and mix bands. At that time, production was becoming less and less about tape machines and boards and more about Pro Tools. With the DAW revolution, it was understood that everyone was soon going to have a studio in their bedroom, so there was a lot of concern around a career as a music engineer at that time. There was also concern because of the increased number of schools teaching this stuff.

I stuck with it, and the opportunity came up to be an assistant at the advertising firm Chiat Day. They had a post-production company in house with video editing, and they were looking for an assistant. I had never seen an Avid system before, but I was able to figure it out. They got a sound booth, and we recorded some voiceovers in house. Most large ad agencies have these kinds of facilities with varying degrees of success.

The nice thing was that I was working with someone who was very experienced—he had done Super Bowl commercials. We had a pretty modest setup that included a reel-to-reel and a couple of mics. I started doing more and more of this, as well as doing some sound design. Eventually we got a Pro Tools rig, and I started mixing commercials, and I loved it. All told, I worked there for about four years.

Did things begin to get a little stale there after a while? What drove you to the next step?

After four years it became obvious that I wanted to spread my wings. I also wanted to take my experience with me and move to Chicago, where I'm from. I got employed with another video post-production company, a place called New World Editorial that serves outside ad agencies. They had audio post-production and needed an engineer. I worked there for three years until they closed down.

From there I went to Red Carr, another big post-production company based in Chicago with five or six offices and about fifteen to twenty people. They were only doing video post-production, and when New World closed, one of the owners went to Red Carr, so that was my connection. I worked there for three years, and I was the only audio engineer.

After three years my contract was up. I'd been working at all these video places and thought someday I'd like to have my own studio so I could do this stuff the way that I really want to do it. After all, by this point I'd been doing this for 10 years and had the credits to my name. I realized I had the ability to convince someone that I'm worth investing in. I decided that I wanted to open up a boutique facility entirely focused on sound design and mixing.

That seems like an enormous risk nonetheless. What was going through your mind around this time?

I'd been in town for six years, so I had plenty of people I'd worked with. It was a big risk, especially when you consider that we hired the top architects in the world to come in and build a studio for us in Chicago. We'd never owned a studio or even a business before. I was cocky and confident that we were going to make this work, and I had a partner who felt the same way. We knew we could get the money—the cost of opening a studio had come down significantly from where it was just five years before. However, the cost of architecture and construction had remained the same or gone up. It was a little bit of a "build it, and they will come" scenario, but I was well connected and ultimately knew it wouldn't be a problem.

How important were your network and connections at that point? It seems like a frail time for you.

I knew I had enough connections, and there were enough people in the industry telling me that they had confidence in me. I also had a pretty decent reel at the time. Many potential clients had expressed a serious interest in working with me, and I had the attitude of, "I'm going to make this work because it has to." In the back of my mind, I knew that if it didn't work I wouldn't be ruined because I'm still fairly young, and I still have time to crawl back up, regroup, and get back at it if I have to.

What was your personal situation like during this time? Did you have a family?

I was married at this time with no kids—our son was on his way. I really felt that I wouldn't be happy until I did this. If I had waited, I would've been *less* prepared because my lifestyle would have become more set in its ways. I would have more dependents and would be disrupting more people than myself.

Did you ever say, "Hey, wait a minute…there are people making triple what I'm making in audio and struggling a lot less?"

I don't want to think about how much money other people are making doing things that are probably much easier to do than this career. This is what makes me happy. This goes all the way back to a conversation I had with a career counselor at Millikin about wanting to do this as a career. I was like, "Who *does* this as a career?" He totally understood the passion of the people who go after this line of work. Other people don't really quite get that—it's not easy, and there's nothing particularly lucrative about it.

What kinds of qualities have enabled you to persevere and see your passion through?

I'm very persistent and independent—a couple more reasons why I am willing to inflict this pain on myself. But it's refreshing—every project that comes around is a little different. Some projects are easy, some are hard, some are super-cool and creative, some are straightforward and less so. Music made me more prepared for this career than anything else. I also now realize that there was so much luck involved in getting to where I am now.

Obviously it's not just luck. You have to be able to latch onto opportunities and see patterns in your career, right?

You've got to be able to see two steps ahead and understand when those opportunities are coming up so you can capitalize on them. You also have to be able to work with people. Having the basic talent and chops is only the starting point because, after all, nobody is going to give you the time of day if you're not giving them a halfway decent product. From there its about being intuitive with clients, building relationships, and encouraging people to come back and work with you again and again and again.

So can you walk me through what a typical day might entail?

This morning I had a three-hour voiceover session for an hour-long show. This client is putting the finishing touches on a bunch of shows. They use the same two people for this series, so over the next two weeks we'll be doing lots of voiceover work. Thursday we'll mix with the director for the documentary. Earlier today I was doing some bids for potential new business—a radio spot and some scoring.

Of all your skills, what do you consider yourself best at? Are these skills valued by your clients?

Sound design is my forte and also my biggest interest—typically, commercials involve sound design. However, commercials can be seasonal and a little slow over the summer. I also like to do work on movie sound design, which is a little different.

Is your job highly stressful? How do you handle the day-to-day pressure?

There is stress from an ownership point of view. When you are a regular employee, it's hard to understand this pressure. As an employee, you get bored or you get time off! But as an owner, just four hours go by and you think, "Gosh, I hope someone calls me again!" That's always a stress. You feel like you have to keep talking to people, taking them out to lunch, finding out what's going on. You also have to keep up with equipment and maintenance in your facility; otherwise, you fall behind on what the clientele feels is the cutting edge.

What about directors? Are they the source of a lot of pressure?

Some directors give you pressure; others are very hands-off. I did a film last fall for a writer of a very well-known TV show. This is his first film, and he invested his own money—he plans to go direct. I never once talked to that guy. I maybe had a few email exchanges and dealt with his producer and editor—he was so laidback. With other people, you have to handhold them every moment and get them to relax.

I would think that your career choice of owning a business has led to a difficult work/life balance. Have you been able to maintain a normal family existence?

My hours are pretty normal—that's one great thing about post versus music. Post-production professionals aren't vampires. Most of the people I work with have 9 am to 6 pm deadlines. Of course when the chips are down and there is a deadline, they might have to work all night; that does happen. But generally speaking, we keep normal business hours around here.

Things do come up and change our schedule, but the best way to handle that is to not let it get to you and to be flexible in your lifestyle. I'm not going to sweat planning a vacation the two weeks in July. I will instead say that I want two weeks in the summer when the schedule looks like it opens up—this approach is easier as an owner.

What about money—what can someone expect just getting into this field, and how can that develop over a longer career?

Twelve years ago, my first job paid $25,000 per year. The same job now probably pays around $30,000. Most of the people we work with are part-time or freelancers because we can't afford to pay people's healthcare. A higher salary range for employees in post might be around $65,000 per year if a facility is pulling in their own work. People who aren't affiliated with anyone and who are repped can easily make six figures. They're like rock stars.

What about being a business owner like yourself? What are you left with after all your facility and overhead expenses?

If you're really rocking and not getting creative fees, revenue for a small-business owner with one room might be around $500,000. But then you have to look at your expenses. Do you have bills left on construction? What is your rent? If you are a partner in a facility, you might have $250,000 and more coming in the door, but then you have your nut—your bills, your rent. It's a very expensive business.

How about maintaining an outside life? Have you found your career to be all-consuming or have you developed other hobbies and interests?

I'm in a band, and we make CDs. I have a pretty nifty microphone selection, and I enjoy making records for myself and others. I also have a family and two kids, and that takes up my time! We live in a bungalow in Chicago, and we do lots of renovation work, which we like.

Is there any special moment during your career that has been especially rewarding?

It was pretty fun to sit down with John Storyk and have him doing drawings for me at an AES show—that was cool. Also, one of the sweetest moments was when one of my old employers became a new client. They turned out to be a great client, too!

If you could provide a few words of advice for recent graduates going into this field, what would you say?

The number one thing is the attitude—you have to be able to work with people. Also, you need to realize that there will always be somebody hotter than you. If you want a career, you have to be someone who people love working with. Be humble—go intern or assist someone who you respect and admire. See what you can learn from that person, and don't be afraid.

Does this feel like a market that is expanding or contracting lately?

It still feels like the market is growing. The major markets are still New York and LA for post, but if you want to work on movies there is only one place: Los Angeles. That's where it's all happening. For a wide array of post projects and diversity, New York and Chicago are good, though the market in Chicago is shrinking. Some of the work in Chicago has moved to Toronto.

Any other advice?

We are seeing web and web content grow—Pro Tools is without a doubt the best thing to learn in terms of tangible skills. People should take comfort in this field—as long as there is picture, there will always be a need for sound. The medium might change, like web or whatever, but the picture always has to tell a story, and audio has a permanent role in that.

A Closer Look: Peter Fish and the Composer's Role

Peter Fish is a composer for Howard Schwartz, a leading audio post-production company based in New York City. Prior to working at Howard Schwartz, he owned his own post-production company for 25 years. In speaking with him, I sensed that he became very self-assured at an early age and was extremely focused all along on one discipline: composition. As he became more and more successful, his confidence—and client base—only grew. Now he is one of the top composers in the business and is in extremely high demand.

Peter Fish.

Peter, can you tell me how you got started?

I was a performer with a record deal, and I settled in New York permanently because there was so much opportunity to write music. The first job I ever did was an industrial, and I'm not too proud to tell you the title because it's hilarious. The title of this industrial was, and I quote, "Engine Fudge: Myth or Reality?" It was a corporate industrial for an oil company, but it was married to picture. Gradually, I realized that, and I wrote and recorded the music for this thing.

What level of technical understanding must you have as a composer?

I know what is going on from a technical point of view—my analogy is that I know how to drive the car, but I don't know how to fix the car. I have a strong technical background in that I can tell you what is going on, but when stuff isn't working, I'm not your guy.

What is a typical day like for you?

Seventy percent of what I do is under the broad heading of television—it could be themes for TV shows, which is a very big part of my business, or it could be underscoring for a series or commercials. The next thing down is feature films, and then everything else. I enjoy film work the most, but for an East Coast guy, the film work is smaller. [Film work is] not necessarily as lucrative as television jobs, but it is more creatively rewarding because you get to sit with something that is bigger and larger and see it through to the end. I guess the first film of any size I did was 10 or 12 years into my working career.

What is your educational background and what traits have helped you succeed?

I am a high-school dropout. I am not the most talented guy, but not the least talented guy. I think I have perseverance and an ability to work very, very fast. Most importantly, I am not afraid of different styles of music. I have a tenet or a theory that I hold onto very strongly: There are 12 notes; we've all played them. There are only so many ways you can break up time—we know what all the time signatures are, even the odd ones. There are 2/4s, 3/4s, 4/4s, 5/4s, and 6/4s. There is no mystery to this, and I don't get too hung up on anything except for realizing that if there's a sound and if you can listen to it, you can absorb what that sound is.

What is your proficiency as far as reading music is concerned?

I can read and I can write—it is a really helpful skill. I know guys who can't read or write who do just fine, so it's not imperative, but it's a good skill to have. It helps me be versatile, and the key to my career has been versatility. This morning I did a 30-second Devo-esque spot for a commercial, and in the afternoon I was doing some Gerswhin-eque songs written by me for an HBO film. As soon as I'm off the phone with you, I'm working on a thing for CBS News. The key to my career is to go from thing to thing to thing; it's all music.

Photo by Jeff Touzeau.

Voiceover booth.

Are you able to balance your personal life and your work life?

If you ask my wife, the answer is no; if you ask me, the answer is yes. It's difficult because you can't turn work down. I can't say to you, "Call me back on December 15th, and I'll be able to work on your project," because by then you've called the next guy on your list. So I rarely say no, and I find a way to get it all done—sometimes it means long days, sometimes it means weekends. You try to maintain a life, but I guess I am guilty of failing at that simply because it is hard to say no.

There are four stages to someone with a career like my own. Have you heard of the four stages? The four stages start with Stage One: "Who is Peter Fish?" Stage Two is "Get me Peter Fish." Stage Three is "Get me a younger, cheaper Peter Fish." Stage Four is "Who is Peter Fish?" The key to the game is to stay in Stage Two as long as you can.

Another thing I remember is the famous catcher, Yogi Berra—who is much more famous for saying things that don't make sense but somehow make sense anyway—once said back in the '50s, when he was playing, that everyone suggested they were going to go out to dinner at this bar. And Yogi said, "Nah, no one goes there any more. It's too crowded." Of course everyone knew what Yogi meant. It's true that if you get the perception that Peter Fish is too busy—don't call him; he can't do it—then the phone stops ringing. No one will call. So you have to say yes for as long as you can. And the day when the phone stops ringing—and it most certainly will—you can say you sucked that dry as long as you could, and hopefully you put enough money in the bank.

I am salaried by Howard Schwartz, yet my livelihood is dependent on the fact that people call me to work. Fortunately for guys like me, composers make royalties. The more stuff I have on the air, the more money I make outside of my salary. So it's sort of a combination of the two. I don't care what field you are in—if you're not bringing home the bacon, you don't have a job. It doesn't matter who employs you. It doesn't matter if you are self-employed or employed by General Motors.

Do you work out of your home? What equipment do you have there?

Here's what I have at home. I have a 7-1/2-foot Steinway grand piano. That's it. I have nothing at home, and I bring nothing home. Occasionally I compose at my piano, which is a beautiful thing, but the minute I record it, it's into the studio.

What advice do you have for foks just starting out in audio for video?

It is much easier to get started in this field now because budgets have gone down. A lot of companies like the idea of young and inexperienced people coming in and giving ideas on how to do things very quickly because they can pay them less. So it's easy to get started as a recording engineer if you get a gig as an assistant. You'll get your experience very quickly, but then it's tough to move up. For a young composer, here's my advice: Get a client. Get one stinkin' client—it doesn't matter who it is. Even if it's your father's brother-in-law's best friend who happens to own an advertising agency. Once you have one client and you have a piece of work to show, you can probably get another client. Just build it a client at a time; that's what it's all about. It's about having people say, "Yeah, he can do that, because I heard him to do this."

A Closer Look: Ryan Collison and the Art of Foley

Ryan Collison is a Foley artist for Sound One, based in New York City. He entered one of the most competitive areas in sound for picture—Foley—by being at the right place at the right time. He started at the bottom and has worked his way up through perseverance and love for what he does. In speaking to him, I appreciated how he stuck it out and has been able to reap the rewards of his efforts. He seems to be very much in line with what he originally set out to do.

What attracted you to this whole field?

During my last semester in college, I suddenly became interested in film following a documentary filmmaking course I took. From there I went to the New York Film Academy just to try and make a film myself. I ended up making my own short film, and then when I was finished with that, it was on 16 millimeter. I wanted to have it transferred to show all my friends what a cheesy student film I made, so I came to Sound One to have it transferred. They were able to do it all in the course of a day, so I just hung around and noticed posters of all these films I had seen. After they were finished with the transfer, I asked them if they were accepting resumes.

Ryan Collison.

They said, "We need you to start today." I said, "Really?" And they said, "Yeah. It's not the most lucrative position—in fact, it doesn't pay much at all. But if you're interested, this is usually how it works. It's a stepping-stone type of job. You'll be a messenger, and you'll run around getting coffee and delivering FedEx packages to clients. Pretty much doing whatever they need you to do." This was about 10 years ago. I did that for a while and got to know people here, as well as to know their clients. After a while, I noticed they had a Foley stage. So I started to hang around there and got to know those guys.

By Foley stage, you mean simply a dedicated recording room for sound effects?

Yes, with Foley pits. I didn't really know what Foley was until the day I was going in for my first day of work here. I met a friend on a train, and he was in engineering school at the time. He was telling me all about Foley. Because of him, I hung around the Foley stage and showed interest in doing this—and they decided to train me. That friend who told me all about Foley now works with me every day. I got him a job here shortly after, as well as about 10 of my friends who have come and gone over the years.

What have some of the more rewarding things been for you while working in Foley?

At times it is hard work and a pain the ass. The best part about it is that I am part of something very creative: making a film. It's not just a single brush painting a portrait, or a photographer taking his camera, or even four guys making a song together. This is thousands of people participating in something creative, everybody working toward one piece of art.

The role of Foley artist is kind of hidden, but it adds so much dimension to film.

What we do is very covert. And believe it or not, the less noticeable it is, the better it is for the sake of the film itself. We don't want people to say, "That sound was not done on location." We want it to blend in and to be seamless.

It's just like all the other aspects of the audio in the film. You don't want it to interrupt your conscious flow. We want it to sound real in the sense that it is not intrusive to the ears. You have to work fast, too, which is the tough part. You don't have a lot of time to just sit back and play with the sounds—we have to keep moving. We have an entire film to do and usually a very short time to do it. We are between picture editing and mixing itself, so the second-to-last in the production process.

What is the job market like out there now and how competitive is it?

It probably is competitive. I think in New York there is a smaller market, but these things do work in cycles. In Los Angeles, there are probably ten or twenty times the people working in Foley, whereas in New York, there are only about three or four working stages. Foley artists all seem to work well together—it is not too cutthroat.

What kinds of personality traits are important in your line of work?

Many things you would expect, the basic things. You have to show people that you are a serious worker and that you are friendly and enjoy spending time with clients. This is how you develop a rapport with clients and why clients will continue to want to work with you. So you should be friendly, focused, dedicated.

What critical skills do you need to bring to the table just to get in the door?

You definitely have to know Pro Tools in this day and age. Even though I am very happy I graduated from college, I probably learned everything I needed to know just by being here. You definitely have to start at the ground floor in this business and work your way up. I've seen a lot of young kids come and go because they expect to start with a higher position than they are starting with, or they expect to move up the ladder faster. The most successful folks, though, have patience and perseverance.

How are your workflow and workload? How are you able to balance them with your personal life?

Usually I'm either really, really busy or really, really not. It's mostly seasonal. From the end of August to the beginning of November is usually very slow. But once you get into November and December, that's when all the studios and producers start scrambling to get their movies done by the Academy Award deadline in case they get nominated. Then you have your Sundance deadline.

Do you ever handle anything else besides Foley in your day-to-day work?

My primary role is recording Foley, but in this day and age you have to be somewhat flexible. So if they need me to record ADR if someone is out sick, I can jump in and do that. I always try to find an area where I can be helpful—the best way to survive is not to be a one-trick pony.

What brings you the greatest pleasure in your work?

The more creative we have a chance to be, the better it is. If it is just a film where people are walking and talking and not really doing much—a dialogue-oriented film—it can be a little boring. But when we can add design, we can really blow people away, especially when it comes to comedy, where we can make things bigger, funnier, and noisier. That's when it is worthwhile.

A Closer Look: Robin Beauchamp and Sound for Animation

Robin Beauchamp is chair of sound design for Savannah College of Art and Design. Every day he teaches students how to put their best foot forward and prepare for the exciting world of sound for picture. It struck me that Beauchamp really tries to impress on his students the importance of understanding the content with which they are working rather than just imparting one's technical expertise. Beauchamp is also author of the spectacular book *Designing Sound for Animation* (Focal Press, 2005).

One doesn't really hear too much about the sound for animation. How does one go about pursuing this path?

It's not as predominant, either. I would say that anyone interested in pursuing a career path in sound for animation should really follow the live-action career path for sound because the needed skill sets for live action are greater than they are for animation. The workflow is much more complicated for live action, but it is also inclusive of what is needed for animation. So you'll find the guys at Skywalker or Blue Sky are working on live action for the most part, then they get this animation, which they are dying to do. The main difference is that you have to construct everything in animation, as opposed to live action, where you are trying to take the production audio and enhance it.

What is the typical lifecycle of an animation project?

First of all, a project in animation can run for three years, as opposed to nine months for live action. So they bring you in early, when they are doing motion tests of the basic drawings. If they are doing musical numbers, pencil tests, or animation drawings, they at least need temp versions of the musical numbers. The idea of temping out your sound effects in animation is very common, as opposed to live animation, where they don't do any sound on it until the picture gets locked. The animatic in an animation represents a nearly completed version of the film. It is a really accurate first edit and is usually edited down from 13 hours to 2, as opposed to 70 minutes of animation edited to 120 minutes.

Very often when they do a motion test to see how a character looks like he is walking, they put sound to it to see if the sound reveals any other flaws in the animation. You don't do that in live action. You might record somebody doing their lines for dialogue so that the animators can do a rough lip-synch animation, but then you have to come back and record the big-name talent that is really going to be the voice for it—then the animation needs to be adjusted to that.

Can you delineate the differences between how sound is handled for animation versus how it is handled for live-action films?

There is a lot more involvement in the pre-production and production stages in animation, whereas there is more involvement in the post-production phase for live sound production. Compared to how many live-action films are made, though, there are, as a percentage, very few animations made. So to sustain your career, you're going to need to do both.

Most of the animation houses are outsourcing their audio. They may have somebody in house to do temp stuff, but the final stuff is going to be done at a major post place, like Skywalker, Game Tracks, or any big post-production house. Any big audio post house will have clients who do live-action film—one client will be doing animation, another will be doing games. So those are your target places for you to have a job. They have the resources, the recording studios, and the credibility.

What kind of people are going to succeed in animation?

The people who are willing to work long hours, and people who are going to look for opportunities rather than wait for them. To my mind, you don't become a sound designer until the director tells you no, and you respond in a positive way. When you make something that you feel is really awesome, you show it to the director, and he says, "No, I want something else." If you can handle that in a positive way, you have a chance at being a sound designer.

Are technical skills important?

Most importantly, people need to understand what a picture is about. What is the core of the film? That is the key. If you simply have a skill set, it can be outsourced. If you have a creative understanding and the ability to realize that creativity, this is not outsourceable, and it is ultimately going to sustain your career. People will think, "I don't want to risk my film not having that person on there." A lot of people are great at Pro Tools, but the technology needs to be totally transparent, and you need to be able to take it a few more steps than the next guy. More often than not, people will find that they have fewer tools than they need to get the job done. But can they get the job done anyway?

Tell me about the work/life balance people should expect.

There is lots of stress in this field because the date of delivery is non-negotiable. The film will be taken away from you at this date, so what's done is done. There are people in queue who are going to do what they do that day. You get six weeks of post-production time, the film gets turned over to us two weeks later, and you're still expected to deliver it on the same date. They almost always expect it earlier, and usually they are over budget. It's feast or famine, and when it's feast, you've got to go—you're working 14- to 16-hour days, and you've got to put away that money because there's going to be a famine while you're waiting for the next gig. You can't spend a lot of time looking for the next gig while you're working on the current gig because you don't have time, and you have got to get this one done.

5 The Audio Publishing/ Audio Trade Media Market

Any fully developed industry needs to keep its professionals and market informed. The audio industry is no exception. Across many countries, including the United States, the United Kingdom, Germany, Japan, Australia, India and many, many more, audio industry trade journals and magazines cull together heaps of valuable information about the business, its components, and what keeps it ticking. Books on the audio industry (as opposed to audio books) continue to educate, inform, and entertain as well, with their titles only increasing over the last several years.

Although on the surface it looks as if the studio industry has been suffering, if you look a little deeper, there are more people than ever who want to get involved in the audio industry. There are home recordists, teachers, studio and equipment professionals, and so many others. These audiences number in the hundreds of thousands, and with an industry that is changing so rapidly, there has never been a better time for information. Whether that information is disseminated via a magazine or online journal or through an RSS feed, the content continues to drive the medium—not the other way around.

Market Viability

The audio publishing world has been impacted by the gradual transformation of content to the Internet. Overall circulations of physical publications, however, has held its own because nothing can replace a magazine sitting on a supplier's table, and it's nearly impossible to conveniently leaf through the Internet. This might change at some point, but for now, publications typically rely on a hybrid model that includes both print and online content, with print still being the dominant force.

One could easily make the argument that the audience is only increasing—the home recording boom, which occurred just over a decade ago, has left thousands of enthusiasts, many of whom are now professionals, clamoring for information on new products, recording techniques, product specifications, and other practical content. Although everyone agrees that the entire industry is redefining itself, now is the time when people require more information, not less. This ensures that the trusted magazine and book publishers will be the first to expose trends that are afoot and what the future holds.

musicetc.

by Jeff Touzeau

Crowd Pleasers

Clap Your Hands Say Yeah is (l-r): Tyler Sargent, Robbie Guertin, Lee Sargent, Alec Ounsworth, Sean Greenhalgh.

Last year was quite a good one for Clap Your Hands Say Yeah. The Brooklyn, NY-based group's self-titled debut album, financed entirely by the members of the band, startled the independent music community, leaving a long trail of ecstatic music reviewers reveling in its wake. Much to the dismay of many an A&R rep, Clap Your Hands Say Yeah remains independent and completely in control of its own destiny, selling out shows wherever they set their feet.

Pro Sound News caught up with lead singer, Alec Ounsworth, just as the record topped CMJ's new music charts and as the group launched its first Japanese and European tour.

On Life Before Clap Your Hands Say Yeah and Remaining Independent:

I live in Philadelphia. I was renovating a house in Philadelphia doing carpentry, construction kind of stuff. I would go home at night and work on songs. Everybody else was doing design work generally, up in New York. Tyler was doing computer web design-type stuff, for example.

As far as I'm concerned, the idea of being independent and beginning independent or remaining independent is keeping the idea of how you started in the first place. Our sudden success only seems to be the case. It's skyrocketing from certain people's perspective, which is to say that other—or more—people are listening. But as far as I'm concerned, it's still always an independent relationship between the musicians and the music.

On Touring:

We're in London now, and the audiences are pretty similar. We were lucky enough to get an enthusiastic welcome on our first tour of the United States and so far, it translated over to Europe pretty well. We started in Japan at the end of January, came over to Paris, and now we're in London. We're legitimately starting the tour tomorrow in Belfast. So far, the reception has been great. I think we're coming back to the U.S. around March.

On Getting on with Writing New Material:

I'm adjusting to it [the business side]. Ac-

tually, it's a little disconcerting because it happened a bit fast, you find yourself a lot busier than you used to be. I was used to working on songs all the time, and now I'm just working with the guys and trying to execute on stage. It's a different game. I don't have much time to write at this point, but I have enough for the next couple albums if it goes so far. [The songwriting process] starts off in Philly where I live, because I put together a tiny studio just to kind of get down ideas. When I hear something in my head, I bring it up to the guys and just run through it in the practice space. Everybody is talented and creative enough to take the suggestions and run with them.

On Working in the Studio:

We did a lot of the basic tracking with Keith [Desouza, of Machines and Magnets, Providence RI], and it was about trusting what was in his studio and what might come out. He didn't really say much, like, "You really nailed it that time!" but he had really good ears. It was my first time in any proper studio, so I was getting adjusted and pretty much working on an instinctual level. I was there the whole time during the mixing and tracking process.

Adam [Lasus, of Fireproof Recording] was great; very accommodating and very open to suggestions, which I am pretty strong about because I have a pretty good idea of how I like it to sound. The important thing of working with somebody like that is to make it through the translation, I think. We did six or seven basic tracks at Machines and Magnets; then we started mixing and doing over-

dubs at Fireproof. While we were there, it turned out we wanted to tack on more songs to make a full-length album so we also tracked maybe four other songs in Brooklyn. It was a great drum kit that Adam had that Sean borrowed.

For vocals, we used a variety of mics. We tried different mics for each one of the songs, and for the backup vocals as well; we tried a bunch of different stuff. [For the backing vocals], on some of them, I had the idea before the song was tracked, and sometimes I recognized a certain hole in the song and just sort of filled it spontaneously.

On Establishing the Feel of the Record:

Some of the basic techniques might have involved leaning on room mics a little more, ala Pixies albums like, Surfer Rosa, on a couple of tracks. For me, though, it was always a matter of sound more than saying, let's use this for EQ or this for a compressor. We had a limited amount of time, and that might have had a lot to do with how the overall sound of the album came about.

Some of my favorite albums I look to are like The Velvet Underground's White Light White Heat, and some of Bob Dylan's albums, where you can just tell that everybody is sitting around trying to figure it out as they go along. The idea of spontaneity is a strong one, and I think we've started off on this album concerned about trying to preserve a certain degree of spontaneity based on the fact that everybody was learning as they went along.

The album sounds nice and wide-open. I like that sort of live quality to an album, and

that's something to hold onto. And I always savor the room microphones rather than the close mics for certain things because they always seem to bring out and enhance a certain aspect of a recording. Fireproof was big enough that if you wanted to lean on a room mic for a big sound, you could. As far as I'm concerned, I'm not exactly sure what's going to be on the second album, so it'll [whether we record differently] have everything to do with that.

On Sonic Reference Points:

I remember bringing some early albums from The Rolling Stones, trying to convey certain points about compression on some of the songs. The idea that you had to make sure that you compress the hell out of certain things to enhance the sound, say the tambourine, for example. I'm not sure whether I played Scary Monsters or Low [David Bowie] for Adam, but in the song, "Scary Monsters," I think it's [producer Tony] Visconti that worked on that with him, and I'm not sure what they used to make his voice flutter in such a way. They might have run it back through an amplifier or something like that. It's important as far as instrumentation and color is concerned to have certain precedents to rely on, but not too closely. That's a whole part of the translation; especially with someone you just don't know and who has no idea about what you're bringing to him. So I brought some of the demos that I was working on which was kind of the groundwork for the songs themselves. It was pretty speedy the way it shaped up, because I had a pretty clear idea initially. There are a lot of things that were drawn on to make it work.

This feature column in *Pro Sound News* is written by the author of this book each month.

Job Profiles and Career Opportunities

In publishing, there are typically two silos of functions: editorial and publishing (or the business side). The editorial side is responsible for writing and gathering the content that readers will care about, but that will also align with advertisers' interests. Although the audience is very important and makes the publication relevant, the ability to sell advertising pays the administrative bills. This is obviously not true with books, who look to serve mainly the readership—albeit at a more expensive price to the consumer. (The price of the book must support many more pages of printed material, a cover, and an entirely different chain and approach to distribution and marketing.)

Sample Career Path in Publishing

This illustration represents what a career ladder might look like in publishing.

Within each silo of functions, there are many different roles—including some roles that actually bridge both silos. The editor-in-chief is not surprisingly at the top of the food chain on the content side, and the publisher is in charge of the business domain and must report facts, figures, and performance aspects to whoever owns the magazine, be it a holding company, a board of directors, or another individual.

While publishing definitely falls under the "less pay" category—and this is true both inside and outside of the audio industry—there are six-figure salaries out there, though they are few and far between. Because media itself is going through arguably a larger-scale transformation than the audio industry, people who are able to identify the "next medium" will be sought after and will have a far greater chance to succeed than those who are simply going along for the ride. Therefore, assuming you are interested in entering the publishing industry on the content side, it makes sense to gain an understanding of not only how to write, but what possible media you have at your disposal to carry the message. A mastery of these media commands more dollars: RSS, blogging, web 2.0, wiki, and every other new communication vehicle that has emerged. Here is where the younger generation definitely has an advantage over its older counterparts. At the time of this writing, it is a sure bet that those at the very top echelon of audio publishing—book, trade magazine, and otherwise—do not have as good an understanding as many recent college grads. This is worth money.

Editor-in-Chief ($65,000 to $100,000+)

The editor-in-chief is responsible for the overall look and feel of the publication, as well as its content. He or she is responsible for the overall direction and voice. Sometimes the editor-in-chief will contribute his own content or articles, but most of his time is spent ensuring that the staffers are hitting the mark with both their assignments and their overall quality of output. After all, the editor-in-chief must answer to the publisher, and whether the publication gets read depends 100 percent on the content that is included.

The editor-in-chief is looking at the big picture and must see the 50,000-foot view—what is the overall business purpose of the magazine? How do the articles or the book serve the readership, and are they in line with the overall vision of the magazine or publication? The editor-in-chief needs to be able to not only communicate clearly to the readership and advertisers, he must also be able to communicate to his staff and the publisher—plain and simple, he is the enforcer of the vision. The editor-in-chief has limited responsibility as far as quotas, profit and loss, and budgeting are concerned—these tasks are primarily left to the publisher.

Managing Editor ($60,000 to $80,000)

Beneath the editor-in-chief—figuratively speaking, of course—is the managing editor. The managing editor is one of those individuals who bridges the content and publishing side. He or she ensures that the piece has enough words and pictures from all the contributors. If a piece does not have all the required elements, he circles back to the appropriate person to make sure that the piece gets them. This might mean calling up a freelance writer and asking for more words or specifying a caption. In his role, the managing editor communicates on a regular basis with the production staff because they determine whether there may be a word shortage or a layout problem. The managing editor is also often responsible for divvying up payment to freelancers and other contributors.

In the case of a book publisher, the managing editor ensures that the book titles and content reflect the overall business goals of the publisher. For example, if a book publisher is focused on technical training manuals, it might not make sense to do a book on the history of the electric guitar. Additionally, once a book deal has been signed and a project is underway, it is the responsibility of the managing editor to manage each book through its production course. At a small publisher, this can mean managing anywhere from five to ten titles; at a large publisher, it can be well into the hundreds.

The managing editor at a book publisher generally deals with both acquisitions editors and project editors, whose roles are detailed in the following subsections.

Acquisitions Editor

Typically, several acquisitions editors report to the managing editor and publisher—these are the people who exhaustively research the market and determine what new book titles may be required. Once they come up with an idea for a book, an author is sourced to write it either through assignment by the acquisitions editor or through randomly submitted proposals. If an acceptable proposal is given, the acquisitions editor then puts the project into play and sets the book into production.

Project Editor

Project editors handle all the intense details that comprise putting together a book—ensuring that manuscript submissions occur on time and coordinating with copy, technical, and development editors as well as layout techs, proofreaders, and other professionals. The project editor is the hub who ties all the loose ends together in the throes of book production. A project editor may be working on several books at a time, with different acquisitions editors. They are also very often freelancers who work for many different publishers.

Staff Reporter ($35,000 to $55,000)

Most magazines and newspapers have different columns or sections, and typically a reporter will be assigned to that particular theater of the publication. Staff reporters are responsible for—just as they say in journalism school—the how, what, where, when, and why of a story. If an article *can't* answer these five questions, it will very likely have little bearing for readers or advertisers. Staff reporters also obviously must have an excellent command of the English language and communicate clearly and effectively—this is a prerequisite of the job: Don't expect to pass Go or even be invited into an interview unless this is a demonstrable skill in your toolbox.

Beyond that, depending on the approach of the magazine, a good reporter will have a sixth sense for what a story is. Just because a new product is introduced, that doesn't make it news. How will that product impact the business or process flow? Will it make any other players or products less relevant? These are the kinds of questions a good reporter will have to uncover and answer before the market does. The editorial staff typically must help in proofreading and doing background checks on content, as well as being the last line of defense before the article goes to layout. This means that attention to detail and accuracy are key ingredients in an editorial staffer's arsenal.

Production Manager/Graphic Designer ($35,000 to $60,000)

The production manager falls on the content side, albeit at a relatively technical level. He or she ensures that the final layout of the magazine or trade journal will reproduce faithfully in print. Just like the reporter, he brings his own toolbox of skills to the party—namely print production, color management, and a knowledge of printing processes and proofing methods. He is also responsible for managing the printing budget and ensuring that the project comes in within range.

In some publishing arenas, the graphic designer actually flows the articles into the layout using a platform such as QuarkXPress, InDesign, or an equivalent. The graphic designer must also have a good eye and a working knowledge of programs such as Photoshop and CorelDRAW. If there is a problem with word count or an image, the graphic designer will notify the managing editor, who will then fix the issue with a staffer's help. Typically, the graphic designer's role isn't industry-specific, meaning he or she can come out of just about any other magazine with transferable skills and still be efficient from the get-go. In this day and age, it goes without saying that a graphic designer's success rate will be greatly increased by his or her command of web-related technologies and layout programs.

In the case of book publishing, the individual who flows the book into the layout is generally referred to as a *layout tech* or *compositor*. The layout tech coordinates with the project editor on any layout issues. The key concern in this context is that the publisher has allocated a definitive page count for the book, and it is up to the layout tech, in conjunction with the project editor, to ensure that the book doesn't run substantially over or under the target page count. This means keeping close tabs on words and images. In addition to handling the book's layout (again, typically managed in a program such as Quark or an equivalent), layout techs also manage print production and color management—therefore, they must have a good command of scheduling as well as proof reviews. In this day and age, the role of layout tech is largely freelance.

Book publishers often use graphic designers as well, but they typically don't manage layout—rather, they are usually focused on creating illustrations or cover art for each title. Layout is done by the layout tech/compositor.

Entering and Succeeding in the Audio Publishing Market

To succeed in the audio publishing market, communication is the largest prerequisite. That said, nothing can substitute for good industry knowledge; therefore, it makes sense for any aspiring audio journalist or writer to get out there in the business somewhere and cut his or her teeth. If you are able to bring a good business sense to the job—a sensitivity for what the underlying issues are in different audio silos—you will be far more valuable than somebody who only can write quickly and accurately.

As mentioned previously, the publishing industry is notoriously low paying. However, if you can bring tangible skills to an employer—specifically, an understanding of groundbreaking dissemination vehicles or even connections—you will increase your value substantially. Quite frankly, most audio publishers do not take people right out of college except in positions such as graphics or other functional roles. A better way to gain entry to this field might be through freelancing or as an intern.

One of the most important attributes of a reporter is reliability. Meeting the publication's deadline is of the utmost importance because many, many other people count on having the article in place—all the way from the editor to the layout artist to the printer. Failure to deliver an article is not an option, though you can often negotiate a schedule up front, just as you can negotiate a fee (if you are a freelancer).

Before you accept a position in publishing, be sure of what your end goal is: Is it to cull experience to move on to another publication or another role? Is it to grow within a certain company? Make sure that the publisher has a very defined growth path. If you don't take responsibility for answering this question up front, you don't deserve to question why when you hit a ceiling later.

One of the most obvious tactics to gain employment in audio publishing is to grow, cultivate, and maintain your connections—just as in all the other career fields in audio. But remember: You can and should only use connections when you can walk the walk. If someone else opens a door for you, which happens very frequently in this industry, you owe it to yourself *and* the person who helped you out to do the best job you possibly can. That person's reputation is on the line, too, as is your ongoing relationship with him or her.

The audio publishing industry's ecosystem contains almost every aspect of the pro audio world. If you do a good job, you could easily move into another role with a manufacturer, a production company, or a related services company—assuming you have the core skills to find your way forward.

Traits Valued in the Audio Publishing Field

I've already discussed many of the traits valued in the audio publishing field, but I'll reiterate them here: good communication skills, reliability, a personable nature, and a strong work ethic. It also helps if you are highly organized and a fast writer. Things such as sources can become confusing when you have more than four for a single article, and it can be difficult to juggle five articles that might be due in a week (or in a month if they are features).

Flexibility   Accuracy
Communication Skills
Focus   Writing Ability
Organization
Reliability   Curiosity
Technical Knowledge

Here are some basic traits that may be valued in the audio publishing industry.

Companies in this field also appreciate flexibility—receiving an assignment at the last minute is an all-too-frequent occurrence, and sometimes the impossible appears to be routine. Have a thick skin and don't let criticism of your work get you down, but grow from your mistakes because you will most certainly make them. To quote a famous philosopher, "The only difference between stepping stones and stumbling blocks is how you use them."

Benefits and Drawbacks of Working in the Audio Publishing Market

Folks working in the audio publishing market usually have fairly normal hours. This has immeasurable benefits if you value your time away from work or you have a family. Many, many areas of pro audio simply cannot offer this benefit, and as a result, many people in the industry are sorely lacking the necessary dimension of personal time in their lives. Add to that basic health insurance benefits and sometimes even 401k plans—remember, these audio publications are often part of larger corporate conglomerates that have the muscle and interest to offer employees a basic benefits package in the interest of enticing their talent to stay. This is not the case for freelancers, though, and one way publishers reduce costs is by offloading work to freelancers who are typically responsible for getting their own benefits.

Benefits and Drawbacks of
Working in Publishing

Relatively Secure Career	Relatively Low Pay
Highly Transferable Skills	Future of Distribution Uncertain
Opportunities in Web 2.0	Can Be Political
Pride of Ownership	Must Do Your Time
Influence Published Pieces	Lots of Deadlines
Exposed to Lots of Great Content	Difficult Authors/Writers

Another obvious benefit is that you get to write about a subject you (presumably) love. If you love what you do, you will succeed. Imagine being able to write about technology every day, or interview your favorite artists/producers to learn their techniques—the knowledge you cull can be applied in your bedroom studio later that day! Another benefit is that as a reporter or an editor, you can vastly increase your base of professional contacts.

One drawback is that publication environments can make for a droll day-to-day existence. Unless you are out in the field, life can get boring pretty quickly, regardless of the illustrious staff that might be on your team. Add to that the mediocre pay and the pressures of meeting deadlines; this deadline-driven mentality might make you feel as if you are indeed "working for the man."

All that said, the environment of publishing is still highly desirable compared to that of an engineer who needs to work 16-hour days just to make ends meet—and then has to explain to his significant other that he just doesn't have time for her.

Is the Audio Publishing Market Right for You?

If you have a knack for writing and you like a fast-paced environment, audio publishing might be a suitable market for you. We all strive to communicate our passions, and there is no better outlet for audio enthusiasts to do this than audio publishing.

A Closer Look: Frank Wells and the Audio Media and Publishing Industry

Frank Wells is Editor-in-Chief of *Pro Sound News*. In speaking with him, I realize how many audiences he must be sensitive to as an editor. Readers of his publications consist of not only technology aficionados and industry influencers, but also advertisers. The reputation of his magazine, which is among the finest in the industry, directly correlates to how professional and informed its writers are.

Frank Wells.

When were you first exposed to audio technology?

I actually started doing military electronics out of high school. I caught the tail end of the GI bill to get funding for college and was trained as a radio communications tech. I did my four years in the military.

Did you have a natural interest in electronics?

Yes. I had taken a couple of classes in high school, so when I took the military aptitude test, it was easy for me—I had already been exposed to it. We had an ex-military radio guy who taught a couple classes in a Department of Defense high school I went to in Okinawa—my dad was Air Force. So I had my pick of jobs available at the time when I went in, and I picked the one that had the biggest tech school, thinking I'd learn the most. I ended up working on point-to-point transmitters for the military—long-haul communications kinds of stuff. When I came out, I went into Tennessee State University to study mass communications, figuring I could combine my electronics with a broadcasting degree.

I then interned under the chief engineer at the radio station at WMOT, a 50-kilowatt public station at Tennessee State University. He happened to leave right at the time I graduated, so I basically was able to walk right into his job—primarily based on my military electronics, and not what I had learned at school. I did that for six years, and my better interns were from the recording program on campus because most of the broadcasters really didn't care about working on the gear. The recording students did, though.

I took one recording technology class in college, and that was my total exposure at the time to recording studios, signal flow, and the equipment. While at the radio station, I became very familiar with tape machines, alignment, and consoles, albeit on a smaller scale. One of my interns from the recording program had gone to work as a tech in Nashville—he was up for jobs at a couple different studios. He took one at Masterfonics and eventually made an introduction for me. I ended up migrating to recording studio maintenance with no real experience. I only understood signal flow and the electronics, and this was a very intense mixing and mastering facility.

What kind of advantage did your technical understanding give you?

It was a great time to get into studio maintenance because digital was just happening. Masterfonics had already been doing digital mastering for a dozen years before I got there. They also had a great reputation. We added a tracking room in the back room where Vince Gill's first couple of gold records were cut, and a whole bunch of other projects. We eventually added another freestanding facility that was dedicated to tracking and mixing. I got experience in building rooms, maintained all the gear, and was responsible for all the technical aspects of the facility.

It eventually grew from myself, two mastering rooms, and a mix room to two studios plus the mastering room, mix rooms, copy room, and editing room. I had a staff of three when I left there.

Where does publishing come into play?

Pro Audio Review called because we had bought three Apogee UV-1000s. There were four of them in the country—they asked if we wanted to do a review of ours. They asked the owner if he wanted to do it, and he said, "Nah, see if Frank wants to do it." My first entry into trade journalism was writing that review. For the next two years, I had at least a bench test or an article or two in every issue.

Coincidentally, *Audio Media* out of the UK had decided that they wanted to do a US edition of their magazine. A good friend of mine that worked for Sadie referred me to them. They looked in the US and decided California would never be on the same time zone and New York was too expensive. As a major recording center, they thought Nashville was perfect because it didn't have a competing media presence.

I ended up walking straight out of my tech shop into the editor's chair, having had no experience editing a magazine whatsoever. They told me, "You know your industry and you can write a complete sentence. We'll teach you the rest." In the end, I think my understanding of technology was what really sold them. *Audio Media* was a very technical magazine and was constantly reviewing big SSL consoles and tape machines. I could play the role of technical editor and editor at the same time. I had real-live experience in what the market was about. All of those things kind of came together and played into my favor.

Did you have a natural aptitude for writing?

Yes, that just kind of fell to me. I'd always read a lot—I think that helps, just reading other people's words and trying to understand how they're put together. Although my first couple of articles must have been pretty bad [laughs]!

Pro Audio Review was a feature review book, but the review side of it was very natural because I'd been doing it for a couple years. As a consumer of these magazines, I kind of knew what they were about and what I wished they were about. The technology aspect of it was core to anything they wrote about. If they were writing about a studio and a production, or a production technique, the technology was always at the forefront of that. It was always built around the tools. It wasn't too much of a stretch to take the writing I had been doing and get more into the feature writing.

Were you comfortable when you made the leap?

The offer sort of landed in my lap [laughs]! It was pretty painless, and it wasn't even like I was making a deliberate move. I was happy at Masterfonics and I got to do a lot of fun things. During the period I was there, we had spent three million dollars building a tracking room and we were really focused on this new room. You come out of that, and there's a little bit of a letdown—it's a change in pace, and you're back to the routine and drudgework aspect a little bit.

I wasn't really burned out, but I had been on call effectively for 15 years. With a radio station, you're on call 24 hours a day—if something goes down and they run into a problem at 2 a.m., you're going to get called in. Pager and telephone at the ready, I had been on call for 15 years and had my share of getting up in the middle of the night and driving in to fix something for somebody and handling a lot of crisis maintenance. During that time, my family time definitely took a hit. I had two kids, and the lifestyle changes were attractive. I figured, "Well, heck. Let's give this a shot. If it doesn't work out, there will still be plenty of gear broken up and down

Music Row, so I can get back into the maintenance thing if I need to." As one of my friends put it, "Nobody is ever going to call you at 2 a.m. and tell you an article is broken."

How long before you had that sense of confidence that you had made a good decision?

I would say within the first year. Some of it is just ignorance—you go into something and you don't know you can't do a good job at it, so if you don't go into it fearful and you stay confident, you can get there. It took about two or three issues before we had a good flow and we knew it could work.

Beyond the technical understanding, what other things helped you pull this off?

Well, the networking aspect is important because through Masterfonics, which is a very high-end facility, I had good contacts with a number of manufacturers from top levels down. I knew people at SSL, Otari, and many other places. When you are at a facility like that, there is always somebody coming by to try to sell you something.

Attitudes were also very important. Our tech department always had a can-do attitude. We treated people on the staff just like they were important, too. In return, almost everyone in the company would do things for our staff, too. We would have interns from a number of different colleges, and most of them had very good technical knowledge. But the ones who succeeded also had a great attitude and a willingness to do whatever it took to get the job done. You take that attitude and transfer that to whatever situation you are in.

Trade journals are a funny thing because they are totally advertising-based. Nobody in *Pro Audio* has to pay for a subscription to anything, and the business model is not based on that. It is based on being supported on advertising. You have to learn to serve two or three masters—you have to take care of your manufacturing partners and make sure the magazine is serving their needs and goals, but if you do that and ignore your readership, you won't be in business very long because people won't fill out the renewal cards.

Looking back now, are you glad that you invested the effort in these relationships you had? It seems they influenced things in so many different ways.

Absolutely. I always told my crew to treat the second engineer as well as the first engineer because maybe the second engineer is lower on the totem pole, but if you build a good relationship with him, everything will go smoother. If you dissed somebody just because you believed he was in a lesser position, and then he graduates up to first chair, you will have soured that relationship from the start. You never know how important those relationships are going to be in the long term, but the point is you never know, so you treat everybody right.

My dad was always an incredibly conscientious guy and never cut corners on anything he did. In addition to being in the military, he was also a woodworker, and working in the shop with him, I learned that you don't cut corners—you go the extra mile to do something to make sure that it's going to last and to make sure the solution is satisfactory. He was in command-post operations and he was always looking for people who were conscientious but at the same time didn't give a damn. Part of that is taking your ego out of the equation, and that's definitely true in the recording studio—you've got to stay focused on the goal.

Were there any obstacles that followed that you had to overcome?

If there are obstacles, it's just learning how to juggle and how to prioritize. Anytime you've got a large, complex system like a recording studio, you've got more than one thing needing attention. Figuring out how to prioritize those things to keep your clients happy is a big part of that situation. The same thing comes along in a trade journal: You're going to have someone who is unhappy with a review because maybe it's honest and maybe their product is not quite where it should be.

So you have to learn to make as many people happy at a time as you can, even if their goals are somewhat conflicting. A reader wants an honest review so he can know exactly what he is getting in a product, but at the same time, somebody else is making their living off of creating that product. I've often said that sometimes writing a review—you can't call anybody's baby ugly. So it's a diplomatic dance to try to serve all those different masters. This is true in whatever role you are in, especially the studio.

The hardships in publishing are rarely in doing the job—it seems the pressures are due to external pressures. For example, the effect 9/11 had on people's advertising budgets—figuring out how your title can address a downturn in the market to keep your fair share of advertising base and advertising revenue coming in. You have to figure out new services and new ways to keep your revenue coming in.

How would you characterize the overall health of the audio market now?

In terms of opportunity to get your voice heard, there are more opportunities than ever before. For jobs it's relatively healthy, but you have to remember, there is a whole generation of people coming up who get their information in different ways than we did. I was in a conversation with a younger guy about some of the ways that people disseminate information, and the subject of email came up. He said, "Email is dead." I live and die by email every day, but for this individual, email was a nuisance and a distraction. His information was gotten through interactive websites, IM, and those kinds of things. For many of these people, email is too slow for how they work.

Magazines are still a very effective way of reaching a controlled audience. We're not standing still and ignoring that the Internet is forcing the dissemination of information to occur differently. Almost everybody who has figured out a way to make money disseminating information on the Internet, at least in publishing, generally has a strong core print element to that. The thing that gives you the staying power on the Internet, for those who have developed a successful online presence, is credibility. You have to figure in the reputation, the value, and where that information is coming from. With an outlet like *Pro Sound News*, you have credibility: 25 years of experience, a professional staff, a consistent voice, and a journalistic approach. We bring credibility to the content that you don't necessarily get in other outlets.

How can someone best prepare to enter the audio media industry with all these changing communication vehicles?

If we're considering a new staffer like we were recently, you're looking for someone with solid writing skills. Those fundamentals are something that have to be included in someone's repertoire, however they get it—through reading or organically, like I did. You obviously have to have a basic skillset there. But beyond that, we could find plenty of people to write for *Pro Sound News* who have a solid journalistic skillset, but if they don't have the industry knowledge, then I'm not going to necessarily consider them. People can grow into their subject matter, but if I can find a person who can combine both, that person will have a much better chance of getting in my door because I don't have to explain to someone what a compressor is, where it fits into the signal chain, who the players are in the industry, and how they interact. I would strongly prefer someone who has a grounded knowledge of the industry in terms of the technology, how it affects business, how it works, and how the business of professional audio itself works: who are the various players at each stage and who controls the purse strings. This kind of knowledge makes you instantly useful the minute you walk through the door.

Learn as much as you can, do as much as you can so that when you're writing about it, you can come from an informed base and a perspective that can be more readily identified by the reader.

Do you have any thoughts on the value of a liberal arts education and getting a good journalistic approach?

Writing is one of those things that improves with age: You want to write as much as you can. That experience might not come from experience of writing for the target market, but you can always translate that to the specific market later. A liberal arts education is good because the more you know and the more rounded you are as a person, the better you are able to communicate with other people. It just gives you more perspective.

Your writing background doesn't necessarily have to come from journalism school or necessarily a strong English major, but those elements certainly can help. You can dangle participles in front of me all day long, and I might not recognize them, but I can read a sentence that makes sense and fix a sentence that doesn't. If I do a double-take on a sentence when I'm reading my article, then I figure my readers will, too, so I will rewrite the sentence.

How important is geography these days?

I think you can be pretty much anywhere; I work out of my house. I'm plugged into the Nashville community still, but I could work out of my house most anywhere in the country. I wouldn't be able to interact as much with people who are active in the music industry in Nashville, though. I think it's more important that you be involved in an active market at the front end of your career than later on. Otherwise, you'll just not have the experience base if you are in Polaski, Tennessee, where nobody has a studio unless it's in their bedroom. If you are around a New York, L.A, Atlanta, Nashville, there are major music facilities where people are doing lots of work. You should never underestimate the importance of interacting with your audience and learning from them, but the physical parts of doing the job are requiring you to be in a certain geography much less than they once did.

What are the typical positions on a staff and the respective salaries? What are the ranks and divisions?

At a magazine like *Pro Sound News* or *Audio Media*, you have a content staff, an editor-in-chief, and some number of assistant editors. Typically in our industry, you will also have contributing freelancers.

The editor is responsible for the overall look and feel and scope of the magazine and its journalistic approach. If you're going to cover a story for *Pro Sound News*, for example, we want you to cover the business angle as well as the technical angle—how people are keeping their clients and why it was important to buy a piece of gear, as well as what the gear actually does for them in production and workflow. I'm the one who sets that model for the magazine. I will have a certain amount of responsibility in the content myself, but I am managing other people who are producing content, reading things as they come in and asking for rewrites or revisions if something doesn't fit. You may be doing a heavy amount of rewriting content to maintain the core vision.

Your staffers will handle various tasks: They may handle your news side of things, your different sections if you're sectionalized. For example, we have a live section, a post and broadcast section, a recording section, a front-page news section, and we all contribute to the web. I manage the technology section. Our managing editor, Fred Goodman, handles the people and other news and products pages in conjunction with me.

The role of the managing editor is kind of that bridge between the editorial staff, who are all about content and words, and production—layout and graphics. The managing editor is that gatekeeper for the flow of content over to the art department to be laid out. He makes sure that the photos are the right resolution and all the other elements are in place to make the story. As things come back from the production department, then all of the editorial staff participates in proofing, fact checking, and making sure we're re-reading things again to make sure that everything goes out on the page right.

On the production side, you typically have layout artists who are working in Quark or some other desktop publishing program. They are telling you if you have too few words or too many to fill a space. Then editorial comes down with something to fit or suggests another photo to help fill a space.

You also have someone in a production manager type of role who acts as the interface between the production team and the printer. That person is taking the pages that were laid out by the art staff, gathering the ad material from your advertisers; they're making sure all of those pieces get together to make sure the printer has everything they need and managing that back and forth.

Then you have the publishing team, who are ultimately responsible for the market of the magazine and who your audience is. That is a very economic role if you have a publisher like I do.

They are very involved in making sure we serve our clients and serve our industry. They have to make sure that the vision for this magazine is useful to its readers, but at the same time make sure we keep the magazine responsive to our advertisers in a way that is a useful vehicle for them, too. The publisher and her team turn around and actually sell that space to the advertisers. They are also responsible for working with the circulation departments to make sure that you have the right combination, number, and balance you need for your readership and to sell advertising.

You've got to maintain that balance but at the same time not have such a large circulation that the advertising budget needed to maintain the physical mailing and the cost of printing and staff is unsustainable.

How much of a finance background must the editor have? Does the editor ever look after business aspects, such as profit and loss?

It's pretty much the publisher's job to worry about that. The editor will have a small budget in comparison to the total budget of the magazine. There are some budgeting issues—I have so much I can spend on a given issue on freelancers in addition to the articles that are coming in from the staff, so I've got to make sure that I keep within that budget.

So you don't need a really strong business background for this?

You don't have to for this one. Sometimes a publisher will grow out of someone in an editorial position, but it's actually more common for them to come up from the sales side, where they have been more exposed to quotas for advertising and hitting those quotas—dealing with the numbers side of it.

What about stress and work life? It's deadline-focused, so how do you deal with that?

We have moments of high stress, but it's fairly manageable as long as you have realistic people who you are working for as publishers. If they understand what it takes to get the job right and they allocate adequate resources to get the job right, it's pretty manageable.

What about hours?

[They are] relatively normal. You have exceptions to that—trade shows, for example. When we are covering trade shows, it can be fairly brutal. The press conferences may happen before the show opens, there are parties and events that people are expecting you to attend. You need to make an appearance at these things and maintain the relationships with many different folks. If you have four people who are expected to cover 500 booths at an AES show, and you turn out a daily newspaper for it, those can be highly stressful days. Sometimes you have to start production early, and getting the magazine to the printers can be a little grueling. In general, though, you can maintain it as fairly routine. If we're covering concerts, you have to make allowances for those sorts of things. It's balanced across the whole team, though, and everybody pitches in to help with different tasks.

Are there standard health benefits?

One of the benefits of doing this as opposed to working in the production flow: Most people in the production flow are self-employed, and they don't have benefits unless they are paying for them themselves. They usually don't have paid vacation time. You also have more time to yourself and a schedule that is more normal—there is value to that. Typically, if you are working for a publishing company of any size, you will have something in the way of an insurance benefit, and depending on the size of the company, 401ks and retirement plans. I don't know of any studios that offer that sort of thing.

If you are trying to make a living freelancing, it is pretty tough. There are lots of people trying to get their names into print and who are willing to write things for you. So if you are willing to sometimes take something that you may have to edit heavily, you can get it pretty cheap. If someone is looking to make a living doing $350 to $850 articles, they will have to do lots of them in a given month. So a lot of your time is selling yourself as well as writing. This needs to be factored into what you are able to do to make a living. In a freelance capacity, many people are doing it for fun money and for supplemental income or for income when times may be lean in other sorts of their work, rather than freelancing for a living. The number of people who can make a living writing strictly for audio trades is fairly small.

That said, there is a limited number of full-time jobs in this industry, and there are people who make it. I would say that for starting salaries, you are going to get low-balled by some folks. Twenty-thousand dollars is not unheard of for a walk-in-the-door position. If you are in NYC that's pretty tough, but in Nashville it may not be so tough. Salaries can go all the way up to the triple digits, but I would say there are not many of them out there.

So what other positions are above you? Whom do you report to?

I'm diffused to these positions to certain extent, as most things can be worked out at the publisher's level. Above the publisher is the vice president of publishing, and he handles new projects or new initiatives or projects that may overlap multiple titles or multiple groups; I will consult with them on specific projects. They don't deal with the day-to-day audio stuff or the content—they are looking to make money. They are saying, "We're coming up on NAB. Should we do a publication on surround audio? What would we talk about and what is different? What manufacturer partner participants does that open the door for?" They are looking for a purely monetary goal of theirs. They are exposed to other pressures.

The best attitude an editor can hope for is a publisher who cares about their industry and wants to see their industry grow. Hopefully, they aren't just concerned about the bottom line. The best position an editor can be in is if the publisher cares about the content and can validate the direction.

In our case, we are a trade journal—we serve an industry, and being plugged into that industry is part of it. You can't just milk it for something and be on the outside and looking in. In the case of CMP Media, they are saying, "We're giving you a certain number of beans every month and we want you to give us more beans back. So go grow us some beans." How you do that and what you write about—at some level up above there, they could care less. Because they have shareholders who are investing in the company who are asking them, "What are you doing to grow my investment?" For those guys, it's all about the beans.

A Closer Look: Orren Merton and the Audio Book Publishing Market

Orren Merton is acquisitions editor for Cengage Learning (formerly Thomson). He has worked in both the magazine publishing environment and for a book publisher. Speaking with Orren, I understand how important a publisher's instinct is, and why it is so important for publishers to be surrounded by good talent: production staff, editors, and of course writers.

Orren Merton.

What are some of the key differences in writing for magazines versus books in the audio publishing world?

I would say that a book publisher is far more concerned with the long view than a magazine publisher is. A magazine publisher by design has to be incredibly deadline-oriented, focused on immediate trends and immediate results in the sense that they have to come up with stories that need to be written quickly and that are hot. A book publisher really has the luxury to develop a project that will have legs and be on shelves for years to come. It will likely have value for a longer time—which isn't to say that all magazines are just disposable, but if you are trying to put together a shootout on microphones, you know that in a certain number of months, there will be other models, and some models will become obsolete.

Many of the books we do have a certain shelf life intended. For example, if we are writing a book on a particular version of software, we know that the software will be updated, at which point the book will be obsolete. But very often you have at least a year or two before the software is updated, so you are still writing for a longer horizon than just a magazine article. Books that talk about trends in the industry, artists, or general musicians' interest topics can very often dive in deep and aren't going to have a limited shelf life. They can survive quite a long time and continue to be interesting.

Can you break out the key roles and groups within your ecosystem? What are the different departments?

There is production services—they are the ones who handle the actual layout and design of the book as a product itself. They bleed into editorial in the sense that production is usually in charge of hiring freelancers, including freelance editorial. That's where the overlap is. I am in editorial services, where titles originate—we brainstorm, research, and come up with book ideas, or we are the ones to whom outside authors pitch. Agents don't really play a big role in technical nonfiction—it is usually the authors themselves who pitch ideas.

How much control do you have over your own destiny in terms of content? Are you driving the ideas?

We are. The PTR group is very autonomous—I like to joke that we are the cool kids, the cool group, because we have the fun titles: the music, the animation, the digital photography—the cutting-edge, interesting stuff. Cengage Learning as a whole is one of the largest academic publishers in the country. In fact, I would say that in any college student's life, they will likely own no less than a dozen Thomson/Cengage-branded learning books. Course Technology is a little bit more end user-focused as opposed to student-oriented. In our PTR division there is more of that—we are retail-oriented, and our main mission is retail. Because the company as a whole is mostly set up for academic books, as long as we are making them money, they leave us alone.

What typical backgrounds are in your group? What kind of mix is there?

There are two people that are acquisitions editors for the music line: myself and Mark Garvey. He comes from a long publishing background and was originally acquiring songwriting titles for *Writer's Digest*. Then he worked for a publishing company called Muska and Lipman, which was absorbed into Course Technology. But before all that, he was a musician and an engineer. In my case, I was a musician and did years of freelance writing, including writing books and editing for Course Technology. Mark finally suggested I apply for a position, which I ended up getting.

There are six or seven other acquisition editors within the PTR group who have widely varying backgrounds. A lot of them have a long career in publishing—the joke in the MI industry is that everyone working in one of these companies at one point or another wanted to be a rock star. They finally ended up as a sales manager for a guitar company or whatever—you may find similar things in photography and animation. These are people who are so into it that they found a way to integrate their passion with their skill sets and make it work—others, not so much.

What are some of the personality profiles that tend to succeed in book publishing?

I think first and foremost, people have to be able to project a sense of mastery of what they are talking about. Even in my position, the people above me who hold the purse strings want to be able to trust me. I also think the ability to work on deadlines is really important. You have got to be able to meet your deadlines.

Part of doing what I do is that you have to be able to balance the personal and the business and know what it takes to be a curator. What I find, especially in the younger writers, is that they can be incredibly talented and nice people, but often they are just a little bit over their head or a little bit insecure. Sometimes a little pat on the shoulder goes a long way. You've got to be able to relate to people.

What about stress and work life?

One of the things about being an acquisitions editor is that as the years go on, you are able to work from home. So on the one hand, working from home is great, because being at home you have inherently less stress than being in an office, where you have a stressful commute and other people to deal with who may be stressed out about deadlines. On the other hand, if you are someone who takes your work seriously, there is a very real danger of being in the office 24 hours a day. In our case, the danger is regulating the time so that you are very specifically working 9 to 6 or whatever. You must give yourself time off, including on the weekends, so you are not always on call, checking email, putting things into databases all day and all night. Some people do get stressed out, but overall, the people who can do this are able to regulate their time efficiently.

Is this business seasonal?

In general, there tends to be a bit of a bump after a trade show—we may have a bunch of ideas for new titles or authors, so there might be more work after a trade show like AES. But generally it's pretty even. However, internally, every corporation has a fiscal year, and we find it tends to be busier toward the end of the fiscal year as far as reporting, spreadsheets, and all that.

What about the income potential for someone coming in the door versus someone with a more fully developed career?

So much of that depends on where you live geographically. The entry level for an editorial spot is about $30,000. Once you start getting into more senior titles, executive editor, or general manager, you might get into the $60s or $70s. You're never going to get rich in publishing.

If you get too high, though, you aren't as close to the content you love, right?

The number of ranks available in any given company really depends on the size of the company. Cengage Learning is enormous, and there are many different levels in editorial. You can go to senior acquisitions editor or executive acquisitions editor. At a smaller publisher, they wouldn't have all these different distinctions. The acquisitions editor might be doing what a copy editor might be doing. We also have a lot of freelance positions that are outsourced.

What have some of the highlights of your career been?

Maybe I can walk you though a successful acquisitions experience. I will be reading the trades or a magazine and I will get an idea. Let's say I read about how bands are using MySpace to reach an audience. I will start talking with my boss and say, "There's a lot of traction here with musicians being interested in MySpace. Maybe there is a book there or an opportunity to help musicians navigate this." So I will look for an author and find one or more people who I can talk to. If we can understand each other, I'll work with an author and I'll collaborate with them and get an idea together. We'll then get a proposal, take it to our editorial board, and the project gets green-lighted with the author under contract. I like to see how the book is going along and then take it all the way until everything has been submitted. The cover and text are done, then it's all off to the printer. I see it on shelves and have it sent to me. I read it and usually think, "This is pretty great. I'm proud of this."

Can you take me briefly through your professional career and how you got into this?

After college I wanted to make it as a rock star. I had a Goth band, but my day job was teaching English part time at a local community college. While I was gigging with the band and song-writing, I was getting into computer music to record ourselves and gear. All of that coalesced along with the Internet, and I just started writing tons of reviews. I did them all for free—before long I ended up as a moderator on Cubase.net and knowing all these people in the business. Eventually, I was paid to write for *Computer Music*.

So the network for you was very important.

Yes. If there is any advice that I can give to people, it is to know the value of what you do, but never be afraid of doing something for free if you know it is going to help you. Because that is how I got where I am. Eventually, I started beta testing for Emagic, the company that made Logic, and then I was hired to write some of their website text, whatever they needed. That led to even more freelance work, which led me to write my first books on Logic for Course Technology. To go back to what I said earlier, I was able to project a mastery of my subject area. I was finally hired as a freelance development editor.

So you got one thing at a time, one brick at a time.

It took years—I don't want it to look like I did this overnight. It took a few years of writing for free before I got my first paid gig, and a few years of freelancing writing before I got my first book. The people who hired me see how I could fit, but they were concerned that I didn't have years of experience in editorial—however, I had the drive and the passion.

What is up around the bend for Orren Merton?

On a personal level, I have my musical project, Ember After, out there—we have a new album out. It is industrial metal. On a personal level I would like to see that do well and sell some records and keep doing it. It is a fun and rewarding sideline. Professionally, I love my job. I would basically like to move up in what I am doing but remain doing what I'm doing. I'd like to keep doing what I'm doing.

6 The Live Sound Market

Live sound is an enormous area of opportunity for anyone seeking a career in audio. When you think about the audio market, it pays to think of it as attached to other mediums of content delivery. In this case, audio is inextricably tied to transmitting sound to the masses. The implications of this are wide-ranging and only limited to the imagination. Consider any conceivable venue with more than 300 people, anywhere in the world, delivering any kind of content that needs to be heard. Think concerts, lectures, drama productions, musicals, religious services, political events, parties, or anything else where a large gathering of people needs to be entertained or addressed.

Although sound-delivery technology has changed drastically, with changing file sizes and innovative delivery mechanisms, delivering live sound to an audience will always have core requirements that include physical speakers of some size and dimension, a sufficient amount of power to drive those speakers, and someone or something to control the levels and output of the audio signal.

Market Viability

Not every vertical industry in live sound will appeal to everybody—without a doubt, live sound touches more vertical industries than any other aspect of audio. Schools, conference centers, cruise ships, community theaters, museums, resorts, churches, theme parks, and casinos all have a need for live sound technicians. Each industry may contain differing ranges of career growth and ability for advancement, but rest assured that if you learn how to mix live sound, you will have a highly translatable, evergreen skill that will always be in demand. This is not true for many other aspects of audio.

In this case, it makes sense to highlight some of the most popular and perhaps most promising aspects of live sound.

Job Profiles and Career Opportunities

Live sound engineers—no matter who they work for or who is receiving the live sound—all have a common goal: to ensure that the audio is heard by the appropriate people, at the right time and at the highest possible quality. If you can learn how to achieve this on a consistent basis, you will be able to write your own ticket in this wildly diverse field. As with any career, however, your talents will be spotted and put to use more successfully in some environments than in others. If you are the AV tech for a single conference room in a hotel with no other locations, for example, you might limit your chances to be exposed to interesting musical content and have limited career-growth opportunities as well—unless the hotel in question has a predefined career track for AV techs. For conference and event work, most of the good work is in the warmer climates: Las Vegas, Orlando, San Francisco, and Phoenix.

Basically, there are two broad categories of live sound technicians: touring and non-touring. Within these two categories, there are entry-level low-paying jobs and senior-level high-paying jobs. The pay generally correlates to the vertical market (such as the education or hospitality market), rather than being tied to any predefined scale of pay in the audio industry. That said, there are many unions available to live sound engineers, and if you join a union, employers are legally obligated to adhere to a scale of pay.

Photo courtesy of Edge Audio Services.

Literally every stadium, concert hall, nightclub, community theater, and auditorium requires a sound technician and/or engineer. Even if a venue's primary income stream is from touring acts, there still needs to be someone on hand who knows how everything is set up and understands the system. Typically, venues need to be able to accommodate a variety of acts; therefore, the engineer needs to be flexible and able to rethink the wiring and sound design for any given setup.

Generally speaking, the smaller the venue, the lesser the pay. However, this is by no means the rule of law. Smaller places that command big names, such as some of the famous jazz clubs in New York City, will deliver higher wages than many other larger venues. It is safe to assume that live sound engineers for the country's largest stadiums are making well into the six figures, because the more people who attend an event, the more liability is on the promoter or other show sponsor to make sure that the necessary conditions are in place to deliver a high-quality performance.

Photo courtesy of Edge Audio Services.

If you are touring, you need to establish a good understanding of a venue's facilities well before arrival. Although many venues have common technical specifications, such as a monitoring position, a front-of-house (FOH) position, power, consoles, and other basic elements, you cannot assume that your setup will run sufficiently on the venue's infrastructure. If there are shortcomings, you need to plan for them and address them well in advance. The touring professional also needs to make sure that sufficient human resources are in place at the venue—specifically, a person who understands the host system and can point to a solution should a situation arise.

Setup and Breakdown

One of the most time-consuming yet critical roles of both monitor and FOH engineers is setup and breakdown. Depending on the scale and duration of the performance, this task can take anywhere from a few hours to a few weeks. For this reason, it is absolutely critical that someone handling the role of a live sound technician know the ins and outs of power, cabling, signal routing, mixing consoles, outboard gear, and speakers. Basically, live-sound folks need to have an understanding of equipment from head to toe—often including instruments, because if there are not dedicated drum techs and guitar techs, live sound engineers can often find themselves filling in for these roles as well.

An important note on skill: Live sound is an area in which it is very important to be up to date on the equipment of the day—the latest digital consoles, monitoring systems, and sound reinforcement gear. You should try to understand and operate as many systems as possible, because this will be part of your vocational "currency." If you have experience on up-to-date, often digital, gear, you have a better chance at getting the gig—and possibly a long-term opportunity.

Following are some of the common roles available in live sound that, for the most part, cross all vertical segments. Importantly, salaries can be much lower in clubs and smaller performance venues, which often pay by the hour or by the gig. Also, depending on the size of the venue, the FOH may have to cover monitors *and* sound design.

Monitor Engineer ($35,000 to $60,000+)

The monitor engineer needs to ensure that the performers are able to hear all aspects of the performance. This is obviously a very important job, because if the performers can't hear where they are in a song or in a performance, it will impact the quality, timing, and delivery of the material—ultimately creating a negative experience for the audience, which will result in decreased revenues...bad for business all around!

Typically the monitor engineer, who is situated near the stage, sets up monitor speakers and wedges in positions that will not interfere with the stage design and the performers, yet that ensure all the performers involved will be within audible range of one of the monitors. He also sets up all the racks, submixers, and power devices. The monitor engineer works closely with the stage designer and sound designer to accomplish this and needs to be very familiar with available equipment choices and technologies. There are many more equipment choices available to the monitor engineer nowadays to achieve success, including wireless in-ear monitors from innovative companies such as Shure, Sennheiser, and others.

Monitor engineers go through a similar sound check regimen as the FOH engineer might go through, albeit on a much smaller scale. Typically, the monitor engineer needs to make sure performers arrive for a sound check at least an hour and a half before show time. The process entails ensuring the monitor system powers up and delivers clean audio to all speakers. It also entails achieving a proper gain structure or audio level for each individual performer. The monitor engineer can have anywhere between 8 and 96 channels going at once, depending on how intricate the performance is.

In a live performance, the monitor engineer typically receives a feed from the FOH engineer, who is most often first in line to receive the signal. Seamless communication needs to occur between the FOH engineer and the monitor engineer to ensure the monitor position is receiving the required channels. A dedicated talkback system also needs to be in place between the performers and the monitor engineer so that the performers can indicate whether a given sound source is audible enough.

Sample Career Path in Live Sound

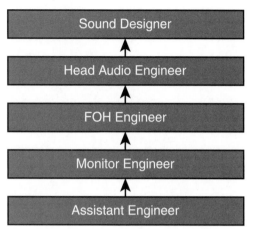

This illustration represents what a career ladder might look like in the live sound market.

It is extremely beneficial for a live sound technician to gain experience at the monitor position because almost every other position in live sound requires an understanding of the monitoring system's role in achieving a good performance. After a monitor engineer masters the skills at hand, typically the next stop is the front-of-house role.

Front-of-House (FOH) Engineer ($60,000 to $120,000+)

The front of house is the "brain" of the performance venue, at least as far as sound goes. Indeed, the FOH engineer is situated in the middle of everything, where he can get a balanced view of the sound and the stage. As mentioned, the FOH engineer is the first to receive the audio signals from the performers. It is not unusual to have up to 96 channels coming into the front of house. The FOH engineer is then responsible for sending any required feeds to the appropriate places—for example, the monitor engineer needs a feed, but maybe a recording truck or a broadcast booth also needs a feed. The FOH engineer needs to coordinate closely with all these destinations, because some might simply require a stereo output while others might need very specific individual tracks. This is one reason why digital consoles have become so popular in live sound over the last decade, and why companies such as Digidesign, who got into the game in 2004, now see this as an opportunity they can't ignore.

The most important responsibility of the FOH engineer is to ensure that the audience is receiving a quality, balanced signal in every possible listening position. To achieve this, obviously the FOH engineer needs to be working in an acoustically suitable environment. He must also have an adequate sound system in place that is capable of delivering the goods. Mixing sound for a large venue is a different game than mixing in a recording studio. Someone once said that the room determines 90 percent of the sound. If this is true, then there is a very substantial difference between a recording studio and a live concert venue.

Photo courtesy of Edge Audio Services.

Any FOH engineer will be able to testify that sound behaves very differently in different rooms. The FOH engineer must not only make sure that the decibel level is adequate, but also that the frequency response is sufficient throughout the venue. Because low-frequency waves are larger and travel farther over a given period of time, the FOH engineer has to be sensitive to whether listeners in the rear of the room or the upper tiers are receiving a balance of frequencies across the equalization spectrum.

The FOH engineer is usually in charge of the sound check for all systems—at the end of the day, the buck stops with him, so if there are any anomalies, it is his responsibility to identify them and troubleshoot accordingly. The FOH engineer relies heavily on a competent team of audio professionals who can handle their respective roles. Because the FOH engineer is at the brain of the audio system, it is usually he who interacts with other roles, including the stage manager, sound designer, and production manager. If a problem emerges during the performance, the FOH engineer will dispatch communications to the team and provide direction for a resolution.

Sound Designer ($80,000 to $120,000+)

In live sound, the sound designer is the first in command of the audio portion of the performance. The sound designer's role is much like an architect's role, as he provides detailed plans of how the performance's sound will occur. The sound designer provides detailed specifications and requirements of the audio system with this in mind. Is surround sound a requirement? Will there be a lot of special effects? Is there an orchestra pit that will have live performers? Do any microphones need to be hidden in and around the stage?

Photo by Jeff Touzeau.

The sound designer is the one with the vision of how the event will play out—all the other roles support this effort, and once the whole machine is finely tuned, hopefully the audience will be on the receiving end of this vision. The sound designer may not have a day-to-day role—instead, he may only be involved at the beginning stages of a new performance or at a critical juncture of an existing one, such as when the performance is being taken overseas. The sound designer is the primary reference point for all the other sound technicians and serves as both a creative and a technical guide to move the project forward. The sound designer usually reports to the event or performance producer.

Entering and Succeeding in the Live Sound Market

Live sound is one of the easier skills to access and master because it is so ubiquitous. There are a lot of jobs out there, as illustrated in the earlier discussion about vertical markets. If you are ready to lend your skills hauling and setting up equipment, most people will welcome having you around. Live sound is not restricted by geography—in fact, wherever you live in the United States, there is likely a local venue that has some degree of sound reinforcement where people congregate. As you move into the larger metro areas, you will also begin to see the larger performance halls.

One good piece of advice is to try to surround yourself with a good team. In live sound, success is dependent on a chain of many people, and (forgive the cliché) the chain is only as strong as its weakest link. Work with people you can have a laugh with and who you can stand working intensely with for several hours a day. You should also be highly tolerant of different kinds of music, because you might have to mix a polka act one night and a punk band the next.

Don't be alarmed if you have to start at the bottom of the food chain. There are many nominal tasks you may have to perform before actually mixing anything. These tasks might include tagging and inventorying the gear, re-padding touring cases, wiring racks, organizing and counting cables, and running occasional errands for the FOH or monitor engineers. If you keep your eyes and ears open while you go through these seemingly routine tasks, you will learn and eventually be in a position to apply your knowledge.

When you have grasped the basic principles of sound reinforcement, you can move into a vertical market that suits your interest or perhaps your music style. And when you have developed an understanding of how sound systems are set up and operated, chances are you will be in demand as a live sound engineer. There may be work at local community theaters or town performance halls, or if you live in a metro area or near a large city, you can offer to assist in a larger performance space.

In terms of skill sets, it makes sense to understand video. This is becoming more and more important in live sound as visual displays become more common in large venues. An audio technician who knows how to work with video people has a valuable skill that will translate onto the event floor and can therefore command a higher salary.

There are many job boards and other leads for professionals in this field, including placement services from audio schools. Most of the individuals I spoke to for this book indicated that networking was vitally important in getting to where they are. Therefore, there is a higher probability of success if you start with people you know and work your network, however large or small.

Another obvious, but perhaps less employed, tactic is to read the trade magazines (there are plenty in the live sound field) and simply get in touch with one of the quoted live sound professionals. These professionals very often have accessible contact information, and anyone who has helped further someone else's career—even at its early stages—will admit that this can be a very rewarding endeavor. First ask these people for advice and, if appropriate, ask them for leads later.

Once you are in the business, you might find that your career becomes naturally propelled by who you know, who you have worked for, and how competent you are. As with any career, you must learn to spot opportunities and align yourself with conditions that will be beneficial to you over time. This includes placing yourself within an environment that has the elasticity to support your own growth.

Traits Valued in the Live Sound Market

If you plan to get into live sound, prepare yourself for long hours and not much sleep. Live sound is very much a field in which you need to pay your dues, and unfortunately there are no shortcuts around this. Therefore, one of the key traits valued in live sound is perseverance. To make it in the field, you have to stick with it. You also have to be a hard worker, ready to employ more muscles than just your brain. It is not unusual (and in fact it is very common) for live sound professionals to be their own roadies and haul their own gear around. So if you are adverse to physical labor, long hours, or not much sleep, you might want to consider another area in pro audio.

Confidence   Physical Capacity
Hard Worker
Strong Constitution
Perseverance   Resilience
Emotional Tenacity Problem Solving
Independent Thinker

Some of the traits that the live sound industry might find valuable.

Another pair of traits you need to be successful in live sound is a thick skin and a strong constitution. Almost every live sound engineer experiences a moment of failure, which can negatively impact a live show. You'll need to be able to swallow your pride and pick yourself back up, even when you have experienced the deepest humiliation in front of your colleagues.

The live sound market values one's ability to pick up and diagnose sound problems—if you have a sharp ear that can detect a hum coming from a floor tom mic, you can quickly gain respect from both your colleagues and the talent.

If you are a touring professional, the live sound market values emotional tenacity. Moving from location to location can be a lonely and draining experience. It can also prohibit you from laying down your roots in any one geographic location. So if you require the sensation of being settled, once again, you might want to consider another area in pro audio.

Benefits and Drawbacks of Working in the Live Sound Market

The biggest benefit to working in live sound, as mentioned, is that you have a highly translatable skill that will allow you to work almost anywhere in the world. Another benefit is that as a live sound engineer, you will be able to experience an enormous range of live events limited only to your imagination. If you are interested in travel, you can doubtless set yourself up to see all corners of the globe with a touring outfit or even a cruise ship—most of which require live sound technicians. It might also interest you to know that most of the top destination resorts in the world require audio technicians. Therefore, it is quite possible to land a full-time job in your version of paradise, whether that is on an exclusive beach, on a faraway mountaintop, or at a world-class ski resort.

Benefits and Drawbacks of
Working in Live Sound

Exciting, Creative	Can Involve Incessant Touring
Offers Immediacy Recording Cannot	Very Often Late Hours
Collaborative Environment	Not Conducive to Family
Highly Transferable Skill	Must Pay Your Dues
Very Secure Industry	On-the-Job Health Risks
Union-Structured	Often Unpredictable Work Environment

If you pursue live sound, you will be part of an international community of professionals and will always have resources at hand to help you in your growth. The live sound market is much bigger than the recording market, and there are many blogs, message boards, and online communities in which you can develop relationships, in addition to the many folks you meet in person. Unions are commonplace working in live sound, so it may benefit you (it might even be required) to become affiliated with a union—this is yet another venue in which you can develop relationships and contacts.

If you are a touring live sound professional, it can become extremely lonely on the road. That said, if you are touring with an interesting group of people, it can be fun and a great opportunity to develop lasting friendships. Craig Cassidy, the FOH mixer for Broadway's *Mamma Mia!*, met his wife while touring—for him, this "benefit" has clearly outweighed other benefits that are more commonplace in the field.

Some of the drawbacks we have already covered include possible loss of sleep. When doing live sound, your own personal time clock becomes the performance's time clock. Load-in occurs early in the morning, sound checks occur in the early evening, performances occur in the evening, and tear-down occurs in the late evening. This is very much a routine, and one around which you will need to schedule your life (unless you are working in a stationary environment that doesn't require equipment changes). This intense schedule has the ability to wreak havoc on your personal life and your family's. If you don't have a family, a live sound career can play a part in seeing that you don't start one, if you aren't careful.

Is the Live Sound Market for You?

If you appreciate the immediacy of live performance, and if you feel more excited at a concert than when listening to a CD, consider working in live sound. However, if you are someone who needs balance in your life, consider that a career in live sound may be all-consuming. It requires intense hours and intense energy expenditure, both mental and physical. If you are someone who has a lot of stuff going on all the time, you might not have the time in live sound to devote to outside hobbies and personal relationships that you might have in another line of work.

If you are determined, persistent, a hard worker, and an audio nut, there will be a place for you in live sound, and you could find it highly fulfilling. Someone who is creative, intelligent, and a quick learner can literally write his own ticket.

A Closer Look: Craig Cassidy and Doing Live Sound for Broadway

Craig Cassidy is the head audio engineer for Broadway's *Mamma Mia!* He has had a love for theater at least since he was a teenager. Craig is one of the few I met doing research for this book who had a laser-focused goal: to work on Broadway. Although the road was a rocky one, as my conversation with him indicates, it is clear that success for him was all the sweeter for having set such a clear goal for himself at the outset.

Craig Cassidy.

What is your role in live sound?

Right now, and what I've been doing for the past 15 years, is I'm a production mixer on Broadway. I freelance—I'm in the union, but I work from show to show. Basically, each new show is a new production company, so I go to work for them. There is not one particular company I am working for; I move from show to show. I've been here at *Mamma Mia!* for five years, and previously I did *Phantom of the Opera* for six. So I've been lucky to get on successful shows that run for a long time.

What do you do at *Mamma Mia!* and what is a typical day like?

I actually mix the show every night, front of house. When we just have one show in the evening, my show call is at 6:30. What we do is fire the system up, do a system check. We go through every mic in the pit, walk the room, check all the speakers and check every wireless microphone. On this show we are using 36 wireless mics. So we spend about 45 minutes doing that. We hand the mics out to the actors, and if there are any system problems, we deal with them at that time. This is all done at 6:30 for an 8:00 p.m. show. Once that is done, we hang out until show time at 8:00. My assistant and I will then mix the show. My assistant will be backstage, and if there is a problem with a wireless mic or any other sound anomaly in the pit, he will deal with that.

Can you walk me through how you got started in audio from the beginning?

I started doing film and shows in high school many years ago. I was very interested it. I did my high school productions. That's what I wanted to do, but there was really nowhere to go to learn those skills—this was in Maryland, and there wasn't really a place to go learn this craft at the time. It was in the early '80s. So I went to the local community college and got involved in the theatre department there. I learned how to build scenery and do the lights. Unfortunately, the theatre I was in at the time only had 200 seats, so there wasn't a need for any sound reinforcement [laughs]! It led me to work at a local theatre, and they put out a small tour, which I joined them on. We had 10 wireless mics, and you were lucky if three of them worked on any given night.

What was it about drama that drew you in? Clearly, you have been passionate about this since high school.

I guess it was because it was a continuation of what I was doing in high school. Also, I wanted to be involved in sound, and I had a little idea on how to do that. When I was younger, I was interested in doing rock shows and things like that, but I got my foot in the door in the theatrical end of it and made my contacts there. I just kept working at it and working my way through the industry.

So you've been in drama for your entire career in audio. Not many other folks in the business can say they've stuck with one silo.

Yes I have. I had some time when I was first starting out in between shows when you'd work for a sound company and you would do everything—monitor mixes and so on. But the bulk of my career has been mixing shows.

Are you self-taught?

I really had no formal education at all. Even in community college, it was really nothing to do with sound. That just taught me the basics on how theatrical productions work. I went out on my first small tour, and it was a really small tour, small system. We did primarily one-nighters for 10 months. Everywhere I went, the house sound guys that were there would teach me a little more. I picked up a tremendous amount of information that way. I was just a 20-year-old kid who didn't know what the hell I was doing, and they helped me along.

Did you have any kind of mentors along the way? How important were other people in helping you along?

As I moved up, I got to work on the bigger shows and with successful NY designers. Abe Jacobs, who originally did *Chorus Line*, *Evita*, *Cats*, and *Jesus Christ Superstar*, really got the whole "sound design" concept going for shows. When I was starting out, he was designing a lot of the big shows in New York at the time, and I think he was one of the first people to come up with a system concept for theatre. I eventually got a chance to work with him, and he was great. I also got a chance to work with Martin Levan for 10 or 15 years; he handled all of Andrew Lloyd Webber's shows in Andrew Lloyd Webber's heyday. I learned a tremendous amount from both of these gentlemen.

What areas of your background, which you either were born with or developed, were most important in achieving your success?

The first thing is that I've always been a really hard worker and always willing to learn and listen to other people. These things are very important. You can't let other people's opinions get you down. You can't let what other people think about how it should sound really bother you. You have to listen to what people say and decide whether it's a valid point. Especially in theatre—this is a really collaborative environment. I work with the conductor and the music director quite a bit. We work together to try to improve the show all the time.

What are personalities like in general in theatre? Are people difficult to work with?

There have been some difficult situations, but for the most part, everyone works really hard together to make it right. I think a big difference between doing sound for theatre or a rock show and recording is that there are compromises. For example, in a theatre production, you can't get the mic in front of the mouth [laughs]! Or the costume designer wants them to wear a hat—this can impact the sound. So you always have to work out a solution around things like that.

Is working in the theatre location-dependent? Do you have to have your sights set on New York, or can you work anywhere?

I started out touring, and I think a good many people do that. They work their way up through the ranks that way, but eventually you get tired of that. It's a good experience, and I had a great time doing it, but eventually you want to sit down and be somewhere. If you're doing theatrical shows, New York is the place to be. Vegas is getting that way now with all the Cirque shows and the other shows that are going out there now. But there are tons of regional theatres you can start out in. There are a lot of job opportunities that way. This is kind of the pinnacle of my field, getting a Broadway show.

What is the hierarchy like there? Who do you actually work for? Give me an idea of the organizational structure.

Sure. As a production engineer, I'm working directly for the sound designer who designed the system. He usually will have an assistant or an associate to look in on the show and give me notes. Our conductor or music director will come out and say, "Can we try this?" and we'll work together as well. The show has stage managers who oversee everything, but they really don't give us notes other than, "You didn't have somebody's mic on." For a lot of it, you are on your own.

So you really have to be a self-starter and not wait for people to tell you what to do?

Exactly. When I come out to mix the show, I've got nobody telling me, "This mic comes on now." It's all on me at that point.

Is there a lot of pressure in your job?

When things start breaking, it can become stressful [laughs]! Especially if you get on a show that has been running a while, you get in a groove. That's why we come in at 6:30 and test everything. We don't just come in and turn the system on and say, "Oh, it's going to be good tonight." We check everything that we can check within reason. And more often than not, we get through the show without a hiccup. But gear fails, and you have to work your way around it. We don't stop the show; the show keeps going!

Who works for you? What kind of help do you have?

On *Mamma Mia!* we have two people in the sound department—myself, who is the head of the department, and I have an assistant. We have it set up where he mixes four shows a week and I mix four shows a week. Then we switch to backstage.

That's a really good way of having your assistant learn the ropes, by putting him front and center. Right?

Absolutely, but the guys we have as assistants aren't just starting out. They've been around for a long time and they have great skills. It's great. That way you don't get so fatigued, and it keeps the show fresh. Plus the show is protected. I've worked on shows before where it's just me, and if you're sick, you just have to suck it up and do it.

When you were learning the ropes, you probably didn't have much of a personal or family life, right?

No, I did not. Well, I can't say that. The good thing about being on a theatrical-type tour is there are always a lot of girls in the chorus [laughs]! And that's actually how I met my wife. This is great—she's not doing this anymore, but she understands how the business works.

So this is almost like a little community of people.

It is, and the longer you are in the business, you end up working with the same set of people, especially as you move higher through the pyramid.

What kind of hours were you doing when you were touring? Were you doing 12-hour days?

Twelve-hour days were short days. When I started out, a typical day was load-in at 8:00 a.m., sound check at 6:00 p.m., show at 7:00 p.m., load-out until 1:00 a.m., then do it all again the next day.

So it's like being on the road like a rock star, but you're the roadie and you're doing everything else, too!

Yeah—it's the rock star without the rest! You have to move your own gear on these shows. You get on a bus, travel to the next city, and sleep. That's on a tour that's doing one-nighters, one week stops. There are tours out there that do four cities a year, and those are great, but those load-ins take longer. They take like a week, because the show is bigger.

When you are done with a tour do you get a break? Is it cyclical, and is there downtime?

The touring slows down in the summer for theatre. Usually they will go out in the fall and shut down in June or so. Then you look for a new job for the fall. You have to be ready to look for the next thing; otherwise, you're not working and not getting paid. The first couple years when I was doing it, I would tour probably eight months, then do something else with those other four months—I would just go from job to job to job. Then, as I moved along in my career, I would stop having those four months and try to figure out how to get a week off here and there.

How would you rate the overall health of this market for someone considering this field?

It's absolutely healthy and still growing.

Now that you have all this experience, what kind of advice would you give people in hindsight?

I think overall, a good way to get into the field would be to look into regional theatre and see if there is anything you can get involved with to just get your experience working shows. The schools now will teach you how to be a sound engineer, and then you can just apply that to the theatrical world. I think many of the schools have reinforcement programs, and the way digital desks are going now—for example, Digidesign is very heavily into live sound now—if you know Pro Tools, you can almost do live sound. Back in my day, you had to kind of find your own way.

How important has networking been during your whole career?

Well, that's how you get your jobs. Basically, as I worked my way up through the field, other people were working their way up through the field in other departments as well. You kind of stay in touch, and they go, "I remember Craig; he was good. Let's get him to do this." I still do jobs for people who I worked with 25 years ago. Having a good network has opened doors for me. I've gotten to do some neat things in my career, like going to Japan, Korea, and Germany to set up shows in all those places. We took the whole rig over to these places—it was interesting working with another culture and making it work. It was a really great experience. I also did a production with *Phantom of the Opera* down in Mexico City, where I was associate sound designer. I oversaw the load-in, set up the rig, trained the mixers, and went back and looked in on it.

You have to make sure the staff is all confident and the whole show is running up to spec, right?

Yeah. In Mexico City, it was difficult because they really hadn't had any experience doing something like that before. We ended up bringing people in from the U.S. and Britain who knew how to do a show, and they trained the locals once we got the show up and on its feet.

What is the best way applicants can break into this field?

Obviously, they're not going to break in and get a Broadway job or one of the high-profile tours. Find a company you can work for or a small theatre company just so you can get experience. Broadway shows don't do internships, but some of the local theatres will let you work for free [laughs].

What kind of pay can someone entering this as a career expect?

I know people who mix Off-Broadway shows do like $300 or $400 a week, maybe less than that. Out in mid-America or the 'burbs, it might be less. When you're starting out, you're not going to make a lot of money. You've got to pay your dues.

And what about a fully developed career?

Somebody touring can probably make between $80 and $100,000. If you're touring, that's it—that's your job, with no chance for other freelancing. While I'm doing *Mamma Mia!*, I also do some design work on the side. That's one of the nice things about being here on a long-running show. They are great about letting me go.

How long did it take you to break into freelancing?

It wasn't conscious. A friend of mine needed help and he called me. He kept having me come back, so I've done a couple shows for him for five or six years now.

What's been the most rewarding aspect of your whole career?

I think just getting here. This is my dream. As a young kid starting out, I wanted to mix a Broadway show. I remember when I first got to New York and was mixing *Joseph and the Amazing Technicolor Dreamcoat*. I remember thinking, "I made it!" It was cool and everything, but then I thought, "Now I need a new goal [laughs]!"

You're really living your dream.

Yes. I'm very fortunate and doing exactly what I wanted to do. It makes it a pleasure. At some point this show will close, but I'll just move on to the next one.

What excites you most in the theatre?

When it all comes together, it's quite spectacular. When you're doing one of these shows, it's 60 to 80 people coming together with one goal—to put on a good show. When the show is new and you're getting it all sorted out, there's a big rush, and it can be really exciting. But once you've done it as long as I have, it's kinda like driving to the store.

Where do things go next for you?

I really still enjoy mixing shows, so it would be hard for me to transition out of that. I have been doing more design work, and I hope to continue doing that in the future.

What is typically involved in design work?

For one of these shows, you come up with a system that is going to achieve your sonic goals for that production. Then you meet with the director to find out what kind of sound effects will be required. Then you get together with the music director and find out what the pit setup is going to be. In theatre we have to design a communication system, a video system. Since we were the last department to come around in theatre, and since we were really small and didn't have a lot to do, anything else that needed to get done in theatre kind of got dumped on us—so that's how we ended up with video and communications.

Do you have an outside passion, and have you been able to cultivate an outside interest?

Yeah, my family and I enjoy sailing. We've been doing that for the last 10 or 15 years. It's funny— I know a lot of sound guys who do that. I think during my 20s and 30s, I was just consumed with moving my career along. Once I achieved my goals there, I had the opportunity to pursue other interests as well. I think it helps a lot to get away from it and just clear your head.

A Closer Look: Rich Mullen and Working in Live Sound

Rich Mullen and his business partner built Edge Audio Services from the ground up. While Rich always had a love of music and audio, the backbone of his success has always been built on sheer determination and having a solid understanding of how to run a business. Rich is all about preparation, and for him, focus is the name of the game—in fact, he believes that most of the work on a job actually occurs *before* the crew is on site.

Rich, what were your first experiences in audio?

I spent a lot of my early years in studios—I think that's a good background for any facet of the audio business. The reason is that working in a studio, particularly on the inside of the glass, gives you that left-brain/right-brain mix that you need to know how to use gear, mic things up, get the right sounds, and also bolster waning confidences on the other side of the glass. It is a great background.

Photo courtesy of Edge Audio Services.

Rich Mullen.

What did you study in college?

I got an undergraduate degree in finance and worked in that field for a while. I didn't go to college right away—I waited for two years and played out a lot during that time. I don't remember exactly why I went to business school, but my father was a businessman and had at some time, unbeknownst to him, made some impression on me: "You should go to business school." That sears into a young boy's brain. I got through that, I did very well in college, got out and got a job. After about six or seven years of doing things like accounting, point of sale, and inventory control, I got the idea that I wanted to start a business. I was still playing as a guitarist in a band this whole time—in fact, there were times I was playing 280 dates a year, so it was almost as if I had two jobs. I realized I was much happier doing the audio stuff.

I got a business plan together for a rehearsal studio north of Chicago—we built the recording part of it in the other side of the building. As the business developed, we were doing a lot of rehearsals, and the project studio we had developed into a mid-level studio. Live sound was another component we added—so in all, there were three components. After about six years of that, the live sound kind of dominated.

So things started to take hold and the business was viable?

It was a real business. I wasn't making the greatest money, but my wife and I were able to struggle through it. She has always been very helpful, and most of my success has been based on that support. After six years of running a mid-level studio, we realized we were going to have trouble. The DAW stations were coming out, and the ADATs were fading. The market was not good, and we had a very limited upper end in terms of what we could charge. The same was true for the rehearsal studios. If you have four or five of them, what is the most you can make? There is a ceiling to it.

So after six years we left that business model, and my business partner and I, who is also a very close friend, changed the business model to be just live sound production. It was a difficult year. Two years into it, though, we started to see significant growth, and we have had that ever since. Now we are a pretty big company.

Did this make you feel more secure in your career?

I still don't feel like I'm secure, and I don't think anyone who owns a business ever does. I first started to feel like this was a career when I started to do a couple of jobs for theatrical comedy groups that had corporate training arms where they go around and do corporate events. We ran into them once, and we did a really good job. I made it a point to keep going after them, asking them to recommend us. All the business we initially got was through people I knew and repeatedly mentioning what we did. These people knew I was a decent and honest guy.

So initially, your work was based more on your drive than on your talent?

No question about it. There is the initial "it's not what you know, it's who you know" adage that holds a lot of business. The early years were about making personal connections and trying to wring as much out of that as I could—then you learn as you go. Based on the kind of person you are and your tolerance of risk, you decide how far you want to reach into a given situation. My partner and I tend not to reach too far out of our core competency—we go for help when we need it. We train our people during slow times because I fear that one major failure can diminish your chances for success.

What do you see as your niche in live sound?

When someone hires us, we can be successful. I don't really care whether there are bigger event producers in town. They don't have to call us all the time—they only have to call us when it matters. Eventually, you see live sound in the field, but the success happens in the warehouse and in the preparation. It is essentially a warehouse business, capturing details early on in advancing the process of the show. Then it is about disseminating that process quickly and simply to the operations staff who get the equipment prepped. We can produce as many as 10 shows in a week, and we have lots of equipment. These things have to turn around quickly—there is a lot of stuff.

Where did the business background come in handy?

When my inventory control background came in, I started to realize that we could do this better than other people once my business partner and I realized we could split roles. I could take the business background and create an operational system to help us capture details around a show; this helps us get prepped quicker. I also structured all our expense and capital expenditures in our financial systems, making it a business. Once we were able to make it a business with structure, job descriptions, and all the other things, I realized we were so far ahead of many of the other companies who were just going out and doing "rock 'n roll sound." I have a love of sound, but I realize also that history is littered with good sound people who couldn't run a business. Those companies are now defunct—the same is true for studios.

Walk me through a typical process from client call to execution.

First, there are different levels of clients. There are major event producers who do this all the time, and these folks know exactly what they need and want for their productions. They know how to communicate this to those who execute the show and provide a technical rider—a document that communicates the needs of a show. A less educated client might call and say, "I'm having a show or a business meeting." I ask them how many days, how many people, is there PowerPoint, what is the room like, how many mics they need. I literally have a checklist, and I ask them about all these things. I will then draft a quote, and if we receive a second call, our estimate to contract is about 90 percent. The contract gets signed and is confirmed in our system.

Then we do site visits, and often a floor plan will get drawn up in CAD. This is to provide the clients with an idea of the scope, but it also serves as a secondary piece of information to the operations people as well. Speakers go here, screens go here, cable runs go here, front mixing console goes here, that kind of thing. After CAD drawings, we schedule loading times with the hotel or convention center. We will then stage and prep all the equipment, usually a day before it is delivered. Then we schedule a truck delivery based on what time is in our system and send at least two of our guys as well as some freelance labor.

We will set up, and then do a rehearsal for the client before the actual event. The operators then stay for the duration, and then we load out and do the next one. Then the process gets repeated. Last year we almost did 500 shows.

What are some of the key things to keep in mind during all this?

In all walks of the live audio business, what matters is your ability to communicate to clients. What I call my A1 not only has to be good at operating the digital console or the tech piece *du jour*, but he or she also has to be presentable and know how to communicate. The same is true for topnotch monitor engineers for people who are touring with major artists. Those guys don't get hired because of their EQ skills, but because they are able to talk to and gain respect from that client. They are able to say no to that client in a way that makes them understand. I have a bunch of stock lines I always tell employees, and one of them is, "You can say no to the client, but you have to explain why and do it with respect and a smile."

What are some of the key roles in your business?

We have salespeople and we have project managers. The salesperson goes in and gets the basic quote to the person—without the little details. If the show gets confirmed, the project manager takes it to the next level and fills in everything. Project managers have been out in the field for years, and they have to be seasoned, know all the gear, and know how it all goes together. There are also event technicians—all our guys are event technicians and can do different things. Then there are operations technicians, which is a warehouse position. They fix gear, drive, and load trucks. For us, this is a good "foot in the door" position. They are good with soldering irons—they handle the fundamentals. After all, you are not going to start mixing on a big console—before you do that, you need to understand every wire in the sound system and you need to understand signal flow.

While I started and own half of the company, I don't know how to operate some of the gear that we have. I've been to lots of training, but I've never done a show on some consoles, even though I know what they will do. I can easily communicate to a client as to whether or not they need a certain piece of gear or how best to achieve what they are trying to do. Project managers need to know more than this and get to the nuts and bolts. Even technicians need to use both sides of their brain if they are going to move up to project manager, which is a salaried position.

What makes you proud to be a part of this business?

As my career has gone on and my job has morphed into being a boss running a business, I realize I'm very good at that. I'm good at being a leader and delegating. We've been reasonably true to our vision. As you delegate you have to communicate goals—not specifically how to get to the goals.

A Closer Look: Jim Kerr and Live Sound

Jim Kerr is a live sound professional who lives in Phoenix, Arizona. In my conversation with Jim, I realized the value of sheer determination and hard work. Live sound is not an easy gig—there is a lot of pressure, physical stress, and thankless hours that can make domestic life seem very elusive indeed. One of the reasons Jim has been successful is because of his enormous will and perseverance in the field.

Jim Kerr.

Jim, how did you get into all this?

My father is a disc jockey in New York, so on Saturday mornings I used to go to the studios when he was on air, and I used to sneak into FM2 and play around with the gear and tape machines. I would edit my own bits and spots and pretend to be a disc jockey and be involved in the whole production. I was doing that for like a year when I was a kid. I must have been 10 years old.

So you were creating this whole imaginary world for yourself while your dad was doing the real deal next door.

That's when I first really enjoyed the concept of production and when it became fun. Then came the Tascam four-track cassette, which I got for Christmas one day.

When did you get the sense that you could do something along these lines as your real job?

Early on, I wanted to play music; I wanted to have my hands in all forms of creation of it. During that time, when I was 11 or 12, I was going to a lot of rock concerts, seeing how it was all happening. I saw the Who at Madison Square Garden from the catwalk, which definitely gave me an unusual perspective. During high school, I was into playing music, skateboarding, and girls. I began to acquire some equipment and started recording.

I went to a summer program at Berklee in Boston, and that opened my eyes to other avenue of what can be done with audio and how it can be done. I've been in the industry ever since.

When did the live music part become apparent?

I wanted to become more involved with other people. That was one factor. I did have experience in the studio by this point, but I just wanted to get involved in other things. I went over to the Bottom Line, and the owner, Alan Pepper, was gracious enough to take me on board. I got involved, and that was kind of mind-blowing. There were so many things happening, and I still felt like I was part of the music.

I started out as a stage technician and was really learning all aspects of live sound. I was learning all the standards—dealing with stage blocks, a stage manager, and all those things. Also, you learn very quickly that when it's live, it is a one-shot deal. There is only one chance to get it right. The pace was definitely different, and the timing was really intense.

I learned a lot from that, and then a few months later I hopped onto monitors, where I had actual control over part of the audio aspect. The talent at the Bottom Line was pretty much established acts: You would have Steven Tyler from Aerosmith or Ringo Starr—he would come through. It was intense and a lot of fun.

When did you feel like you had a handle on things and could make a career out of this?

I think it was during a show. There was probably a moment when I realized that what I was doing was absolutely correct and working. I was accomplishing what I thought I wanted to accomplish. This became apparent when I noticed that the bands felt very comfortable with what I was achieving for them sonically. Even my suggestions were very welcomed by some very professional acts—that is a huge compliment. So I could finally sit back a little, and things were really good. I also sensed that I could have a direct impact on making the show better based on what I was doing.

What are some examples of things you knew you had to get right?

Eventually I knew what sounded good, in contrast to how it is supposed to sound to the audience and to the performer. The performer has his or her own perspective, and I would definitely try to put myself into the performer's shoes. What do they expect and what do they want? I was definitely open-minded without being too experimental. With each piece of experience, I would get more confidence and apply new things I learned that seemed to work. I also learned to be able to translate. Some artists don't know how to ask for what they need. I learned to anticipate what they were looking for.

This seems like a very important skill you were learning almost subconsciously.

It's weird because there is a sense of love of the music. It just happens. One time Richie Havens played at the Bottom Line. We had a finicky light board, and I was working monitors at the time. He was playing acoustic guitar, maybe a bass player. We had a nice sound system, all encompassing, and he was rocking. Sometimes, though, the lights would go out, and to fix that, the lighting guy would have to lift the board up about an inch and then just drop it down. It was like the jukebox on *Happy Days*. He was rocking out on "Freedom," and the lights went out. For me, I knew what was happening. I don't know if the audience knew, but I knew the lights had failed. But the music is still rocking on. Nobody flinched. Then the lights banged back on, and the music kept going. Suddenly, Richie is back in the spotlight, and it was almost surreal as he was singing "Freedom."

Artists like that sense of being on the edge a little bit, and you don't really get this in the recording studio unless the producer is really good. Those things happen and can be intriguing—that sense of a great live performance. You can learn to anticipate some of these things, though—for example, the bass player may play softer. The guitar player may turn up, or the singer might sing softer during the performance.

One of the things I have learned doing monitors is the importance of visual communication. It is almost a sense of sign language between the mixer and the artist. There is all this weird body language that goes on that is not really taught but is most certainly used.

What is the best way to get the whole picture in live sound? Is there any recommended path?

Most of it is learning it from other people. There is always a previous engineer working before you who has his own style. For example, this guy says you cut only on the graphic equalizer—they won't boost anything. You tend to learn each person's approach and apply your own variance of that.

Generally, it is helpful learning as a stage tech. You learn that things will be happening that you are not expecting. You can read through textbooks and gain a lot of knowledge, but there is nothing like going through the real experience. As a stage tech, you learn about polarity, signal flow, phantom power, isolation, and so on. Monitors come right afterwards—they are the clos-est thing that is happening to the stage outside of the band. When you are working the monitors, you are working more closely with the band—they want the sound a certain way.

Did you feel the urge to move beyond the clubs? How do you break out of that?

I definitely wanted to grow out from the clubs. It's a little scary because you can get stuck in the clubs. Sometimes it pays very well, sometimes it doesn't. When it paid well, I would remind myself: I just worked with Roger Daltrey. There is a mutual respect—the artist usually appre-ciates what you do, and you certainly appreciate what the artist is doing. The most rewarding thing on working the clubs was that I was able to do something that I have always dreamed about doing.

What strategies did you put in place to take things to the next level?

A lot of it is networking, finding other people who wanted to do other things and had the same thing in mind as me. I would find people who I had worked for, and they would ask me, "Hey, can you record us?" or, "Hey, can you mix us at this club?"

The Bottom Line had closed when I was there, and that was pretty crazy. There were several spin-off gigs that occurred after the Bottom Line, then I went over to work at the Bowery Ballroom—I saw Kenny Lionheart, the production manager and the FOH engineer there. I told him I was looking for a job. The Bowery Ballroom by that time had been a pretty well-known venue, and I told him I could work right away. I got a call a couple days later to come on down.

Things were set up a little bit differently, and it took a little bit of getting used to. One thing I learned is that the routine is so important at a venue. The wheels just run easier if you learn this, and every club has its own routine. I stayed at the Bowery Ballroom for about four years, and that was higher pay. It actually helped because the whole situation was more my thing. There was a lot more hanging out with other bands, and there was a lot more freedom. There are a lot of new, young bands coming in.

That led to really branching out—then I started to do some work with John Hanti in Wee-hawken. I did mixing for rehearsal sessions for people like Lenny Kravitz, who was auditioning a bass player at the time for a huge charity rock concert. I also began doing sound at the 92nd Street Y in New York City—that was completely different. I would mix Hillary Clinton, or Billy Joel talking about his songs. Another time I did a musical there—my sort of "Broadway." That was fun.

So what are you up to now?

I am actually freelancing. I got in touch with the union down here in Phoenix, where I live now. I've taken some jobs from them, and I'm going to see where that goes. I recently got a call to do some work during halftime at the Super Bowl, a gig I got through IATSE [*International Alliance of Theatrical Stage Employees*]. They cover all aspects of production—I have done about three or four jobs for them so far. The cool thing about it is there are all sorts of different people with different skills, and it is a learning experience. For example, you learn about people like riggers. You spend 70 hours working with these people doing it. I was able to put my skills to work with what I know through this union.

Why did you move to Phoenix?

I had been in New York for 33 years and just needed a change of pace. I was at the Bowery Ballroom and I had left when we had finally gotten our big 50-percent raise. That company expanded immensely and they are doing all sorts of work and paid their employees very generously. That was great, but I left them about a month after that—my fiancée and I decided we wanted to try a new frontier. When I came out here, I had a couple of leads and phone numbers to call, but that was about it. It was going a little on the blind side, and I'm taking my chances.

What is most important in live sound in terms of getting it right?

Take the case of Bowery Ballroom: The band comes in and they are saying, "We're playing at one of the best venues in the country." They are expecting a lifetime kind of gig. We help take the pressure off the band and get everything going until they achieve a satisfactory result. That makes all the difference.

7 The Broadcast Market

The broadcast market is an exciting path for many because it provides nearly immediate interaction with an audience. No other field in audio offers this level of interaction, except live sound. Although many tried-and-true broadcasting techniques remain the same, the field has been swept with changes, including new mediums such as satellite TV and radio, podcasting, and web streaming. On the whole, broadcasting has been tremendously impacted, mostly for the better, by the proliferation of the Internet and broadband networking.

Broadcasting is also becoming more segmented and specialized as time goes by. Because newer mediums such as the Internet and satellite have a greater capacity for multiple channels than, say, FM radio, there is an opportunity to work within a very targeted subject area that suits your interests. If you consider all of the content offerings on satellite TV—for example, everything from the Food Network to the Animal Planet to the History Channel—you will soon find that areas of interest are almost limitless, not to mention the potential consumer consumption.

Market Viability

The broadcast market has experienced steady growth over the past two decades, primarily due to the increased number of television stations—including cable and satellite outlets. There is plenty of work in this industry. According to the US Department of Labor, there are more than 30,000 jobs throughout the country, and this is expected to grow at a fairly average growth rate over the next five years.

To remain competitive, broadcasting companies have to stay on the cutting edge of technology. This applies to their entire equipment and technical infrastructure—if this is not up to date, they face a competitive risk. Therefore, candidates who have a solid understanding of DAWs, digital consoles, and various broadcast mechanisms stand a better chance at being employed.

One of the broad trends that puts the field at a slight disadvantage is the consolidation of the broadcasting conglomerates—one of the ways these conglomerates remain efficient and profitable is that they tend to broadcast from a single location over many geographies. This means that fewer technical positions are required to carry out the broadcasts.

Photo by Stephanie Susnjara.

Steve Aprea of WNEW-FM.

As far as the competitive landscape is concerned, candidates will have less trouble in non-metropolitan areas where wages are generally less. Plenty of opportunities will be available in major metropolitan cities, but competition will also be stronger—and folks who pay their dues at smaller stations and broadcast outlets in middle America typically are the ones who get the jobs in the major metropolitan areas.

Job Profiles and Career Opportunities

Broadcast technicians exist to ensure that an audio or video transmission gets to the audience without a hitch—much like a live sound engineer's job is to deliver reliable audio to a crowd. Typically, though, a broadcast technician's audience may be up to millions of people—therefore, there is no room for error. Although broadcast is possibly not as "sexy" as working in a recording studio, it is equally as challenging due to the fast nature of the business. Pressure is high, and the demand for consistent performance is uncompromising.

Some of the common tasks entailed in the technical side of broadcast might include installing and testing equipment, mixing shows, setting up mics, sending and receiving various audio feeds, recording on location, and recording voiceovers and announcements. The prospect of broadcasting music ensembles is becoming less common, though there are still pockets of this kind of work out there for those desperate to have one hand in music.

One significant overall trend is that broadcast companies are expecting employees to have multiple skills. Typically, this means that producer types are also expected to have knowledge of audio, or reporter types are expected to have knowledge of preparing stories for both web and television. Although there will always be valid roles for technicians in broadcast, engineers with ambitions to learn multiple skillsets will have the chance to diversify their talents in a market that is being forced to become more efficient.

Rural operations in non-metro areas are often a good way for broadcast professionals to learn and apply a variety of skills. Indeed, these outfits have smaller staffs and smaller budgets, so where they come up short in pay, they may deliver the goods in teaching you important skill sets.

Broadcast operations require a strong team environment in which everyone is working off of the same page—nobody is working completely independently, and all the production jobs are truly interconnected. Roles in broadcast might not be so obvious at first glance, but if you think about it, everything that you hear on television or on the radio likely has had someone take the time to set up the microphone, get a proper line level, and mix it with other channels or tracks as appropriate.

Sample Career Path in Broadcast

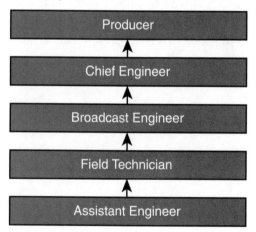

This illustration represents what a career ladder might look like in broadcasting.

In broadcast and television, the career path can be more defined than in other audio fields. You can begin as an assistant engineer, setting up microphones and eventually handling multiple shows as your competency and reputation permit. Let's take a look at some of the various audio positions available in broadcast.

Chief Engineer ($80,000 to $160,000+)

Any broadcast operation needs to ensure that its gear conforms to FCC broadcasting standards and is up to date, technically speaking. The chief engineer decides how this technical infrastructure should be set up—often for more than a single location, given the needs of the business.

As a primary resource allocator, the chief engineer decides what physical space is required for broadcast and mixing, whether digital consoles are required, what DAW platform will be employed, and what the budgets are for equipment upgrades and maintenance. He or she identifies and budgets all equipment expenses, from mic cables to large-format broadcast consoles. The chief engineer also oversees all of the engineering staff—it is a technical and an administrative role, in as much as he is spending time planning and aligning resources in addition to dealing with technical issues. The chief engineer determines how many engineers are required on a specific show and often assigns roles to make sure each shift is covered from beginning to end. He also decides whether audio technicians will be required out in the field to accompany producers doing on-location stories (and, if so, how many audio technicians will be required).

Broadcast Engineer ($50,000 to $70,000+)

Broadcast engineers are always in high demand at television studios, radio stations, and public broadcasting companies. They are the ones who make it all happen technically. In many ways, their job is not unlike that of a recording engineer's—they are responsible for the overall quality of the signal chain, which is ultimately going out over any number of broadcast media that may include cable, satellite, the Internet, or traditional AM and FM wavelengths. However, broadcast engineers can typically experience a much wider range of content than their recording engineer counterparts because TV shows, newscasts, and events can cover almost any conceivable category of content.

The author as an amateur broadcast engineer in college.

Broadcast engineers work in shifts because at most places, there needs to be coverage around the clock—time is not booked as in the case of a typical recording studio. Broadcast engineers are very much in a seniority-driven environment—usually the newbies will end up working the late evening/early morning shifts or the weekend shifts. As they become more experienced and climb the seniority chain, they will encounter more normal hours and find that they are working fewer weekends.

On a typical day, the broadcast engineer will meet with the rest of the staff at a planning meeting, where appropriate resources will typically be assigned for several shows. A multi-feed broadcast that has content coming in at different times and from different locations and that is an hour long might require more engineers than, say, a simpler interview-based broadcast that is only a half hour long.

Before any broadcast, the broadcast engineer needs to assess his resources with sufficient time before the production begins. This means making sure that he has the correct mics set up, getting together all the tapes and other material that may require playback on the show, and checking all the levels. An actual production will almost always entail bringing in other content from the outside at the appropriate time and intermingling it with other live content—possibly from a newscaster, a reporter, an interviewee, or other on-air talent.

Outside content can come into the board from a telephone, ISDN, satellite phone, or almost any other imaginable medium. All of the music breaks and commercials are most often pre-recorded, as are the billboards, or the short segments you hear at the top of the hour.

The broadcast engineer typically has an adequate control room from which to operate, usually with an accompanying vocal booth for the on-air talent.

Broadcast engineers are expected to get it right all the time. Consistent performance is just the beginning, and live air has no room for slip-ups. Therefore, reputations become very important among broadcast engineers, and if you have a very successful track record, you can command higher-paying positions.

Field Technician ($35,000 to $50,000)

An assistant engineer (see the following section) typically graduates into the role of field technician. Field technicians provide a critical dimension to broadcasting because news and events can happen literally anywhere in the world. And in this day and age of satellites, wireless, and Internet technology, there is nothing stopping information in the field from getting to the studio.

The field technician typically accompanies a producer—who is responsible for the story or the reporting—to provide all the required conditions to capture the audio (and often these days, video) that will be fed back to the studio. The main responsibility of the field engineer, apart from ensuring that the audio comes in cleanly, is allowing the producer and reporter to focus completely on the content. There is a trend in broadcasting in which companies are now forcing producers to handle engineering tasks, too. This ultimately has a negative impact on finished content because producers can't be expected to adequately handle these wholly different tasks, both of which are critically important.

Field technicians need to be aware of the subject and location from which they will be expected to capture the audio and plan resources appropriately. For example, if there is a broadcast occurring from the Jersey shore, chances are it may require a shotgun mic with a heavy-duty windscreen. If it is an indoor campaign event, perhaps a small diaphragm condenser mic is more appropriate. Whatever the case, field technicians need to have rugged gear at their disposal— gear that will not fail. They have to plan for sufficient power as well, since in many cases power receptacles mght not be available.

In addition to allowing for clean audio-out signals, the field technician also has to ensure that the on-location reporters and producers have adequate monitoring. This is typically handled with unobtrusive, portable in-ear monitors. The producers and reporters in the field need to be aware of any communication from the studio—both on the air and off—so their segments will sync accordingly.

Being a field technician often means that you are not leading the cozy life. Assignments can send you to a wide range of physical locations—some more demanding than others. Travel and sleep often are not the best of bedfellows, and sometimes you can drive or fly several hours just to capture a segment that is less than a half hour in length.

Assistant Engineer ($25,000 to $35,000+)

The assistant engineer's role in broadcast is pretty much what you would expect—making sure the broadcast engineer has everything he or she needs to get the job done effectively. This can mean setting up for sessions, warming up the recording console, pulling playback segments that will be required for a given program, and even ushering the talent into the booth.

The assistant engineer is very often on the receiving end of the grunt work and also the non-desirable hours—unless he has a penchant for having breakfast at 7:00 p.m. and working the night shift, weekend hours, or the Fourth of July. This is part of the dues-paying cycle, and unfortunately there is no easy path around it for most entering the field.

Even though the assistant engineer is at the bottom of the food chain, there is a lot to be learned just by listening and asking questions. Very often broadcast houses are not sufficiently staffed, which means that the assistant engineer can perform the tasks of a regular broadcast engineer and very often get paid at a corresponding pay scale.

In the role of assistant engineer, it is very important to demonstrate self-sufficiency. Nobody wants to handhold or babysit someone—there are simply not enough hours to go around for this. The assistant engineer who takes the initiative to read manuals, align himself with a mentor, and work hard at supporting his technical colleagues will be most successful and highly regarded by his peers.

Entering and Succeeding in the Broadcast Market

There are many ways to enter the broadcast market. First, there are plenty of job boards and message boards in the field. There are also events that are full of industry professionals, such as the annual NAB (*National Association of Broadcasters*) event held in New York City. Aspiring broadcast engineers, as mentioned earlier, will find that their prospects for employment (at least initially) are substantially improved outside major metropolitan areas. Major markets, such as New York City, Chicago, and Los Angeles, typically only hire experienced talent, often importing them from the suburbs of middle America. Also as mentioned earlier, broadcast is very much a "pay your dues" business—as is live sound. You can expect low salaries starting out, but as Stuart Rushfield notes in the case study later in this chapter, there are exceptions when you factor in the possibility for overtime and union wages.

It may come as no surprise to you that there are many more jobs in television broadcast than in radio broadcast—for the simple reason that video is very quickly becoming the dominant broadcast medium. In terms of required education, most of the audio technical schools have broadcast silos that will help you come to grips with the gear found in a broadcast studio. Often they are common Pro Tools setups or DAWs such as Cool Edit Pro—any common skills you learn on DAW platforms will be widely applicable in a broadcast job.

Many folks start their careers in broadcast quite early, in high school or at their local community college, helping out with school radio broadcasts or the local cable TV show. If you have worked in an environment such as this, even if it is an amateur studio, that will carry some weight during the interview process and perhaps will put you at an advantage over another candidate who only has experience from, say, an audio institution.

Traits Valued in the Broadcast Market

If you enter the broadcast market, you have to have resilience and a strong backbone. There will be plenty of bumps and frustrating moments when you'll wish you had chosen another line of work. The industry values people who stick with it—hard workers who can earn their own wings instead of having them handed to them. Be prepared to "serve" in multiple geographies— it is extremely uncommon to be able to build a fruitful career in a single location.

Flexibility   Accuracy

Curiosity

Communications Skills

Hard Work   Resilience

Reliability   Collaboration

Technical Skills

Here are some basic traits that may be valued in the broadcast industry.

Because a broadcast can be so unpredictable, the field also values people who can go with the flow and recalibrate their approach at a moment's notice. As mentioned earlier, perhaps what employers value most in this field is not making mistakes on the air.

The field also values people who can multitask. When one show is wrapping up, another is starting; therefore, there is often very little time to plan. If you can "get into character" for each show or production quickly, you stand a better chance at succeeding. Also, setting up monitor mixes for people in the field, while receiving other incoming content that needs to be broadcast, can be logistically challenging and stressful if not done correctly, so multitasking will serve you well in this scenario, too.

As far as audio is concerned, the name of the game is clean, audible audio. In broadcast, the value of colorful preamplifiers and esoteric microphones is much less, and performance, transparency, and reliability are key. EQ is applied only to make the signal more clear or audible—not to enhance its personality. This is a different way of thinking for most audio engineers, and those who recognize the importance of audio integrity will gain the respect of their peers.

Benefits and Drawbacks of Working in the Broadcast Market

If you are in broadcast, the content can be highly diverse and exciting. You can be exposed to many colorful characters and personalities—broadcast can be similar to audio books in that sense. Another benefit is that the broadcast market is highly unionized, and this ensures that employees working in relatively similar ranges of responsibilities are compensated fairly. There is also the adrenalin rush of broadcasting to the masses. For many people, this can raise the level of performance and lead to a unique feeling of accomplishment, or a "high." And once you are a known entity and have a good reputation, you can also enjoy a substantial degree of security, maintain an excellent salary, and possess a highly transferable skill that can play in just about any geographic market.

Benefits and Drawbacks of
Working in Broadcast

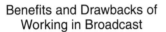

+	−
Diverse Content	Relatively Low Pay
Highly Transferable Skills	Erratic Hours/Schedules
Growing Market	Content Can Be Tedious
Unionized Workforce	Long Promotion Ladder
Relatively Secure Career	Pay-Your-Dues Mentality
Adrenalized Environment	Companies Trimming Resources

Because seniority plays such an integral part in the field of broadcasting, most of the drawbacks are for entry-level or junior-level employees. Negative aspects include the hours, which can be sporadic, and unpredictable shifts. For someone with family interests, this can be highly disruptive, and it can make you a stranger at home to other family members. Junior-level employees are expected to work on weekends and on holidays when everyone else is off—there is simply no way around this.

Very often, unless you land in a particularly interesting company, content can be boring. At a news station, for example, listening to news broadcasts day in and day out can take its toll—especially considering that news is not usually all positive. But from an interest and content perspective, there are many places you can work in this field, so it makes sense to try to be somewhere that aligns with your interests. If you like cooking, it can't hurt to send your resume to the Food Network, for example.

Is the Broadcast Market Right for You?

If you are resilient, quick on your feet, a master of multitasking, and ready to handle many simultaneous tasks, this may be the career path for you. If you are looking for an environment that is predictable and doesn't have much pressure, chances are you should look elsewhere.

It is important to understand that music doesn't often play a substantial role in broadcast, so if you are passionate about recording music, you might have to have to plan on scratching this itch in your home studio or during off hours. Many audio schools these days claim that everyone can be gainfully employed as a music-recording engineer, and as this book clearly illustrates, this is simply not the case in today's market.

A Closer Look: Stuart Rushfield and Public Broadcasting

Stuart Rushfield is a senior engineer at NPR. He is another example of someone who has known more or less exactly what he wanted to do since he was little—become a sports announcer. Although he never got a job as an announcer, he did develop a very successful career on the other side of the mic as a broadcast engineer. Speaking with Stuart, it is clear that developing and maintaining your relationships with colleagues over the course of your career is key.

How did you fall into this career?

I think the thing that led me into the business was that I was a big sports fan when I was a little kid. I was a big Mets fan and used to watch them all the time. They had these three announcers who were with them from the very beginning. I really wanted to be a player, but since I wasn't that good of a player, my friends and I would stay on the sidelines during recess and pretend we were broadcasting games. My own intention was to go into announcing, and I eventually did that in college. I followed this through high school, which had a TV studio, which would periodically do local cablecasts of our football and basketball games. I was all over that, and I still have the tape somewhere.

Then I went on to pursue that in college—communications. I majored in production at Hofstra out on Long Island, and I loved it.

So you really listened to your heart. A lot of people don't hear that, or they listen and ignore it.

Oh yeah. It probably started when I was eight years old.

Where did it go after college?

In college, I did tons of sports play by play and that kind of stuff. My goal was really to be a sports announcer of sorts. When I was getting near the end of my time in college, I started looking for jobs in radio and I kept finding that basically the jobs you could get were at these teeny-tiny radio stations in teeny-tiny towns for teeny-tiny salaries.

I was on my way to my last final exam in college when the phone rang at the radio station. It was somebody calling from WABC who had actually been a student at Hofstra and worked at the radio station years before that and kept in touch with the general manager, who was a guy who had been there forever. She called and said they were looking for some engineering help for vacation relief–type people. She asked if he knew anyone who might be interested. The next thing I knew he handed me the phone, and a week later I had graduated college and was sitting in the lead engineer's chair at WABC.

That shows you have important networking is and how it comes into play. That is a whole dynamic that people miss. No doubt about it.

So were you thrown into a technical situation?

Yeah. The job was strictly engineering and had nothing to do with on-air stuff. It was tough to do, but at the time I basically had a choice between two things. [I could take the WABC job or] I could take a job at this station in a small town called Eunice, Louisiana, where I was going to have to do both morning drive and afternoon drive—on the air. You had to be there from 5:00 a.m. to 9:00 a.m., then back again from 3:00 p.m. to 7:00 p.m. Plus, you had to do whatever other local stuff was going on.

So with radio, you really have to be prepared for weird hours pretty much anywhere you start?

Yeah, I think that's pretty much the situation. The kicker at this station in Louisiana was that the salary for a year was something like $8,400 for the entire year. This wasn't that long ago—back in '89. I didn't take it, but a friend of mine did take it and left after about two years because he just couldn't afford to make a living out of it.

The base salary for an engineer at WABC was $18,000 when I started there. That was kinda like the going salary for somebody starting right out of college. So I started there, they really liked me, and I was enthusiastic about working insane hours or whenever they wanted me to work. I was doing really good work, and they liked me. There was a sister station in New York called WPLJ. We were all on the same floor, and the head production engineer from PLJ was going on maternity leave, and because of the union contract that they had, they asked me if I would be willing to do her job for the summer; this was also in '89. She was a Group 7 in their union contract. Most of these engineers were union, and this is still mostly the case for radio.

It was more of a supervisory role, so she got paid a whole lot more. Whenever I did her job, I got paid on her payscale. Everybody there who worked a certain amount of time had to join the union. This is pretty much the standard for most technical people, although there are places who are not union.

Bottom line, by the end of my first year out of college, despite the fact that my base salary was only $18,000, I actually made like $72,000. I was working crazy amounts of overtime, and a lot of it was under her payscale. So all that overtime really added up. In a nutshell, that one year got me so used to that level of compensation that I was like, "How in the world can I go into any other field?"

Like the golden handcuffs.

Yeah, I was already pretty advanced in my silo. I made my bed, now I was ready to lie in it. Not only the field, but it was like, "How can I even go back and start fresh in on-air, knowing I'm only going to make like $10,000?"

Were you able to keep that level of compensation from the outset?

No. Unfortunately, it took me years and years and years before I reached that level again. It was a great year, and I was able to set some money aside, which I eventually used to buy my first condo, a car, stuff like that. I really did get used to that level of income, though. But I have to say, to this day I still regret not pursuing my dream of on-air.

How do you end up at NPR?

I wasn't actually at WABC very long, but it was actually through another connection. It's all connections, now that I think about it. There was another engineer who'd been at WABC for years and who was also freelancing at another network. Since I was looking for additional free-lance work, this guy got me in the door over there. Then they took a liking to me, and when they moved to Washington, they asked me if I'd like to go down and be the production director for news production.

How were your technical chops at this point?

They were good. I was learning and had learned a lot at ABC. I worked with Rush Limbaugh there and engineered his show. Plus, WABC was the flagship station for the Yankees. I had a great time and loved all of it, but secretly I still wanted to be the guy in front of the mic, and I would always listen to the people I was engineering for and think, "I'm better than this guy!"

Then I'm in D.C. and Unistar gets bought out. One of my colleagues there had been at NPR, and when Unistar was being shut down, he went back to NPR and recommended me for management over there. I got in for an interview, and they hired me as a temp. After a while, I was brought in as full-time staff. Then I left NPR, and an old boss of mine from Unistar had moved on to PBS. They were starting a new talk show with Mary Matalin. My old boss was interested in having me come over there. Rush was good friends with Mary and gave me a nice recommendation. I worked with her for two and a half years, until she had a second baby and decided she no longer needed a job. So I eventually went back to NPR.

What do you think all these people appreciated about you?

I think the thing I hear over and over is that I have a really positive attitude, am friendly, have a good sense of humor, and am good-natured. People like that. They also like the fact that I care about what I'm doing and have always gone above and beyond to make things sound the best they can.

That comes from your own sense of commitment.

Truthfully, there are a lot of engineers out there who are going through the motions and punching the clock. I don't see it that way. While I'm there, I want to do it right.

What is a typical day at NPR?

It kind of depends on what you are doing on a given day. What I've been doing for the last maybe two years is working for the technical director on *All Things Considered*. What that involves really is just a lot of general production during the entire day. The first two hours of my day I am in a different studio, not our main studio. I'm recording interviews, mixing pieces—it could be anything. It's a good-size control room with an adjacent booth, probably 8 feet by 10 feet.

What kind of console?

Most of the consoles that we use are Pacific Recorder consoles. We've gone through a major transformation over the years, like everybody else, from analog to digital. The consoles are actually the same analog consoles that we use for inputs, but we've migrated entirely away from tape, which is the way we did it for years. We used to record on 1/4" stereo, but we also had other studios that did multitrack recording. For the day-to-day stuff, it was stereo. We now run a system called Dalet. It's a very basic audio editing system—the draw for NPR was that it was an easily networked system, so we could tie in all our facilities. We could have lots of different workstations looking at the same server. It started in D.C., but they have since rolled it out to our other satellite locations in New York, Los Angeles, and Chicago.

We are the headquarters here, and NPR has about 700 employees around the country. I can tell you that we have somewhere around 100 junior members who are engineers. We make up probably 1/7 of the overall staff of the organization.

How important is the union?

Truthfully, the union is a requirement. We have a contract with NPR, and if you are an engineer with NPR, you have to be with the union. So if you're not a union member, it's kind of a formality, and you just join.

How often do roles change? Do job openings occur often?

We went through a long period of time where there was really little turnover. We've only had the union arrangement for about nine years. Ever since the union came in, there have been major cost-cutting initiatives. So they are kind of marching in that direction.

What is your feeling about the future viability of the things you're doing?

The particular stuff that we do, we all feel like the end is sort of near. There is definitely a finish line somewhere. It's not that we aren't valuable or can't offer value to the company, but things are really going heavily into digital.

If you were just getting out of college now, what kinds of skills would you consider important for getting into a company like NPR?

I would say web-based—computer, web design, that kind of thing. That's where the jobs are clearly going. There are still plenty of people who do audio stuff, but they are not trained engineer types. There are many people who have been trained to use their ears to deliver this high-quality stuff, but sadly their role is diminishing.

It used to be that anytime hosts from our shows would go out in the field to do a story, they were required to take an engineer with them. Typically, they would get great material. Now they say they're not going to send engineers anymore—they're going to let producers go out with the host and tape their own stuff. The producers are frustrated because now they can't really produce. They have to do two roles, so their focus is lost—now they are worrying about the engineering part of it, and they can't put their full concentration on the story.

In the future, people will need to be the one-stop shop. You're going to have to record your material, come back and edit it, you're going to put together a piece on your computer, and you're going to mix the whole thing.

So some of these producers are getting a chance to do the technical side as well?

Absolutely. If you don't come in as a producer, you can still make it as a producer if you are still into the audio stuff and you have a knack for both things. A lot of our engineers now have had experience in both producing and engineering. A lot of us could do that, but we'd have to essentially quit our jobs as engineers to do so.

Does this make you feel insecure at times?

Yes. At some point you have to lock into the fact that this is your job. This is how you support your family and pay your mortgage. A lot of us feel threatened by the fact that they seem to want to shift the work to producers, a lot of whom get paid a whole lot less than some of us do.

Is this happening in the rest of the field? Where would you go if you had to bail?

I have been saying for the last several years that this is more than likely going to be my last job as an engineer. I don't know how it's going to come down—I may be able to hang on for 20 or 25 more years, but I think around here, people do consider us dinosaurs.

There is less of a concern for the quality of the audio anymore. For example, for years we did this series in partnership with National Geographic called *Radio Expeditions*, where our engineers would go out to places all over the world and return with these incredible wildlife sounds—birds, fish—just really amazing stuff. We are no longer involved with that now.

What I've really been thinking about over the past several years is my own upbringing, education, and the experience I got back in high school at our TV studio. I've been thinking about putting together a proposal to create a radio and TV production program for schools. My wife teaches at a private school, and there's about 1,000 kids. It's something that they could really use.

From an audio perspective, what kinds of skills are most valuable in your field? What is going to give you the most mileage?

Whether or not people are going to work as audio engineers in the traditional sense, I think the computer background has got to be the biggest key at this point. The audio will always be attached to another medium now. NPR wants to be known as a digital media company. Now their reporters aren't just filing radio stories, but they also have to write a separate story to go off and be put up on the web and/or shoot video and photography.

What is the hierarchy where you are? What is the structure?

We have a very large management staff. When I got there, there were two supervisors who were basically managing about 40 or 45 people in the audio engineering department. Now we literally have like eight or nine managers managing more or less the same number of people.

I have a supervisor above me, then that supervisor reports to a senior manager. Producers go on a completely different line. I interact with the producers enough that I could make a jump if I ever wanted to. If I did that, though, I would have to come in at a much lower salary level, possibly less than I could afford.

For *Morning Edition* there are probably six people on the morning shift. People start rolling in somewhere around 3:30 or 4:45, when you get a rollover of shifts. You'll have two people in the studio who are "driving" the show, or engineering the live show. This involves finding all the material that we need for playback on the show, making sure it's all in the right order, checking levels, playing music, opening and closing microphones, setting up mics, engineering newscasts, and bringing in interviews from outside, whether they are coming in via ISDN, telephone, or satellite phone. Recording pre-production for the show—of course, they record all their music breaks, station breaks before the show. We also record these things that are called "billboards," which are maybe one-minute lead-ins to the show that you hear at the top of the hour. Then you have the five-minute newscasts before the show comes on.

What is your favorite part of your job?

To me, it has always been engineering the live shows. There is this major adrenalin rush that you get, especially when you consider that there are 12 million people who listen. When you know there are that many people listening, you get really jazzed up and you want to do a great job. Every day you get off the air without having screwed something up, it's a great feeling.

What about salary ranges? What could people expect?

Basically, everything is on a salary scale that has been set up in our contract between the union and NPR. It's a 10-step pay scale, and it would take someone about nine years to get up to the top pay scale. The starting salary is somewhere in the upper thirties, which isn't bad. When I was at Unistar before I came to NPR, I was making $32,000, and that was back in '94. If you're at the top of the pay scale, the base salary is like $73,000, so it's not huge money, but people get paid much better now than they used to. There was a time when the salaries were really small, and NPR would always try to make up for it by offering good benefits.

The benefits are great—NPR has always been generous with benefits. Vacation is good—everyone starts with three weeks, and people who have been there 19 years get six weeks of vacation. The health insurance is also good. You can also earn lots of overtime—they have tried to realign shifts to create the least amount of overtime possible, but it has kind of backfired. We had four engineers quit in a span of two months, so they had to hire new people who weren't up to speed—meanwhile, the team still had to cover x number of shifts.

What about work/life balance? Has this engineering career afforded you the balance you've wanted?

This can be a difficult place to be an engineer if you have kids. You have to be ready to put in the hours. One of the managers would always say to a complaining new employee, "Welcome to broadcasting!" As people get older and have spent many, many years working, they feel like they have paid their dues and they feel like somebody else should be doing the hard hours. It's very much a seniority-based system. On our most recent contract we made some changes to make it a little fairer to the new people, who would typically get drafted every weekend, whereas the folks at the top of the seniority list would never have to work those hours.

What kinds of personality types would have a tough time succeeding at a broadcaster like NPR?

People really have to be team-oriented. There are engineers and producers who have major reputations for being mean or nasty. You have to be friendly and want to put on a good show all the time.

Have you been able to cultivate an interest outside of engineering? Do you have something that takes you away from what you do at work there?

I am married and have two kids. I'm sort of a workaholic, though. I totally need a hobby! No doubt about it.

What about geography? Do you have to be in D.C. if you want to engineer with NPR for example?

There is no reason you have to be in D.C. The newsmakers are here in terms of politics, but the truth is, you could pick up NPR and drop into the middle of Nebraska and do the same thing. The core operations are here, and we've kind of outgrown our building, so we're moving into a new facility.

Does NPR actively recruit?

There is a lot of that. They do a lot of these intern fairs and things. Among engineers, most of the recent college people we've had have music recording backgrounds in college.

NPR has a performance studio with a huge console—a really beautiful recording studio. A lot of people come to our company thinking they will spend their days recording rock bands, symphonies, whatever, but they are kind of shutting that all down. Our people are amazing at recording this stuff and have come from places like Full Sail and Peabody in Baltimore. Unfortunately, they are slowly shutting this stuff down.

It wasn't like that before—this was the last place where you could go to do all this great stuff. Now it's taken on the tone of a much more corporate kind of climate. I'm in an interesting position compared to others—people in public radio likely don't know what corporate radio is like. They want to get as much done for as little as possible.

A Closer Look: Steve Aprea and the World of Broadcast

Steve Aprea is chief engineer of WNEW-FM (New York). Steve's story is an interesting one full of unexpected twists and turns. Of all the people I spoke to, Steve was among the most energetic and resourceful. At almost every point during his career, he was balancing at least two different roles while trying to line up the next opportunity.

Photo by Stephanie Susnjara.

Steve Aprea.

Steve, when did you first gain your initial interest in audio?

My earliest recollections are going down into my grandfather's basement when I was about four or five—he was a Big Band leader. His basement was like a radio soundstage that had been thrown away from the '30s. I used to go down there when I was a kid and play. He had all the microphones and early speakers. My nana used to be a pioneer at Bell Systems—she was one of the first 10 operators hired and she used to bring all this gear from the early days of the phone companies. A lot of the early public address stuff came out of Bell Laboratories.

So that must have gotten your imagination going, right?

Yeah. I used to go down there and break the stuff when I was about four or five. By the time I got to be about seven or eight, I tried to put it back together. This interest in gear has taken hold of me to this day.

When did you first become interested in audio as a career?

When I was in college. There was a college radio station there, WSOU. By going to the station and meeting some of the people in classes, I could see how my skills and interests would complement what they were doing. That turned into a beautiful relationship between myself and a group of people, some of whom I am still involved with today—27 years later.

Fortunately, the people at my college radio station were very serious about it. That led to us being the most successful noncommercial station in the United States. I started out as an engineer and worked my way up to program director. I was at SOU for three years and professionally employed in my senior year as program director, and then I went to work with Infinity; this would have been around 1990.

What kinds of things are expected of you now as chief engineer at WNEW?

I am responsible for making sure that the commercials are on the air. That is the bottom line. If the station is on the air, it is because I am doing my job right. If it's not on the air, I'm not doing my job right. I'm responsible for making sure the station stays on the air. For me, it's a one-man team 99 percent of the time. If I am ever in a situation where I need help, my engineers at CBS FM, 1010 WINS, WFAN, and CBS AM all come together. These guys are incredible.

So it is a tight-knit group and they are nearby?

WINS and myself are in the same building, CBS FM is about 10 blocks away, KROCK is a couple avenues away. We all work together as a team and collaborate on studio designs.

Give me a sense of the technical complexity.

It depends. You could have a transmitter go down. If you've got a control board with a bad cap, you've got to find out where that is. I've got miles and miles and miles of wire. I've got antennas on the Empire State Building, antennas on top of the Viacom building, transmitters in all locations, and multiple formats of radio coming out of those antennas.

What are some of the most important things you picked up over the years?

It still comes back to the same thing as when I was a kid. Don't be so cocky that you can't ask a question. There are plenty of things that I encounter that throw me a little bit, and I am not going to be so ego-ed out that I am not going to ask for some help and get some of the brain trust on it. The Internet is a great resource to have, but most problems can be solved intuitively or by looking at the service manuals for the schematics.

What kind of background is important in this field?

You'd be looking for a communications program, and you should be drawn to things that other people take for granted. If you are curious about why things happen versus just letting them happen, you have the right mindset. There is an incredible amount of pressure. You talk to technical people who are at the companies designing the new generation of gear; you talk to listeners, carriers. I don't know if I manage it well—sometimes I explode. Some days it is just too much.

What is behind all this pressure?

Part of it is knowing that the station cannot go off the air. When you are in broadcast, it's live; you are always on the air. The wrong button pushed, the wrong cross-connect, the wrong moving of a wire can cause a domino effect technically, which will result in the commercials not getting aired. Commercials in a major market are incredibly expensive, so the amount of pressure on us to make sure they are always on the air and being properly monitored is enormous. They are going to a whole new ratings system now, which is based on the new protocol of embedded tones in the music as opposed to the old Arbitron diaries. So we've opened up a whole different world on top of the digital broadcasting world that they put on our backs. We now have a new world of technology that relates to how ratings are generated that we need to be responsible for.

How do you stay ahead of all these issues?

Well, that's it. Having been a student of history you learn to anticipate. Looking at my grandfather's basement, they went through so many revolutions back then in thought and theory that it caused a total rebuilding of the infrastructure so many times over in a short period of time. Then we coasted for a while and there wasn't a lot of change. Right now, there are technical revolutions everywhere, and it's like one of those hotspots on the timeline. I am kind of mentally prepared and can feel the history of the moment and realize that this is a great time. I want to hold onto all these things that are old and good and incorporate them in the new world.

One of the most important things I have learned is that you do not drop your old friends to embrace new ones. Technology that served us well for 20, 40, 60 years will not be easily abandoned, even though we look at new technologies and learn to integrate them.

How important is confidence in other people so your situation isn't compromised?

There is a community of standards among us in terms of how we would leave a job and how we communicate with each other. This set of standards allows us to be safe and protect ourselves as well as ensure stability.

What are some of the downsides and risks in your role?

Long-term exposure to RF can cause any number of health issues. In FM broadcasting, that is the unspoken dirty word, and you need to be sensitive to this. Also, you are always on call—it doesn't matter what time of day or what day it is. It is never say die when it comes to keeping the station on the air, and you have to get that part quick.

What are some of the best things about your job that you really like?

Radio is a really special thing and a unique medium. No matter what happens with the other media, radio will have a unique place because it allows us to do anything we want to do while listening to it. It is portable, and you are impacting so many listeners at a time.

Where is it all going?

I think it is going back to the beginning. Radio started with the theater of the mind, and I think that a lot of the great, wild, wacky things that were done with radio in its infancy will be done with many other new things in the future. Radio has a lot to offer.

Do you see careers opening up or are things becoming more competitive?

Many of the things that we do will just be done on the computer. Most of the infrastructure will be rented from companies like Sprint and Microsoft. The big broadcast companies will just be content providers as opposed to broadcasters. But there will always be signals they want to propagate on waves and mass distribute. There is no better way to put it out than on a carrier wave.

Where are some of the opportunities now?

There are lots of international opportunities opening up. They are trying to put together for Beijing; radio stations in India; my buddies are opening stations in Alaska, Uganda—this is going on around the world. America is one place, but the world needs radio.

What kinds of things would you want to keep in mind if you were just starting out now?

If this is what you want to do, don't let them push you into a sales job. They are always looking for new sales guys. If you are technically inclined and serious about how things work, you should call your local radio station and get involved. Try to get an internship there.

What single thing has gotten you the most mileage in your career?

Mic placement. I used to obsess about it when I was a kid, and it turned out to be something really good to obsess about. It is so important, and microphones really blow me away. I think my true passion for this stuff has shined through. I know a lot of people paid attention to me because of the questions I asked. Also, I listened to their answers—so you have to be a good listener, too. You have to find things that excite you, and if it is the gear, let yourself be drawn into that and see where it takes you.

8 The Manufacturing/ Distribution/Retail Market

Manufacturers, distributors, and retailers have experienced solid, if slow, growth over the last several years. Although the United States still boasts the lion's share of musical instrument (MI) and pro audio gear purchases, growth in international markets such as China is helping bolster overall growth.

Market Viability

Retailers and distributors of professional audio gear stand to gain a lot from such a lucrative market. Guitar Center, a U.S.-based musical instrument retailer, has tripled its size over the last decade and now enjoys revenues of more than $2 billion. Retailers such as zZounds.com, Sam Ash, Sweetwater, BSW, and Musician's Friend have all established a solid online presence where consumers can find almost anything they need—and at competitive prices.

Manufacturer, Distributor, Retailer Relationship

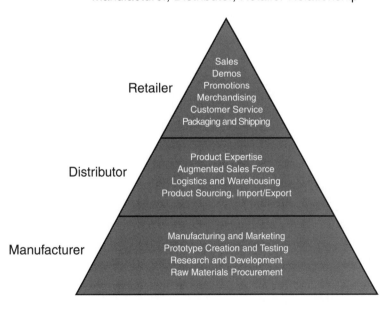

Retailer
Sales
Demos
Promotions
Merchandising
Customer Service
Packaging and Shipping

Distributor
Product Expertise
Augmented Sales Force
Logistics and Warehousing
Product Sourcing, Import/Export

Manufacturer
Manufacturing and Marketing
Prototype Creation and Testing
Research and Development
Raw Materials Procurement

The proliferation of home studios is driving the manufacturing/distribution/retail market both in North America and abroad. Innovations in recording technology and other areas have given the average musician access to features and functionality that would have cost tens of thousands of dollars just two decades ago. Continued innovation of CPUs and circuit boards is also helping manufacturers pack more functionality into smaller footprints, and the appetite for gizmos and audio gadgets doesn't appear to be receding anytime soon.

Job Profiles and Career Opportunities

There are a few core disciplines at the root of many manufacturers, distributors, and retailers, and for professional audio products, this is no exception. Product development and sales are among the most important aspects for these companies. The very simple reason for this is that without new products and innovations, there would not be anything to sell. Without sales-people, there would be no one to bring the products to market.

On a rudimentary level, the manufacturer is responsible for identifying the market need, handling all aspects of research and development, creating prototypes, and finally creating and marketing the product. They are also responsible for sourcing the raw materials, operating the manufacturing plants, and managing product lifecycles. Manufacturers can either sell directly or work through distribution and/or retail, and they almost always enjoy a much higher margin on sales than distribution or retail.

The distributor's role is to move the product out to where it will sell. This involves warehousing, logistics, packing, and shipping to retailers. Distributors can come in a variety of roles—those that simply "pick, pack, and ship" and those that add value to the transaction (or *value-added distributors*). In the case of the pro audio market, value-added distributors might have particular expertise in high-end microphones, compressors, or preamplifiers—and for this expertise, they may earn higher margins.

The function of distribution in professional audio evolved from dedicated sales organizations that functioned as an extension of the manufacturer. As the industry grew and needs such as importing, exporting, and off-site warehousing became more and more important, the role of distribution began to take hold and become increasingly relevant to both manufacturers and retailers.

Retailers have the most public face to the consumer. Recently, the online presence of retailers has far overshadowed their physical presence, which has streamlined and changed the dynamics of how a purchase is completed. Retailers have the benefit of dealing with many lines of pro audio and musical instrument products; therefore, they can have an extremely diverse customer base. Retailers are last in the distribution chain and have one of the most important jobs in the business: identifying and solving customer needs.

Product Channel Job Descriptions

As described a moment ago, manufacturing, distribution, and retail have very different roles in the lifecycle of a product. Vice president–level positions are indicated here to illustrate the organizational breakdown. There are many individual roles and responsibilities in each area beneath these positions, many of which are alluded to here.

Manufacturing/Distribution/Retail

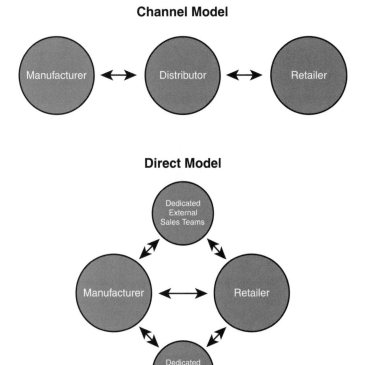

Manufacturer: Vice President of Product Development ($80,000 to $200,000+)

The vice president of product development oversees the entire manufacturing cycle of the product, from research and development, to prototype, to final product. This role entails managing many positions, including materials specialists, technical developers, programmers, testers, and manufacturing plant managers. Perhaps the most important decisions a VP of product development can make are: 1) is it possible to build a product being proposed; and 2) can it be done within a pre-defined timeframe?

Product development is where the more technical areas of a manufacturing organization will lie. These folks are the ones who specify components of the products to make them faster, smaller, and better than the competitors' products. Audio engineers, technicians, and configuration testers all need to ensure that the products will properly integrate with other audio gear, including computers, DAWs, interface hardware, connectors, and so on. In this day and age, it is mandatory that products are built with interoperability in mind, because every successful pro audio environment uses a variety of gear from different manufacturers. An important part of product development is visiting customers with sales teams and providing in-person demonstrations of new equipment.

Manufacturer: Vice President of Marketing ($80,000 to $180,000+)

The vice president of marketing is responsible for all marketing aspects, including branding, advertising, promotions, and corporate communications for the manufacturer. Another important function of marketing is supporting the sales structure. The marketing organization needs to help create the demand for the product in the marketplace and keep the company's identity contemporary and reflective of its product line. The pro audio and musical instrument manufacturers operate in a very crowded market, so it is often not enough to have a unique product—an equally compelling marketing strategy can be just as important.

Some typical activities for a marketing organization might be organizing a trade show presence where partners, end users, and the rest of the audio community congregate at NAMM, AES, or NAB conventions. Their corporate communications departments typically handle the press function—either internally or externally—and time product release announcements and partnership announcements. Advertising departments need to make sure that compelling product messaging hits the trade magazines, online retail sites, and other outlets. They may engage with outside agencies or have a small internal creative staff to handle design, layout, and placement of ads.

Manufacturer: Vice President of Sales ($80,000 to $180,000+)

The vice president of sales manages the entire sales organization for the manufacturer. This can mean in-house sales reps who cover specific assigned territories, as well as external sales companies that might be hired for specific product launches or other projects. The most important task for any sales team, as obvious as it may sound, is to listen to the customer. Professional audio consumers are very sophisticated and can provide incredibly valuable feedback to sales teams, both on where their products will be most effective and on how a company can change their products to become more effective in the marketplace.

It is up to regional sales managers to incite the interest of distribution and retail and book purchase orders, plain and simple. Salespeople in professional audio, as mentioned a moment ago, have a customer base that is typically very knowledgeable about pro audio products. In such a competitive market, products compete by features and prices. Sales managers need to be able to articulate the value of their products both in their own context and against the products of competitors. Because the role of sales is very tangibly tied to a company's success, a good salesperson can be compensated extremely well through incentives and bonuses tied to performance.

Distributor: Vice President, General Manager ($140,000 to $200,000+)

The general manager for a professional audio distributor must have not only a good command of business and finance principles, but also a solid knowledge of audio-related products. To succeed in the pro audio industry, distributors need to do a lot more than just pick, pack, and ship. A good general manager brings focus to an organization, helping them specialize in specific technologies or niche markets. General managers interface at a high level with manufacturers to justify margins, which can be anywhere from 5 percent (for very basic services, such as inventorying and shipping) to 12 percent for things such as providing advanced expertise in a niche market.

The general manager helps identify the overall market need and puts together agreements with manufacturers and retailers. He also builds the distribution team, with all its operational, sales, and logistical components. In a market that moves so quickly, the general manager also needs to be able to identify what products and trends will likely take hold of the market and allocate resources and investments appropriately.

Distributor: Vice President of Operations ($80,000 to $180,000+)

At a distributor, logistics and operations are fundamental to success. The vice president of operations is responsible for procuring, warehousing, and shipping manufacturer products, as well as for standard back-office functions, such as finance and accounting. The vice president of operations interfaces with key contacts at the manufacturer to maintain sufficient inventory levels so they can meet demand.

For this reason, it is very important for the vice president of operations to be in lock-step with the distributor's sales organization. The sales organization provides the sales figures and SKU (*stock keeping unit*) numbers that the vice president of operations needs to balance inventory. Perhaps the most important role the vice president of operations plays is making sure the pipeline is running smoothly—this involves managing vendor and customer returns, placing orders for products, and ensuring the company has enough cash to operate competitively.

Distributor: Vice President of Sales ($100,000 to $200,000+)

In distribution, the vice president of sales has a very different role from a sales position at a manufacturer. For one thing, distribution must typically look after many different product lines, often targeted at different market subsets. However, distribution sales *does* resemble the manufacturer organization in that sales teams are typically broken out by region, and their primary role is to get purchase orders from customers.

This sales role at a distributor entails going onsite to retail locations, making presentations to key personnel, arranging for product demonstrations, providing sales incentives to potential purchasers, and once again, listening. Distribution can play a very valuable role in providing information back to the manufacturer on what customers really want. An advantage a distributor's sales team may have over a manufacturer's is that at a distributor, products manufactured by different companies can be bundled into a complete package and discounted to fit a specific market niche.

Retailer: Vice President of Sales ($80,000 to $180,000+)

At a retailer, it is really all about sales. Whether you are in a brick-and-mortar shop or you have an online presence, the most important thing is moving product and making customers want to remain loyal. In this day and age, customers expect more for less; they expect lower prices, free shipping, fast service, and expert advice. Failure in any of these basic areas can equal lost business. A good vice president of sales will pull together all of these aspects, creating the conditions for a positive purchasing experience to nurture repeat business. Once repeat business is created, relationships can be created—and it is the salesperson's job to build and maintain these relationships, which directly correlate to the success of the business.

Sales in the retail market is very, very competitive, and these days the consumer is very much the winner. The vice president of sales knows his company's strengths—whether it is pricing leverage, integration expertise, product knowledge, or geography. He needs to make sure the entire sales team is working toward these strengths and putting the best foot forward. For example, a small, specialized retailer will not be able to compete on price, but might be willing to come on site and manage a complex equipment integration.

Customer Service Manager ($45,000 to $85,000+)

Customer service starts when a customer first makes contact with the retailer—expectations are set, first impressions are made, and communication is established. A good customer service manager will handle customer calls and retail with walk-ins with the same degree of commitment as a call from a returning customer who frequently purchases big-ticket items. The simple reason? How effective a customer service operation is has a direct impact on reputation, which is a key sales driver. In the highly competitive retail market, there is no room for anything less than a great reputation, and this is the customer service manager's ultimate goal.

Customer service managers help guide customers through the sales experience, which, as mentioned, begins with the first call and ends when the customer is satisfied. Customer service managers often supervise support teams and call centers where the primary goal is to make sure customers are speaking with the correct people—a technician, a product specialist, a salesperson, or a returns/shipping specialist. Calls they field can originate at any point in the sales cycle, and their job is to bring to bear all the resources of the retail organization for the benefit of the customer.

Entering and Succeeding in the Product Channel

One tried-and-true way to enter a major product channel company is through an internship. Most major audio schools provide internship programs, and although internships typically do not pay well, having a major manufacturer on your resume before your career even starts can be a tremendous asset and can increase your perceived equity in a company.

The two most common paths through which people enter the product channel are product development and sales. To oversimplify, product development is the technical route, and sales is, well, the sales route. Many people get their start in the product channel on the retail floor—nothing can replace personal, interactive experience with customers, and being on the front line pitching products can provide experience that manufacturers, distributors, and retailers all find very attractive.

One prerequisite for success is knowing the product(s) inside and out. This knowledge is something that both product development and sales professionals share, for different reasons. For a product developer, having an understanding of things such as signal flow, circuit boards, electrical design, and programming can be very important factors in achieving success. Product developers often have to turn the theoretical into reality; therefore, they rely heavily on myriad technical skills.

As far as sales are concerned, some people claim to be born to sell. There is some truth to this in that selling comes naturally to many who have a gift for gab or to people who have Type A personalities. But selling can be a learned skill as well, and knowing what you are selling is the first place to start. Salespeople need to be able to convince buyers why theirs is the best product—and in the audio field, this often comes back to product specifications, speeds and feeds, and frequency response measurements. Many salespeople get their start as customer service reps, an invaluable training ground that helps them become sensitive to customer needs—and one that teaches them to listen.

There is nothing a manufacturer wants more than visibility and transparency into a customer's desires—therefore, a prime recruiting ground for the top manufacturers is the retail environment. Many product development types are recruited as former studio or live technicians—the people who get the calls when gear breaks. They not only know how to fix gear, but to improve it as well, so it can presumably be more competitive in the market.

The most important background a distributor could ask for is import/export experience; back-office functions, such as financing, logistics, and operations; and sales, since they are ultimately selling to retailers. Many of the people who work at distribution companies have done their time in retail environments—they obviously have a very significant degree of product knowledge as well. From an education perspective, it is no surprise that the product channel values computer-oriented and technical skills—walking in the door with these skills will increase the salary you can command.

Traits Valued in the Product Channel

Word spreads very quickly these days on product quality, good or bad. Therefore, manufacturers, distributors, and retailers all value good communication—people who can be personable and build trusted business relationships with other people. It seems like a very basic skill—an easy one to master—but it is not. Companies' reputations are built on integrity—following through on your commitments and how you communicate them.

Leadership is another trait that will come in handy at any size company and will help you gain the mindshare of others and move ahead of the pack, increasing both your influence and your salary. Leadership means being able to develop a vision, delegate tasks, and deliver results in a business environment. It also means being able to pull together teams—both internally and externally—to work on common objectives.

Team Player   Accountability
Leadership
Communications Skills   Integrity
Ambition
Curiosity **Organizational Skills**
Intuitive Thinking

Some of the traits the product channel values.

Any company in the product channel expects exceptional organizational skills. Product launches, sales and marketing initiatives, and operations all must face deadlines, to-do lists, and often less than adequate resources on a day-to-day basis. A good manager at one of these companies will be able to navigate the way forward and separate the forest from the trees. Just like in a recording studio environment, adaptability is also very important—not just for people, but also for products. And you should be able to switch gears and work alongside many different personality types.

Other traits companies look for include intuitiveness and curiosity. What could make this product better? What makes this other product so good? An inquisitive mind will help a company solve its problems, thereby helping customers solve their problems. Curiosity also helps keep you ahead of the market. People who can't get enough at a NAMM show or people who are "gear sluts" can be a perfect fit for a good manufacturer if they bring this enthusiasm into the workplace.

Benefits and Drawbacks of Working in the Product Channel

There are many benefits to working for a manufacturer, distributor, or retailer. For one thing, you get constant firsthand exposure to the products, which may have a direct impact on what people are able to do creatively—this can be very rewarding. Working at a reputable manufacturer, you get to work with the best talent in the industry: Techs, engineers, product visionaries, and marketers all work alongside one another toward a common goal—making a competitive product. Once a product is introduced, there is pride of ownership among the entire team.

A clear benefit to working in the product channel is that you are able to be in the heart of the audio community because your customers are essentially the driving force. All the significant manufacturers, distributors, and retailers attend shows such as NAMM, AES, and NAB and have the opportunity to build lifelong relationships with colleagues both inside and outside their company.

Other benefits include working within normal business hours (this *cannot* be said for the rest of the industry), which in turn means you can actually have weekends and a personal life. Compensation and health benefits are also very good, especially at the more technical companies, because companies need to retain the best employees, lest they lose them to competitors. Other benefits typically found at a product channel company would be generous vacation, discounts on equipment, 401(k) plans, and disability insurance, which becomes very important if you suffer an illness or injury during the term of your employment.

Benefits and Drawbacks of
Working in the Product Channel

+	−
Exposure to Products	Corporate Politics
Pride of Ownership	Can Be Pigeonholed
Team Environment	Not Creating Content
Reasonable Hours	Very Competitive Market
Good Benefits and Discounts	Limited View of Audio World
Highly Transferable Skills	Technology Limitations

At any corporation, you will encounter politics. Generally, as you move higher in an organization, you are responsible for more people, and therefore you often have to sort out conflicts among team members. These tedious but necessary tasks can take you away from what you originally set out to do—work closely with developing and promoting the products.

Is the Product Channel Right for You?

If you are ambitious and you have a passion for audio or musical instrument products, the product channel can provide a very satisfying long-term career with exceptional compensation. It also provides you with a transferable skill set you can apply to almost any manufacturer—operations, sales, and marketing.

Although you likely will not be making creative content at a manufacturer, distributor, or retailer, you will most certainly be creating tools to help enable the process. All of the innovation that has occurred in the pro audio world during that last several decades has been initiated by the product channel—innovation is the name of the game, and if you think you can keep up, this area might just be for you.

A Closer Look: Bob Reardon and the Audio Products Distribution Industry

Bob Reardon is CEO of Boston, Massachussetts–based Sonic Distribution, LLC. Bob has a classic sales-oriented background and was able to couple his natural business skills with his passion for music and audio. He has been able to succeed as a distributor of audio products partly because of the vast network of relationships he has been able to build—a result of being a great communicator. Bob is also an example of how this industry rewards entrepreneurs who can not only develop a vision, but crystallize it through good planning and execution.

Photo by Jeff Touzeau.

Bob Reardon.

Bob, what is a typical day like for you at Sonic?

Sonic is a distribution company. As a distribution company, part of the day is financial, and that has to do with purchasing and also state of accounts. So part of the day is sales-oriented, and some of the day is marketing-oriented—of course, sales bleeds into that. A little of the day is taken up with sorting out issues with the accounts, and some of the day is dealing with products. So pretty much that breaks down to what any distribution company does—even if you're a manufacturer, for that matter.

How did you identify distribution as a viable area of business and why did you want to get into it in the first place?

Like a lot of things in business, it has to do with your relationships over the years. Let me give you a quick overview. Originally, my entrance into getting paid to do any of this was as many people start out, by making music myself. I was in bands and also got involved in recording—sound synthesis originally gave me the bug. I eventually opened a commercial studio in Boston and ran it for about eight years. This was around the time of the MIDI revolution. The clients I was working with periodically required me to do things that needed other gear than was available in the particular studio that I owned. It didn't make sense for me to go out and buy the gear.

Around this time, I thought it might be better for me to continue as an independent engineer and freelance. So I sold the studio and then worked freelance, because my freelance career had developed to be good in a number of places. That also dovetailed into my working in post.

Did you plan on ever getting into post?

I didn't really seek it out. It hadn't occurred to me to go do that. Friends kind of spotted it and encouraged me to pursue it. I worked for a post house for a number of years and became in charge of music underscoring there. Even though it was fun, the hours were stupid, and the deadlines were insane. Friends of mine in the film-scoring world say that is much the same way. Depending on the project, unless you know the producer really well, toward the end of the project they are over budget and you're essentially in the way. Your commitment is 100 percent, and they own you.

At what point did you start to strive for a better work/life balance? Working those hours takes its toll after a while.

I had a young family at this point, so when I got an offer from Lexicon I decided to take it. I was to head up their workstation program.

That's a big jump from post to the manufacturing side.

I am always impressing on the gang here, "Hey, try to be complete and close the loop on what you're doing; you have no idea where that road may lead." That's how I got on the manufacturing side. Then eight years at Lexicon and three years over at Waves taught me about both the hardware and the software angles. After a certain point, you know enough people and see some opportunities. At this point in our career trajectory, why don't we do it ourselves as opposed to doing it for other people? Generally in the world of business, that's not an unusual trajectory in businesses outside of audio. You get out there, you learn from a number of different angles, then you decide, "Well, I've been doing this for other people; why don't I do my own version?"

So now you move from manufacturing to distribution. When did you spot the opportunity in distribution?

Since I was involved with Europe going back in my Lexicon years, I was introduced to this whole aspect of distribution. If you're only looking at America, it's probably not at the top of your radar screen. However, as I was going over to service folks in Europe as a product specialist, I got very used to this idea. Actually, there is more distribution than you might think in the U.S., but it's not as obvious.

When I got on the sales and business side of Waves, I managed their European distribution for two years, commuting every couple of weeks for a few years to Europe. Classically, there is typically a two-tier model: manufacturer to distributor to retailer to end-user. Some of the really big operations own their own distribution operations, with support directly from the factory, and then to a dealer, then an end-user. So it's one fewer layer. But even in this example, they typically have distributors in other parts of the world.

How important is it for a distribution company to be global?

From a business point of view, you need to think global. It can be a company that has done well in Europe and they don't have representation in the U.S. and they'd like to have a U.S. presence. It really helps in any area you go into to have local people. Unless you are of sufficient size to own your own distribution, like the Sonys of the world, there is a huge benefit to the distribution model.

How would you characterize the size and health of the audio distribution market for people looking to make a career in this area?

Distribution is huge. Coming out of school, you'd go work for a manufacturer and learn about it there. The cliché would be to start out as an e-tailer, but you want to be careful about that. People who just put up a website can have a very low commitment, but this can work two ways. Many companies will shy away from doing business with e-tailers because the commitment is so low. One of the messages you can take from that is you have to spend some time. Even if it's less initial expense than a brick-and-mortar store, it's still going to be a considerable investment in sweat equity. Barriers of entry can be lower for out-of-pocket cash, but you need a lot of sweat equity and a maturity of business savvy to compensate for the fact that you don't have a brick-and-mortar operation established.

What are some of the tangible resources in place that enabled you to have a successful distribution operation?

For me to be able to do this, I needed an existing network of contacts all across the United States. Anybody who wants to do this should have some sales experience. I try to make any of the people who come through here realize that no matter what you do in life, you are selling. It is an interpersonal skill—you're trying to communicate your point of view and make a bona fide case for it. Anyone who is not comfortable speaking with people would be very ill-advised to get into this business. You need to be able to write something well, put your thoughts into a presentation, and be able to communicate.

That said, somebody who may not be a good communicator may be good in the back office side—with numbers and details, for example. This is also a skill that is needed, and everyone has a part to play on the team. You don't have to be the interpersonal star, but you have to be good with at least something. There is more than one personality profile a business needs.

What role does education play in preparing for a career in distribution?

I would encourage anybody to get a degree in something. Does it have to be B-School or a music school degree? Absolutely not; the key thing is developing discipline in how you think and how you present. These days, people start their education in one thing, and God knows where they end up. They may have done five or six other things along the way. My career has been quite varied from a certain perspective, but has a connecting thread from another perspective.

What are some of the other associated roles in distribution that may not be so obvious to someone coming out of college?

Independent reps are huge. The independent reps are key for a lot of the companies, simply because the U.S. is so large. How are you going to service it all? If you are Sony, JBL, or whatever, you have plenty of in-house employees. Everyone has a region and deals with accounts. Independent rep firms, on the other hand, represent numerous lines. This is also a paradigm that exists in many other industries: plumbing, medical supplies, fill in the blank. You need someone who understands the product, and they get a commission on sales—they don't just get it in the store. Say, for example, a manufacturer would like to do business in the mountain states. The expense of flying out there and doing it yourself can be prohibitive—hotel and airfare add up fast. You look at the turnover and the amount of profit you're going to get from the sales and decide whether it's worthwhile. If you are not careful, you may be spending a good portion of your profit if you are a small company.

That's where the rep firm comes in. They can bird-dog the area since they have the local contacts and knowledge. They can make their costs work because they have other product lines besides your own. That is not an uncommon model at all. There are more than dozens of these firms out there that specifically handle audio products.

Bob, have you been able to maintain a life outside of distribution? How is the work/life balance in this field?

Distributors and reps tend to do okay with family life, assuming business is going through and everyone has a smile on their face. For most people, engineering is a young man's game. Many people want to do it, and if you choose to do it, you have to be a bit monomaniacal. From my perspective, engineers have to put in too many hours. It's good to have a realistic outlook for what you can expect. In engineering, or even as an artist, you need more than talent. The people that I know who have "made it" have an intense focus and drive and were willing to make some major sacrifices.

How do you feel about internships, and are they prevalent?

Yes, they are very common. I have been doing the internship thing for companies since the early '80s, and they have become very popular among colleges. They are so good for everyone involved—the school, the students, and the companies. As for Sonic Distribution, we get additional help that helps us tackle projects we many not have been otherwise able to do.

Which is more beneficial, a trade school or a liberal arts college?

There are some great trade schools; my alma mater is Berklee. My daughter, who plays violin, is going to Hofstra, and I suggested she go to Berklee during the summer. I told her to go out and get a good liberal arts education because conservatories aren't there to give you a liberal arts education. I had the advantage of private schools during my high school years, which added up to be the equivalent of college—this was a saving grace for me. A liberal arts college will teach you how to do research, how to analyze, how to do proposals, and many other things. These are very applicable and necessary skills to have.

The state of audio education is better than it has ever been, but the state of jobs to go out from that audio education in the classic sense is not. I don't say that to discourage anyone, but there are more schools saying, "You too can be an audio engineer!" than there are anything like jobs out there. It's only going to be the exceptional person who is going to take that and somehow make that into something.

Would you say that the audio distribution market is limited by geography?

Distribution isn't limited by geography, and you don't have to be near a metro area. In fact, you can make a good case for being in the middle of the country, doing warehousing and freight for both coasts. You could have a better cost of living out there.

How have things changed in this field over the last couple of decades?

I've seen the whole business mature in the last 20 years. Computers have changed everything, but it's not just the computers. If you go back to the '70s and '60s, innovation in audio could have come from some smart guy in his garage or his lab. You could get down to component levels and make a better mousetrap.

As soon as ICs came in, now you have core technology that isn't really coming from the audio industry. Then you have these other audio components that are coming from telecommunications, and further up the road you start having innovation coming from the computer industry. Now even the DSP is getting supplanted by CPUs getting used for DSPs. On the technology side, there used to be a separation between pro, broadcast, and MI, but many of the walls for a lot of that have been falling down. The number of players out there has consolidated, and you've seen the rise of large mass-market retail operations with the likes of Guitar Center.

Does this make the future uncertain? What do you predict moving forward?

I'd say some of the things go back to the basics. You are not going to replace transducers. You're always going to have to capture acoustic energy into some kind of device before you do stuff to it—then it's ultimately going to come out the other end so people can hear it. You're going to have some sort of microphone on one end, some sort of speaker on the other end, and there's going to be stuff that happens in between [laughs].

What are the most desirable qualities you look for in a candidate?

If you are going to be involved in the music products industry, it really helps if you know something about the process of recording music. Playing an instrument, even if you don't do it professionally, gives you credibility; it makes it more real and experiential. There's nothing like the credibility that "this person really does this." You can speak to people a lot more confidently about what's really going on. I would encourage people to play an instrument and get involved in recording.

I generally look for the following attributes in someone. First, they need commitment. This includes the commitment to show up on time and to be engaged and part of things. Second, they have to be willing to learn—you do run into people who are too uptight about it, too proud. You've got to have an open mind. Third, you have to be able to take calculated risks—take a chance and try. I tell the interns here, "You get to play with a net here, and you're not on a tight wire." Lastly, motivation. This is corollary to commitment.

What kind of salary could one expect starting out, then advancing to a more developed career?

Usually people start out around the $30k range. Beyond that, the sky is the limit. Senior people can make $150 to $200k, but typical high levels make $90k plus. People's performance in the higher tiers is usually tied to bonuses.

A Closer Look: Paul Foschino of Sony Professional Audio

Paul Foschino is senior manager for professional audio in Sony Electronics' Broadcast and Production Systems division. Relatively early in his career, he was able to gain an understanding of consumer audio products, coupling that with valuable retail experience. Since heading up Sony's pro audio division, his overall mantra has been to generate demand—something he does by understanding his customers and marketing Sony's innovative products.

Tell me how you first entered the audio world.

I went to a trade high school, Bergen Tech, and I studied electronics. From there, I came out and went to Ramapo College and studied computer programming and also had a degree in business management and environmental studies. While I was going through college, I had a part-time job working at Sam Goody, a record store that also had a hi-fi department. I worked part-time, then full-time. I was selling everything from JBL speakers to turntables, all that technology. They offered me $3.25 an hour, which was a lot of money back then, so I took the job. I found it to be

Paul Foschino.

something that I enjoyed and liked the fact that I was still part of electronics. I was also good at it—I was selling and eventually became their top salesman.

I ended up staying there and working until I heard about a job opportunity at Technics, the turntable manufacturer. The job I took was assistant national sales manager, in charge of the cassette decks. And that was it. That started my career path off in the world of audio.

But suddenly you were on the manufacturer side versus the retail side.

Yes, but I had a lot of sales experience working at retail and found that the problems and issues could be applied to all the technologies we were introducing at Technics. Working for a big manufacturer was a new experience for me. I didn't really understand the ins and outs of working for a giant Japanese corporation, but I did certainly understand retail, and that's the experience they were looking for.

All they wanted me to do was learn everything I could about their technology, then they wanted me to take this information out to both retail salespeople and their own internal sales people. And that's what I did for a number of years. But eventually I started working my way up through the company and became assistant general manager and was responsible for all of the Technics hi-fi equipment, along with the Technics musical instrument division as well as their car stereo division.

So you were managing more product lines while getting more responsibility.

Right. I was traveling back and forth to Japan at least four or five times a year. I was working with all the different factories: musical instruments, car stereos, and hi-fi. We were developing new product lines, and I was working with big dealers like Best Buy, Circuit City, all of them. We were developing products that would be competitive out in the market for Technics.

When turntables were dominant, Technics was very hot. When the CD came along in 1982, the field was then wide open for anyone to take the number-one position. Turntables were the number-one playback device for many years, but this was just about to be changed by something digital. When this happened, we found ourselves in a tight battle with Sony. At the time, I was on the board of directors of the Compact Disc Group, which was an industry group that was made up of record companies and the audio manufacturers. The board represented both hardware and software manufacturers because we wanted to make sure when we rolled out the CD, we did it the right way for the consumer. We needed to explain what the purpose of the product was, what the benefits were, why it was going to cost more money, but how it was going to improve their overall enjoyment of music.

It was in everybody's interest.

Yes. It was in the best interest of the record companies, the manufacturers, and the consumer. We did it in a very strategic and organized way. We organized trade show committees where we launched the format collectively as an industry, as opposed to by competing manufacturers, and were able to convey some solid information. We were able to unify the packaging and design of the jewel case—they had to fit in all the old record bins. All of these issues were addressed. During this time, I got to meet people within the industry. I got to work closely with people like John Brich, the president of the audio division over at Sony. Even though we were competitors with one another out in the field, we were working together in an industry group.

How did you wind up at Sony?

Eventually a position opened up at Sony in around '91. John had known me through this industry organization and decided to hire me. My first position was vice president in the auto sound division for Sony. So I wound up working for Sony in the auto sound group, partly because I already had experience at Technics in the auto sound group. When I got there, the group had a lot of issues, there were a lot of problems, so we changed the image and created a whole new look and feel, new logos and identity. Once we did that, things started to turn around and take off.

Shortly after that, there was a new format being launched called MiniDisc. This was very important to Sony; they were competing against Philips, Digital Compact Cassette. John Brich knew that I had a lot of experience launching formats, so he hired me as Director of New Technology. I had launched the compact disc, and I was instrumental in launching DAT and other technologies, so he asked me to head up the launch of MiniDisc, so I did. Eventually, MiniDisc became the dominant format.

Once we launched MiniDisc and turned it over to the individual marketing groups, like hi-fi group, car stereo group, and portable audio, they didn't really need me to do that any more. So it was kind of up to me to choose another career path at Sony. Since I had already worked in every group, including the professional audio group, I got a feel for what was going on at the professional side. So it was great to get back into a marketing group in audio—that never really left my blood since 1970. I needed to get back into manufacturing, marketing, that side of things. This must have been around '95 or '96, and I wound up going to the pro audio group, heading up their marketing efforts and continuing to promote MiniDisc for professional purposes like radio stations, broadcast applications, portable units, and things like that.

In the mid-'90s, pro audio was based on DAT recorders, mixing consoles, wired and wireless microphones, and an awful lot of penetration in the studio market. Sony pro audio was known primarily for its multitrack recorders—things like the 3348 were the ultimate multitrack tape recorders that every major recording studio had. So I got my feet wet working with recording studios based on the equipment they were using, but also in live sound. Our wired microphones were widely used with a lot of rock bands: The Rolling Stones, David Bowie, and Van Halen were some of the groups using them.

Around this time I began to think about ways we might be able to expand into areas beyond just the pro audio gear. I looked at the MI space, where there were tons of opportunities. At that time, Sony had a guitar processor and a lot of other very expensive signal processors: reverbs and equalizers that were going into studios. I wanted to see if we could open up a new channel that we could expand our business in. We ended up being successful in doing this with things like our headphones: the 7506 studio headphones being a prime example, as well as a half-rack guitar processor we had. So we went to Japan, did some industry research, and found that MI was a $4 or $5 billion industry. We found out where the money was being made, what kinds of products were being sold. I saw a fantastic opportunity in this industry, including the home studio industry. I knew we needed a product to tap into the home studio market, where I really wanted to focus. We needed a product specifically designed for home studio musicians.

I knew we needed to find a way to leverage the MiniDisc recorder as a multitracker for this market that people could use in their bedroom. Everyone got excited and, for the first time, introduced a product aimed squarely at the MI industry—we came out with the MDM-X4. This was a four-track recorder that used MiniDisc, and it did a good job. When we came out with the product, it was right on target.

What are some of the things that helped you get through these challenges?

I think understanding people is a big part of it. This is important throughout your entire career. It doesn't matter what you are selling or who you are selling it to. The goal is the same, and that is to close the sale. If it is with a customer on a sales floor trying to sell them a hi-fi system, you have to understand what that customer's needs are, how much they want to spend, then you need to show the perfect product for them to convince them they need to look no further. Once you get to the manufacturer level, you have to do the same thing. If you are pitching concepts to top management, you have to sell them on your idea and convince them that your idea is the best. You refine these skills over time and apply them over and over again.

It is also important to learn negotiating skills. If you want to get stuff done, a lot of the times you have to negotiate your way through a process.

This is a skill that is developed and not innate, right?

You do have to develop it. This is something that comes up when you are discussing pricing—in the end, both parties have to feel that the decisions that were reached are best to maximize the sales opportunity.

What academic skills paid off and are still helping you today?

You may not actually go to college and come out with a job in that discipline or field. In college, you fine-tune your thinking patterns and learn how to do some thinking on your own. You can go out and get a little bit more creative and do it yourself—solve problems and learn how to communicate. If you are clumsy and awkward, you have a lot to learn. By your senior year, you should be able to know what the objectives are up front and know enough to be able to go out and find the information that you need to make an intelligent decision. If anything, that's what most people walk away with from college, rather than the actual skill set you may pick up.

What is your day-to-day role?

I run pro audio and demand creation. Demand creation is purely a marketing group. All we do is look for ways to build more demand with the customer. This involves people working with people and managing them and laying out their career objectives as well. A lot of my day is spent going through email and phone calls, and then of course meetings. I need to organize many events and trade shows: This requires meeting after meeting after meeting.

What are the three most important things you need that allow you to do your job better?

Understanding marketing. Marketing is a whole science in itself. Everything we do is marketing. How we are going to talk to our customers, find out what their needs and communicate with them so we can sell our products. The next most important thing is to sell, sell, sell. We make our money when we sell our product. So I am constantly looking at our targets and our budgets and seeing if we are achieving them. If we are not, I am getting on the phone with our distributors and trying to find out what is going on out in the marketplace. What do we need to do to bring it up to the next level? After you have identified what your objectives are and they are clear, put in a strategy to achieve your goals. Does this involve new marketing programs, SPIF programs for sales or retail, end-user rebates, long-term marketing programs for retailers? You need to provide more incentive for people to buy your product on a regular basis.

What kind of stress can one expect at a manufacturer?

Every person is going to have to make his own decision as to what he needs to do to balance his own career and his own life. Stress can be everywhere in life, and that really comes down to the individuals and how they deal with their job. You have to figure out a balance for your own life; figure out what is important and dedicate a certain amount of time to each thing. I have a family: I have two grown boys, 27 and 28, and they have their own lives and careers. I have a daughter who is 15 who needs a lot of time and attention, a wife, and a home. I also am in several bands: I am in a jazz group at home, I am in a Sony band at work playing rock 'n roll, and I am in a church group.

Is that balance important?

Yes. Even at Sony, a bunch of other musicians and I get together about once a month before we go home. After a long day at work, playing loud rock 'n roll helps get your frustrations out. It also helps within the workplace: I have people in that group who are vice presidents, lawyers, medical salespeople, every part of Sony. But once we are there playing, it doesn't matter—we are just musicians. A bass player, guitar player, or a drummer. It breaks down a lot of boundaries and reduces a lot of stress that could occur in the workplace.

What about compensation? What areas are going to command higher salaries?

Big manufacturers and big companies all pretty much do the same thing. They look at salary as an equation. They look at the standards of the industry; they look at how much others are being paid in the industry and try to come up with a fair balance. It is not just the salary, it is the whole compensation package: It's medical coverage, dental, vacation, everything else rolled in a total offering. You as an individual have to decide where your career path is going to bring you. If you choose to work in a recording studio, then you may have to work late nights and sleep late in the morning. This may be what you've always wanted to do—that's okay. But if you are a creative type, you might not find that kind of satisfaction working for a manufacturer.

Selling audio equipment, you have budgets, objectives that are clear, people you have to work with and manage, you have dealers you have to sell to, you have inventory concerns to worry about. It is a business, like any other business, so you have to be equally balanced in technology and product knowledge. You also have to have people skills. You have to come up with marketing programs and strategies and be able to work with salespeople.

Who is the typical customer?

This can be defined in a couple of ways. The end user is a customer every day when he walks into a retail environment or visits a website. He will be influenced by something he reads on a website or hears from the retail salesperson to make his purchasing decision. We have to consider the end user first, then we consider the dealer and what is going to satisfy his bottom line.

I have different ways to get product out to the market, various distribution channels. I can sell to distributors, I sell to direct Sony account managers, and some dealers I handle directly myself. A lot of the musical instrument manufacturers sell direct and have their own dedicated sales force working on commission. Then there are distributors who buy the product and resell it.

What expertise do you expect out of your distributors?

One-hundred percent knowledge. My distributors have a dedicated sales force and they are all audio experts—either having worked as musicians or in the audio industry themselves. I want a fine-tuned group of salespeople out there who can answer any question and can sell any system. I have experts out there in the field. I break them out in LGTs—limited geographic territories. I have East Coast, Midwest, West Coast, and Northwest. I do this so they don't compete with one another: They actually support each other. They share program ideas; they share training materials. We work on plans and strategies together and help each other sell collectively.

What is the health of the manufacturing industry now?

I think every industry goes through ups and downs, depending on buying trends and product development. But I think it's very healthy. There are exciting new technologies coming into play. I may not want to start my career working for a console company right now, because you can follow a trend in the industry that will show a lot more of that technology has moved into computers. Companies like Digidesign have moved the essential functions of a console into a computer-based piece of software. Even the major recording studios have Pro Tools workstations—consoles are still in need, but this is an area that has been impacted greatly by computer technology. At Sony, our entire pro audio department was based on how many 3348 tape recorders we sold at one time. That industry is gone completely, and it is all about hard drives now. You have to be flexible, adapt to changing times, and find new products to sell.

The microphone world has never changed. There are still wired and wireless microphones. More and more manufacturers continue to get into the business; better and better equipment can be found for lower prices.

If you were going back and choosing a discipline to be educated in now, what would you choose?

If you have programming expertise, that is huge right now. If you are an audio junkie and want to sit behind a recording console in a glass booth looking at rock stars on the other side of the glass, there is still a role doing that kind of thing and making a living at it. But if you are just interested in working for an audio company, then business and marketing are important skill sets to learn early on.

A Closer Look: Tim Schweiger of BSW Audio

Tim Schweiger is president of BSW Audio, the online and mail order retailer. Tim was enchanted by the pro audio industry early in his career, as he was introduced to college radio. Ever since, he has been tinkering with gear but also trying to help other people make the right purchases in his role at BSW. Of all the people I met, Tim was the one who impressed on me the importance of listening.

Tim Schweiger.

What was your basic career path?

I was about 13 years old and I was very fortunate to get on as an assistant in the A/V department in junior high. That would have been around the early '70s, and I became an audio nerd. I realized at that age that while most people shied away from technical things, I was the kind of person who would take the back off of a stereo system and look at all the parts in there. I would try to figure out how it worked—I had an aptitude for electronics and a love for audio. I just fell in love with the equipment and had a knack for wanting to be around things with wires and sound.

How did this manifest itself in high school and college?

The next phase of that was that I was attracted to broadcasting. While in junior high, I talked my way into the local campus college station at the University of Puget Sound. I had been walking by one day and saw that they had a radio station—I saw the control console and the turntable and the D.J. and just said, "That's it—this is what I am going to do." I talked my way into having my own radio program on the campus radio station.

Broadcasting was my next progression, and I went to Bates Vocational School in Tacoma and got my FCC license so I could take a job in the broadcasting industry. I was on the air as a disc jockey, but was not destined to go off and become a Don Imus or a Howard Stern, so I started hanging around the engineers. It was they who always had the fascinating stuff going on. I eventually took a job in retail at a Radio Shack store, and again I was right in my element. I absolutely loved the interaction with customers and trying to help them out—trying to help them solve their audio needs.

After that, one day here in Tacoma, I answered an ad that became my introduction to employment here at BSW, or Broadcast and Supply Worldwide—it was about 26 years ago. Back then, BSW was a supplier primarily to radio stations throughout the country—it was a very targeted, niche thing. We would get calls from radio station engineers, and I was absolutely in my element. They were intelligent and they really needed advice and help in terms of new technology and gear. I was naturally drawn to it and I was like a sponge—we were always trying out new gear.

People say, "Why would you want to go work for a retailer?" The interesting thing is that the retailer gets the gear before anybody. It is the retailer who gets to interact and work with the manufacturer on everything from product development to applications and promotions, and the neat thing is that you can be part of this new technical revolution. As a retailer it is always the new stuff because we are always selling new things from new companies or new products from existing companies. It is just neat being part of that.

It is fascinating. In my case, I have met some of the most brilliant product designers, some of the most innovative factories and products that have been brought out over the years. Again, if you have the knack for it and audio is your passion, it is not a job—it is a career. It is something you just look forward to every day.

The dark side of selling audio gear is that you can't be so opinionated that you close your mind off to other things and other products. But it's like any other sales position: It doesn't matter if you are selling clothes, cars, or whatever. You are dealing with a retail environment so you have to be people-friendly, you have to follow through what you say you are going to do. You are solving their problems and advocating products.

There are all sorts of entry points where people can get into. Right now, one thing that we could use would be technical writers—someone who can write advertising copy who really likes the gear but doesn't necessarily want a gig selling stuff. There are entry points for people who like the gear but don't want to be the ones selling it.

How is the retail field and market in general now?

It is kind of trying times as it pertains to audio. We find ourselves competing with companies who might specialize in selling guitars and drums. All of a sudden, they are selling recorders and mixers. The problem in retailing nowadays is that it is so much more price-competitive. In this day and age, when you have all this information at your fingertips, customers can be pretty fickle. There is not a lot of tolerance for any kind of error, delay, or high prices. We have to monitor our inventories better; we really have to pay attention to price and figure out how we can compete on an open market with companies that might not need high profit margins—but that is the challenge of being in any business.

Is there a benefit to being specialized like you guys are?

Yes. We don't put it in print unless we can back it up, knowing it is what we've got. We have experts in multitrack recording software, computers, microphone placement, just about every discipline. Everyone has their own expertise individually that we call on collectively as a company. We are careful about the products we carry, though—for example, if a guitar company starts offering mixers, we're not going to just turn around and start selling their guitars. That would be silly.

How important is the physical environment these days?

We used to be a physical shop, but our heritage has always been mail order. When the Internet came along, we didn't have to change a thing. We get tons of hands-on time with the gear that we sell. The manufacturers whose products we buy and represent see to it that our people have an opportunity to touch and feel, touch the buttons, and get an idea of how things work. The second thing is that we have ongoing training courtesy of the manufacturers for our employees. Not too long ago, we had Mike Pappas in from Neumann Microphones, who is a magnificent expert in the industry about microphones in general. We learn about proper mics and usage. The depth of knowledge that our people get just by virtue of selling the gear is absolutely amazing. When you specialize and are working with a customer base who knows what they are doing, these guys can tell you a lot about products and how they are using them—it's just amazing. You need to listen to your customers.

How does the talent break out on your staff?

Our corporation, all the people who are in executive positions, have all been on the front lines at one point or another dealing with the customer base. We have morphed more into the business side. I know a lot more about microphones than I do about the P&L statements, even though I am responsible for them. Our true core has always been about the gear first, and the business stuff always kind of comes second. This isn't true for our back office, though: We hire specialists in accounting, shipping, all the other things that are necessary to make the cogs run more smoothly.

To get into sales, it requires some kind of investment either in schooling or as a recording studio engineer or a musician with other related experience. If someone can embrace the whole concept of selling, they can usually survive.

What is a typical growth path in retail?

Growth can come slower than many would anticipate. It depends on how much you know and whether you are bringing a new customer base over. I think there is going to be selected opportunities on this over the years, and opportunities are not growing as they once were. That said, there will always be room for good people who really understand what it is they are doing and can really combine the sales aspect of it versus an order-taking aspect—this is a very important distinction.

What about geography? Is this a concern? Where does someone get their best start?

The retailers for the professional audio stuff are in the most remote, interesting places. You don't have to be in L.A. You can be in Indiana, most anywhere you want to be. I don't think you can work from home in your underwear, though—you at least have to go into a physical retail environment or a call center. You need to intermingle with your colleagues as well as be trained—training takes place at your major facilities.

What about work/life balance? Can you have a life outside the office?

Oh, yes, absolutely. In our case, you aren't working until midnight. It is a straight eight-hour day, weekends off. We are kind of modeled after the manufacturers and the delivery companies for UPS and FedEx. The web picks up a lot of the downtime when people absolutely need to have stuff. But for people who need to speak to someone, most people are tolerant of the fact that an expert isn't usually available 24 hours a day. The pressure starts coming on if you don't keep up with the technology. You have to be able to answer customers' questions, and when you are selling to competent engineers, you can't put anything over on them. You've got to know your stuff. You always have pressure in a sales position, though. You are competing against your co-workers; you are competing for your paycheck and other opportunities—so that puts some pressure on, too. You've got to keep up with your sales skills.

What kind of salary could you expect?

Starting out at a reputable firm, probably around $35 to $40k if you have decent sales skills. A specialized house requires specialized training and a specialized life skill—at a more general retailer, this specialized skill might be lower, but the pay will be, too. There might be scripts for certain products or buttons to push when a specialist is required.

What about an advanced career?

You could go $100+, especially if you get in at a VP level and you are getting into marketing and product development. Or someone who is in a buying position—someone who knows the gear well enough to know that this product will be a big seller, then they negotiate with the seller in order to facilitate a buy and take a chance in bringing the gear in. Tremendous responsibility on these people who have to make a gut decision on what they think is going to sell, how many they are going to buy. You can do very, very well on that financially in retail at the corporate level.

What is up around the bend in the next five or ten years in retail?

I'm not being pessimistic, but I just don't see a lot of growth over the next five years, to be really honest with you. There are other people who do, but I think we're going to go through a plateau period as it pertains to people. That being said, there are going to be some major opportunities with the manufacturers who make the gear. They have got to be able to get out and train the retailers, especially the retailers that are looking to cut overhead and are looking to be full-service houses. They are going to be hiring the people who don't really know a lot about the gear, so the second phase of opportunity for people would be to go work in the manufacturing side and become a product specialist. If you can demonstrate products at tradeshows, go to retail locations, work on the sales floor of a major retailer as a representative of that manufacturer—there are definitely opportunities for that. Independent sales reps are still around and very functional in our industry—they need people who can go out to the retailers and train them. They may handle 10 or 20 different lines. There might be opportunities as entry-level positions for people to get their foot in the door that way.

What segments are on fire at the moment?

For us at BSW, the most exciting category of gear that we are selling is portable recorders based around Flash technology. It is all going down to the Flash cards.

When have you felt really aligned with your career?

Every single day. I pinch myself every single day and say to myself, "I can't believe I walked into this." I love looking at gear: "Can you just turn the thing around so I can look at the back?" [laughs] You just kind of suffer in silence. Here I am in an environment that not only tolerates this, but expects it. It's like group therapy, and I love it!

9 | Services to Professional Audio

As the audio market continues to reinvent itself and diversify, there are many opportunities to work for companies who serve the audio market in some way. If you break out all of the vertical markets in audio, most of which are covered to some degree in this book, it is apparent that each area benefits from traditional services, such as integration and acoustic design, to innovative services, such as collaborative portals and cutting-edge audio forensics straight out of *CSI*.

Market Viability

Many of the companies that provide services to the audio market are relatively small in size and entrepreneurial in nature. For any of them to successfully serve an existing market, they must have a core competency, creativity, and client infrastructure. They also must be willing to bear a certain amount of risk both to get off the ground and to remain competitive.

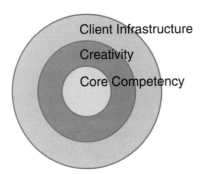

Some of the required audio services that we have identified in this book include acoustic design, integration and maintenance, marketing and public relations, collaborative portals and advanced web services, audio forensics, and audio restoration.

Many services contain elements that are critical to any company's success, such as marketing. Effective marketing, as an example, is built on relatively unchanged philosophies that provide value and can be transferred to nearly any industry. Marketing services require an intimate knowledge of the product or service, the customer, and any number of strategic and tactical mediums to relay the message.

Service Segment Profiles and Career Opportunities

For this section, rather than covering specific job roles within a vertical silo, we will examine the type of service the company provides. We will explore the broad opportunities, required skills, benefits, and drawbacks of each service segment.

Acoustic Design

Despite the well-documented downfall of the commercial recording studio market, some acoustic designers have more work than at any other time in history, because studios are being built across a more diversified customer base and across different geographies. The "second evolution" of the home studio market is already well underway—where individuals began outfitting their bedrooms with digital multitrack capabilities well over a decade ago, now they are taking a closer look at their acoustic spaces and spending the money to build them correctly.

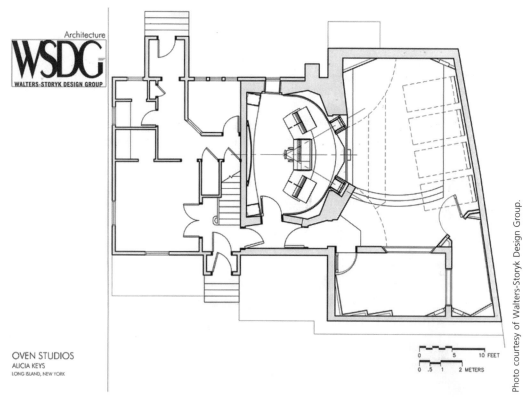

Architectural drawing of Alicia Keys' The Oven studios.

Although there are always do-it-yourselfers who prefer to wing it and build their spaces off of amateur napkin sketches, it is becoming commonplace for musicians, audio enthusiasts, and industry professionals to engage well-known acoustic design firms to take their spaces to the next level. Artists such as Alicia Keys, the Goo Goo Dolls, and Green Day have all built state-of-the-art, commercial-grade studios in the last few years. Companies large and small—many of which are not even in the audio business—recognize the importance of proper acoustic response in meeting rooms, theaters, and other venues. This acoustic trend, which is also common in South America and Europe, is expanding geographically and is poised to grow even further into the next decade and beyond.

Acoustic designers typically have an architectural or engineering background. Any success in acoustic design depends on a fundamental understanding of the physics of sound—something that has not changed since the beginning of time. It is the acoustic designer's job to intimately understand the client's end goal—a post-production house, a live venue, or a commercial recording studio—and accommodate the design to the client's business requirements. Acoustic design firms have the same skills as more traditional architects, but have an extremely specialized knowledge of things such as isolation, acoustic treatment, and designing to very specific technical specifications. Acoustic design firms typically have staff positions that include architects, interior designers, project managers, and engineers, as well as administrative support and back-office functions, such as accounting.

Compensation in acoustic firms can be very lucrative—well into the six figures, especially if you are able to become a co-owner or a principal. There are also opportunities for commissions, because architectural firms are always looking for new work and value new projects and relationships. Benefits usually include health coverage, 401(k), vacation time, and everything else you would expect at a reasonable-size corporation. Acoustic design firms provide a creatively rewarding work environment, but they can be subject to occasional deadline-related stress, which can translate to late hours and off-the-clock weekend work.

Internships can be a very effective way to break into acoustic design, and this field is a perfect example of how a good academic education (versus a vocational, gear-focused education) will put an applicant on a much more solid career growth trajectory. Please see the appendix for a Q&A with John Storyk of Walters-Storyk Design Group, a well-known acoustic design firm that has had a successful internship program in place for many years.

Integration and Maintenance Services

Every professional facility that handles audio usually requires someone to specify the appropriate equipment, as well as handle installation and maintenance. Companies who handle these types of services can make sales margins off of the equipment, including recording consoles, outboard gear, monitors, recorders, and other pieces of gear. They also handle the installation, wiring, and configuration of all this equipment to meet the specifications and objectives of the facility.

Very often, musicians, studio managers, and other people who like to work in recording studios do not want to be bothered with setting up and wiring the equipment. Instead, they rely on studio technicians and maintenance professionals to handle what can be very complicated tasks. Individuals who provide these kinds of services must have an intimate understanding of how all the gear works, including circuitry, wiring, and signal flow; they are well-compensated, and their work is in very high demand.

Photo by Jeff Touzeau.

Professional integration companies handle installing and maintaining complex console installations, as well as racks of equipment such as those pictured here.

The market for integration services is following a similar trajectory to that of studio design—there are more and more studios being built than ever before, but they are being built in places that are not so obvious. Fewer and fewer facilities are staffing their own maintenance and tech crews, meaning there is a greater opportunity for small integration companies and individuals to succeed.

Being successful in integration and maintenance requires that you stay up to date on the latest equipment so you can install it and service it successfully. It goes without saying that manufacturers are changing their equipment design much more frequently than ever before. Computers and networking are playing a more and more predominant role in the audio facilities; therefore, one's ability to both configure and troubleshoot these systems—and increasingly computer networks—can lead to greater opportunity.

Integration and maintenance are areas in which clients place a lot of trust in the service provider. Clients not only require a high-quality and trouble-free infrastructure, they also need a path forward to help them navigate the technology requirements of tomorrow. Clients expect to be sold value and not just product, which means that your choice of monitors, consoles, and recorders needs to have lasting appeal to your customers' own clientele.

The most important skill by far, assuming one already has the required technical competence, is the ability to sell. This is often an innate ability, but one that can also be learned and improved upon. Interpersonal skills and the ability to develop a client base through effective networking are also critical, as they are with any other services segment. Your ability to be responsive following the initial installation will be directly proportionate to your ability to retain clients, which arguably are most often the source of new business.

Key Components of Successful Marketing

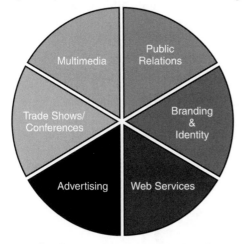

Some fundamental building blocks of successful marketing.

Marketing and Public Relations

Marketing's role in the audio industry (and literally every other industry) is to enhance sales and create awareness. Both of these objectives are critical to the success of any company, including audio-oriented companies of all sorts. Even large organizations, such as Sony, Sennheiser, and Yamaha, rely on the services of outside marketing and public relations firms. These firms are usually paid on an annual retainer and work very hard to help companies gain an edge or increase their competitiveness in the audio market.

Marketing and public relations firms can vary in size from one employee to dozens of employees. Because audio is such a niche market, requiring specialized—often highly technical—knowledge, a company usually selects a marketing or PR firm based on its understanding of this niche and the company's objectives. If the firm is able to deliver measurable results over a given period of time, a company can increase its retainer or extend its contract as appropriate.

Employees of firms that carry out marketing and PR services often have several and any combination of the following skills: branding and identity, advertising, public relations, copywriting, web and graphic design, multimedia services, and tradeshow services. They typically meet with clients on a monthly or quarterly basis to map out objectives and then implement any number of marketing solutions to help businesses meet their goals.

In the web 2.0 environment, social media are becoming increasingly important—even mandatory— for companies to compete. More than any other time in history, consumers are relying on the web to interact and do business. Those companies that are able to market where their customers are—or, in more certain terms, on the Internet—will be in a greater position to deliver value to clients. Therefore, it is absolutely mandatory for marketing companies and PR firms alike to gain an understanding of blogging, wikis, search engine optimization, and social networks, since this is already a multi-billion-dollar industry that will only continue to expand and become even more relevant as time goes by.

Some basic skills that will help a marketing or PR professional succeed in the audio industry include great networking skills (finding and attracting new clients is the very lifeblood of these firms), presentation and communication skills, creativity, and resourcefulness. Because marketing is a skill that is valued by most organizations, it is quite possible to break into the audio industry from an entirely different industry if you are persistent enough and you develop the right contacts.

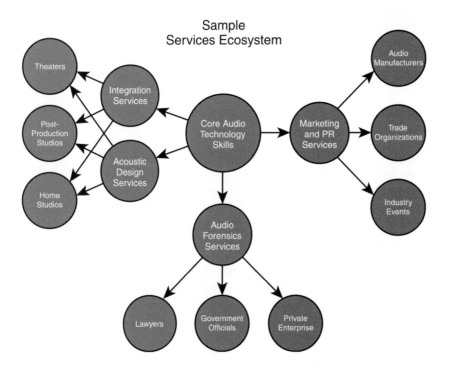

If you are able to demonstrate your value to a company by providing metrics and proof of performance, you can essentially write your own ticket for compensation, but this obviously requires dedication, hard work, and a little bit of luck.

Collaborative Portals and Advanced Web Services

Few people can forget the dot-com boom and bust of the early '90s; therefore, some trepidation is still in order for those charging into the new world of web 2.0– and web 3.0–based services. Although opportunities most certainly exist, there will doubtless be many failed attempts at viable business plans because the market isn't quite ready, or the services haven't been perfected, or they don't provide a meaningful benefit.

However, in an industry that is as hard to read as ever and is undergoing a revolutionary redefinition, there will be almost limitless rewards for those who get it right. One area that looks very promising is artist collaboration. With more personal and home studios going up than ever before, artists, producers, and engineers are looking for more and more ways to collaborate while increasing efficiency and eliminating physical and geographical barriers.

It is no secret that we all live in a world that is becoming more virtual. The thought of employees working remotely a few decades ago was unthinkable, at least in most business professions. Now, if a company does not have a strategy to enable its remote employees, that company's very existence can be threatened. The idea of musicians, producers, and engineers collaborating when they are not able to be in the same physical space is very appealing indeed, as people try to reduce their carbon footprint and especially because they can't be in two places at once.

Companies such as eSession have created specialized web environments that make project management and collaboration a snap. Through their portal, regular musician types can access and engage talent from around the world at very reasonable rates, ultimately increasing the quality standard of the finished product. Other services, such as Digital Musician.net and Kompoz, are integrating a host of other social media capabilities in their portals, such as message boards and feedback mechanisms on which a broad audience can comment on a song or production. eJamming.com provides online education and promotes awareness of diverse music cultures.

These collaboration portals are a relatively new breed of music services based on web 2.0 capabilities that take proven online models, such as Berklee College's online educational offerings, and attempt to find a niche area to serve musicians and other audio professionals. Although the idea of collaboration is certainly not new among audio professionals, these kinds of portals offer promising prospects for taking collaboration into the virtual world.

As new frontiers continue to develop in audio services, online portals will play an increasingly important role, not just in the business models that are out there today, but also in the models that have not been developed or made public yet. The people who can identify what services are required, how to provide them, and who will buy them stand to gain a lot in a market that is constantly trying to come to terms with its identity. Anyone who can become a technical

Image courtesy of eSession.

eSession's home page.

architect of these solutions or who can implement a unique vision for an online service stands to gain a long and rewarding career by doing so.

Web-based technology companies place a very high premium on development talent and programming. If you understand three or more programming languages or you have a unique vision of how technology could increase a company's competitive position, you can essentially name your price. Chief technology officers at these kinds of companies make well into the six figures.

Audio Forensics

Audio forensics is not a new science—just think back to President Kennedy's assassination and the Warren Commission. This infamous event has been examined and re-examined over the last several decades from all possible angles, including the audio perspective. According to audio forensic expert David Mariasy, there was an open radio channel on a motorcycle that was part of the President's motorcade that captured the entire audio of the event—including the gunshots. Since then, the event has been acoustically reconstructed with audio, using microphones and simulated gunshots to approximate the time, distance, and location of the gunfire.

Image courtesy of Team Audio.

David Mariasy of Team Audio, analyzing an audio file.

Not every audio forensics case is as interesting as the Kennedy assassination—or, for that matter, nearly any episode of *CSI*. However, there always have been and always will be plenty of good guys and bad guys, and audio happens to play a very integral role in crime scene investigation. One cannot overlook voice recordings that may be on things such as 911 calls or even planted recording devices on suspects. The audio can often reveal much more than simply dialogue, as the upcoming interview with David Mariasy indicates.

Although audio forensics primarily deals with dialogue and less-than-perfect recordings, it does require very specific skills that go far beyond, say, the typical skills a Pro Tools operator might have. For example, someone involved in audio forensics needs to be sensitive to acoustic environments and how they can influence the interpretation of a crime scene. How do sounds behave differently in a car versus in a dining room? How near or how far are the subjects from the recording device, and what bearing does this have on the sequence of events?

Firms specializing in audio forensics have an established, well-funded, and loyal client base—namely private individuals, lawyers, detectives, and members of the U.S. government. David Mariasy says that people with these kinds of jobs are usually "in it for life," in the sense that they have long careers in these fields—perfect for establishing the kind of client loyalty that most recording studios can only dream about. Obviously, every municipality in the U.S., as well as most other countries, has a local police force and a court system that can benefit from this kind of service. These kinds of clients are willing to pay high prices for quality work that is on time and can influence a case in their favor.

Outside of large government agencies such as the CIA and FBI (often clients of audio forensics firms in their own right), there are very few "large" companies that handle this kind of work on a regular basis. With the advent of the Internet and newer collaborative technologies, audio forensics is a very promising market for audio professionals who don't mind the monotony of listening to, cataloguing, and archiving hours and hours of case-related tapes. Needless to say, exceptional organizational skills are required to be successful in this field, as are interpersonal skills. To spark a career in this area, once you think you are ready, try making an inquiry to your local town court justice or attending a lawyers' conference to gain insight on how you might develop your offering.

Audio Restoration

Over the last several decades, playback formats have changed almost as much as recording formats. There have been consumer reel-to-reel; 78, 45, and 33 rpm records; micro, 8-track, and standard cassettes; all the way to the modern day, in which we have CDs and DVDs. Little to no effort has been made to preserve and protect these recordings over the years, with the exception of a sliver of those that have been deemed historically significant or culturally valuable.

Image courtesy of Team Audio.

Audio restoration involves optimizing files in DAW workstations such as this.

Think of audio restoration as in the same family as photo restoration. A picture of a family member may be important to one group of people, while a rare photograph of a president—or even a Beatle—might be valuable to an entirely different group of people. Every person or organization has recordings that are valuable to them that they will pay to have restored and preserved. Take the Smithsonian Institution, for example. If a rare set of presidential recordings emerge from a former president, it could have a direct impact on how history itself is interpreted. Therefore, it is of paramount importance to a group like this to have any such recordings properly restored and archived, and there is often good money involved in doing this kind of work.

In the professional audio and music world, the term "restoration" can often go hand in hand with the term "remastering." As we move forward in this exciting industry, new tools are being discovered each day that can help restore fidelity to older recordings. Many record companies, such as Sony/BMG, Universal Music, and others, are sifting through their vaults to restore and in many cases re-release vintage recordings. Sony owns its own specialized mastering lab in New York City that is capable of handing tasks such as this.

From a technical perspective, audio restoration is a relatively easy business to break into if you have a strong audio background. A solid knowledge of recording formats, recording mechanisms, and archival practices is required. Common tasks might include transferring 78 RPM records to ¼-inch tape, VHS audio to WAV format, or even microcassette to MP3 format. You will need to document any packaging and label your archived materials with great precision and make them available to your client, often using technology such as FTP (*File Transfer Protocol*).

From a client perspective, breaking into audio restoration can be a long road. The first rule of thumb is to make one client happy and build up from there. First, try your luck working for individuals on family projects that might involve less liability and a smaller scope, and then build up your capability and your confidence to serve larger organizations with more demanding requirements. If you are in business for yourself, you should always make sure you are insured to protect yourself from a lawsuit in the unlikely event of loss or damage of a client's materials.

Is the Audio Services Market Right for You?

There are many areas where you can apply your audio expertise, and the services market seems to particularly value entrepreneurial thinking and new ideas. Very often, people who provide audio services start off in traditional audio fields and spot a need in the market. Skills are often picked up and learned along the way, one client at a time. To succeed, though, you must have a very defined path, starting from what your core competency is and ending with how you can attract and retain clients.

Key Questions for a Service Model

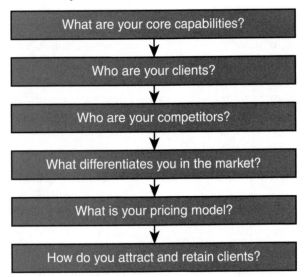

A conceptual map of the different parts that come into play for any service organization—you should be able to answer each of these questions intelligently if you are serious about providing a service to the audio industry.

A Closer Look: Ryan Chahanovich and Innovative Collaboration Services

Ryan is a project manager at eSession, Inc., and is the company's first employee. Educated at the Conservatory of Recording Arts, Chahanovich put his time in at a traditional recording studio before being asked by eSession CEO Gina Saint-Faez to join the company and introduce their refreshing business model to the market. Ryan is also a passionate freelance photographer.

Ryan Chahanovich.

Tell me about eSession.

There are a lot of collaboration sites. There is Kompoz; there's Digital Musician.net. They're really starting to pop up all over the place. We started this because we had an FTP server up at the studio here in Austin, Texas, the live-music capital of the world. We always liked the musicians here, but we also liked working with the professionals in Los Angeles and New York. We would put clients together with talent, and our clients would be surprised, thinking, "I never would have had a chance to work with this guy." There are a lot of other collaboration sites where it's very peer-to-peer. Anyone can jam with anyone, but we want the average singer/songwriter to be able to make a professional music product. That's where we've always stood out and tailored our collaboration that way.

What was the demand like for this service?

People never knew this option was really available to them. So the demand in the lower half of the market, other than the pros, wasn't there because I don't think they ever realized you could collaborate with professionals. How can I get my favorite bass player to play on my record? We've had an uphill battle that way—the one thing we didn't have to worry about is press and getting new people to sign up. We get 100 to 150 new members a week, and we're getting about 3 to 5 new talent members per week. But getting those members to actually convert and really take it to the next level has been a bit of a slower process than we'd hoped. We're doing a lot of sessions now, but it's nowhere near the amount of users we have.

Who exactly is your target market?

It is songwriters and performers we are getting the most interest from. We offer up-and-coming producers the ability to work with other people without having to travel, which can be expensive. Our site not only helps you collaborate, but it is a project management site as well, 24/7. You can set permissions to anyone you want.

What is the potential to get employed with a collaboration-type service like yours?

The market is very nebulous. The beauty of the web is that anyone who is intelligent and entrepreneurial can start and run and operate their own business. Once these kids realize that they can't be the next mega engineer or producer, but if they wear a lot of hats, they can learn some web design, PR, installation skills, everything they can do, they can make a living doing this stuff.

What kind of traits would you be looking for coming out of college?

We are looking for a computer development background, depending on what language we're looking for. For specific positions, there are specific toolsets, but across the board we look for open-mindedness. And if a candidate has done research on us, that really turns us on. If someone has a good knowledge of web 2.0 media, that is also a huge plus. I see people who really aren't savvy in the web 2.0 world, and it's not good.

What would the single most valuable skill be?

People skills, but definitely the ability to write and program are close seconds. You have to be able to do a little bit of everything these days, even a little bit of graphic design.

What is the day-to-day life like?

At a startup or any sort of small company, there is no 9 to 5—it's whenever you are available. The key is to be flexible and be mobile. Have a laptop and a cell phone modem; that's what I do. I am reachable all the time. We've got a pretty good system working—now I have a life outside of eSession. I am a cyclist, and I am a photographer.

What about compensation? What is entry level, then a fully developed career?

Entry-level you can expect mid 20s and low 30s at best, depending on what part of the country you are in and your education. Our CEO doesn't get a paycheck. A high-level developer can go well into the six figures.

What is the structure of your organization?

We are a pretty small shop. We've got our development team, which has a CTO, the highest paid employee. Underneath that there is a development manager, then developers. We've got the Flash guy, we've got the PHP guy, we've got the Java guy. I am artist relations, what I consider to be our back end. The front-end line, we have a marketing guru who is responsible for designing our ads, press, and trade shows. I manage our e-talent user base and manage the e-talent as well—I'm sort of the face of our site. We don't have a sales team, and we are figuring this part out. We also have several outsourced positions with people on retainer: PR and a graphic design firm, for example.

What about benefits?

We have full benefits. We have a great healthcare plan, 401(k), and all that stuff.

What about stress?

It can be very creative and rewarding, but it also can be stressful and monotonous at times.

Are your skills transferable? What plans do you have for your next life?

Absolutely. I think my next life will be in artist relations or PR, when I started out as an engineer. I think the opportunities are boundless. I am optimistic—both for artists and for people trying to make their way out of the high schools and things. I think so many of the schools need to change their curriculum—so many are still saying, "Oh, you can go work in a recording studio—go for it!" They need to change their thought process.

A Closer Look: Dave Malekpour and the Professional Integration Industry

Dave Malekpour is owner of Boston, Massachussetts–based Professional Audio Design, a firm he started back in 1992 when he realized he had the talent to fill a very specialized studio niche.

Professional Audio Design has since become one of the industry's most prominent integrators. Dave impressed on me that to be successful, you have to have resilience, perseverance, and the ability to bounce back.

Dave Malekpour.

Dave, what does your company do?

My company is focused on consulting and guiding clients with the technology they need to achieve their creative goals. We help them choose the equipment, figure out the best way to connect it, ground it, and install it to ensure that it has the best signal path possible. So it's a combination of equipment buying, system and design, and then wiring. We'll offer our clients technical support after they start to use their equipment. People often call us for recommendations on what microphones or monitors to buy, and we help them continue to upgrade their technology as they grow. Often we bring in acoustical architect partners if the client has any acoustic design requirements.

How has your client base changed over the last 15 years or so?

Originally, our primary customer was a professional recording studio, but today most of our clients are actual artists and producers. The people using the equipment also own it more often than not. Back then, there were a few more commercial studios than there are today, but today there are many more people involved in recording than ever before. If you think about it, most people who own a computer have some form of recording capability in their computer. Anyone who bought a Macintosh computer in the last two years, for example, has a recording studio built into his computer. In addition to the client profile changing, the technology has changed, too. Before, $100,000 to $1,000,000 could get you a studio. Today, it could be $1,000 to $1,000,000, but there are so many permutations.

What were your first experiences in audio and what really drew you into this career path?

My first experience with electronics was as a child. When I was 10, my stepfather and I built a power amplifier. This was a lot of fun, and it allowed me to feel more comfortable later on when it came to doing odd jobs like repairing P.A. equipment. Eventually, I would try to take apart tape recorders and rebuild them myself. I also became the guy in my high school everyone would ask to fix the P.A. in the auditorium. By then I was working a day job and playing in a band at night.

At the studio I hung around at night, I learned about the SSL and tape machines. Once I saw this guy come in and change the speakers in the soffit and thought it looked kind of interesting. One day I saw an ad in the *Boston Phoenix* for someone who was looking for salesmen. I had been running an ice cream store at the time and working at the studio for nothing. I convinced the guy that I could do the job and ended up doing that for a couple of years. I then began to develop my own vision for how things should be done and decided to start my own company. I actually was looking for a job, then someone asked me if I had my own company.

I had some good ideas and was only 26 at the time. I had $5,000 to invest when I made my first go at it. I made a couple bad deals and bad choices when I first went into business, so I had to close. But I was able to take that and re-form it into something else—I wanted to start over again but this time do it right. Before, I was doing installations at restaurants, cars, clothing stores, practically anyplace that would buy my systems. The company was called Anything Audio. It wasn't that focused, and the name was really broad. This time I became more focused and formed PAD in 1992.

What personal traits have gained you the most mileage during your journey? What did you learn about yourself?

Well first, I have an incredible memory. I can remember things about people, about their projects, and a lot of details. That has helped me understand my business better because of all the technology. It also helps me remember details on specific projects, and clients appreciate this. My biggest gift is in having a vision for my client. I can see what the future will look like and build toward that. This vision is tremendously important in building relationships with clients and helping them realize the best way to grow. I also have a knack for relating to people and helping them discover what is right for their business. That makes it fun. All told, I am employing all my interests—I love the gear, I love what I do. It's a totally hedonistic and pleasurable thing.

How saturated is the market for people who want a career in audio? Has it gotten worse or has it gotten better?

For technology careers, it depends on which side of the business you want to be in. For what I do, there is a limited market. We are definitely in a niche. We're not a broad market. On the whole, this kind of career is for someone who wants to work with creative people but has a technology knack. Maybe he or she loves the art of recording and music but wants sound, too. It's not a career for everybody, but if you're interested in music and technology, it could be a good path.

What is a typical day for you and what is your office like?

A typical day might entail going into the office after my workout in the gym, then looking at proposals that have to go out. Usually I spend the time in the morning working through active projects, so I have a system of bottom-up management. I have my own brand of chaotic organization that has gotten better over the years—I've been able to systematize what I do.

One of my key roles at Professional Audio Design is to try to make everyone else understand my perspective of what needs to be done with the business and how to work with the customers. I try to explain what the customer's perspective on things might be, so there's a large teaching role in what I do. You have to be able to understand the customer experience from several different angles. You also have to know how to listen, ask tough questions, and provide honest answers. This means that you walk a fine line between being a consultant and a salesperson, constantly looking out for the customer's interest.

Is there a lot of stress in your job? What kind of pressures do you face?

There is stress at certain moments. Deadlines have stress, and client expectations have stress. Being a business owner also has stress because other people's lives are at stake based on the decisions you make. Collecting money can also be stressful.

You need to find a balance in everything, and stress is not necessarily a bad thing. If something is stressful, you have the opportunity for a breakthrough, and you can push yourself to do a better job next time. If everything goes right all the time, you don't necessarily realize what could have gone wrong. So you've got to learn from your mistakes and basically remain optimistic. You need to keep a clear head and not overreact to situations.

How did you develop your self-confidence? This seems to be a common trait among successful entrepreneurs.

A couple of experiences in, you realize you can do things a little better. Someone may say they want this, but your own intuition tells you they *really* want this other thing. Understanding people's needs is key to developing confidence in bringing them a solution—this understanding comes from experience. I do things a different way now, with 20 years of experience, and a person with two years' experience will have a significantly different perspective. As far as confidence is concerned, if you don't think you can do it well, you will never put yourself in a position to perform well. Your personal experience is valuable—it can guide your own actions and help guide the actions of others.

Have you been able to maintain a normal life outside of your career? What kind of personal toll has owning your own systems integration business taken?

It's about choices. You make choices between what you want to do to and what it will take to succeed. If I have a choice between going out to dinner and getting a quote out, I will usually choose getting the quote out—that would have to be my priority. I've made these kinds of sacrifices repeatedly along the way and reaped both the benefits and the negative consequences of this. When you have this level of commitment, not everything will be perfect for a family life, but on the other hand, being driven and knowing what you want doesn't feel like a sacrifice for me.

What advice would you give a recent audio grad or someone trying to gain entry into the field?

If you have a vision of how things could be done differently in any area of this business, go for it. That's what makes our country and our system great. I respect that all the companies out there have their own way of doing things. There are a lot of niches in this business, and that can be very appealing for someone looking for a career in audio. If you're into making wires, there's a career for you. If you're into programming or automation systems, there's a career for you. There are technicians and salesmen, many of whom are producing and playing in bands at night!

What is one of the more rewarding moments you have had during your own career?

During last year we were featured on a couple of *Mix*'s covers, and I've worked with some of the best people in the business. When you help a client through a creative process and then you see it on the cover of a magazine, it's a great feeling.

What can someone expect from a salary perspective, both coming in the door and as a more senior-level employee?

People in integration start at around 25 to 35 grand. A fully developed career might bring you 50 to 120 grand.

Are freelance opportunities available for someone with a skill set like yours?

Absolutely. There are so many incarnations of things you could do with this background. All the opportunities I've had have come from chance meetings. For example, we started working with John Storyk when we were hired independently, working for Aerosmith and Timbaland. We enjoyed working together, so we tried to pair together more often because we both knew the end result would come out great.

When you are interviewing someone, what are the most important traits you look for?

I really want a good presentation. Before they even get in the door, there needs to be a cover letter that reads well and doesn't have typos. You wouldn't believe it, but some of the most basic things are so important: coming in with a clean shirt, being on time or early, and knowing what you're talking about or what the company does. I've had people come into my office and talk about what they want to do, and it has absolutely nothing to do with what we do. Others will come in and ask me what brands we sell. Do some research on the people you want to work for; find out everything about them and study them.

You need to be driven in this industry. Nobody has the time or space for people who need to be babysat. People need to be team-oriented as well, and there is a certain amount of sales leadership that's required.

Dave, have you been able to maintain any outside interests, or has your career effectively consumed you?

I love to cook. If I didn't have a pro audio company, I'd definitely have a restaurant. I also love to work out and travel. Traveling goes well with my business anyway, since I do studios in all kinds of places. Cooking is creative in the same way building a studio is creative. I envision my dinner, think of all the things I'm going to put in it, and maybe it comes out like I wanted it, other times maybe not.

A Closer Look: David Mariasy of Team Audio

David Mariasy is an audio forensics specialist and President/CEO of Team Audio. He has worked on countless crime investigations and cases and is a leader in his field. He currently maintains a client base of loyal customers all over the country. David is an entrepreneur who was able to spot a niche in the market and gradually grow his business, ultimately diversifying into areas such as audio restoration.

Photo courtesy of Team Audio.

David Mariasy.

What does Team Audio do?

We are involved in media forensics. You can divide what we do in half, mainly the forensic end of things. It's mostly audio, but it includes video, too. We enhance any kind of audio recording to enhance the speech recognition and better understand the spoken word. There are instances when the timing of events is crucial. Gunshots, sounds in the background, phones ringing, all types of sounds. The other big half of what Team Audio does is in restoration, which is not limited to crime and is not necessarily time-related. This can involve old recordings, 78 records. Currently we have an assignment, which I can't say a whole lot about because it involves a famous United States president and recordings of him. The restoration things can be buried pieces of audio—we get audio in from broadcast television, where it might be a broadcast interview that is over-modulated. It may have been professionally recorded, but it's got problems.

How did you get where you are?

On a personal note, I never thought that I would be doing forensic audio. I just loved the recording studio. In grad school [Bowling Green State University], I was an assistant for two years, and they basically just thrust me into the studio—a brand-new facility. We had to figure out what we were doing, so I learned from scratch how to solder a patch bay, balanced audio, all that stuff. Then I started designing studios, and we built prototype studios. I was doing this out of the back door of where I was at, in Bowling Green, Ohio. Then we started the original Audio Matrix studios. We would get the occasional call from let's say a prosecutor, police detectives, attorneys. They figured if they had some really bad audio that was relevant to a case, ask the professionals in a recording studio what they thought about it.

There was a key case in town here in Toledo years ago. It was a homicide. The police had a really horrible audiocassette that they had obtained. At that point, we just did what we could for them so they could hear the recording. Right after that, there was a prosecutor involved right in our community; there was another case they had from an outlying town, and another detective was involved. She said, "We have this other tape here from another matter. What do you guys think about it? What can you do with it?"

So it started that way. The light bulb came on—this was around the early '90s. I thought, "There might be something to make of this." It started in our own backyard, very locally. It led me to my first real investment in specialized digital audio, the forerunner of what we use today.

There was this one prosecutor—I got the idea, "Let's take this guy out to lunch and pick his brain." This was before the Internet. We had to do everything analog, so we made flyers, bought lists of police departments, attorneys. We took ads out in very specialized publications. One of the things about this line of work as opposed to the recording studios is that the cops and robbers are essentially in it for life. The criminal justice system—everyone from your local police detective, prosecutors, up to and including the federal government—they are in it for life.

They have lifelong careers—you're in an industry that is stable because there is always going to be crime and crime-fighting.

That's absolutely right. Crime has no season; it's not related to the economy. The other half of my life in the studio is dictated by ad agencies and commercial accounts. They can kind of come and go with the wind.

How healthy is the market, and could you recommend others getting into it?

We're in a funny situation. The notoriety of popular television shows like *CSI* has caused us to put a little disclaimer on our website: "Please be aware of the *CSI* effect." There are things that we can't do. Very simply, there is no magic computer that we have or the CIA has that allows them to get something out of nothing. There is widespread fascination with the whole crime-scene analysis process. I think what makes our organization really unique is that we are all from a professional audio background. We are all musicians on the side and whatnot.

The sonic equation with forensic audio and restoration is upside down from traditional professional audio. In recording, we have basic concept of signal-to-noise ratio. If you've been through analog recording and digital systems, there's always this concept of "we have some noise way down at the bottom." In forensics and restoration, we have noise, and then we have signal at the bottom. So it's noise to signal.

What kind of background will succeed in forensic audio?

I get questions like, "How do I get into forensic audio?" I say that you have to have a real commitment to this sort of thing and you need to be able to back it up. You have to have the time; you have to have the commitment. You obviously need to know how to edit in Pro Tools, but you also need to understand the laws of physics. It is an interdisciplinary-type deal—you have to be able to write. We write reports and document all the time. I have a background in literature, history, and Western art—a liberal arts education. I've never taken a class in criminal justice, but I learn this just by hanging out with the cops and robbers—you get a different kind of mindset.

So you really have to take care of your clients, right?

What is sound and what is the key ingredient? You've got to have air. You start with something really basic like that. There are ways that these things show up in various types of cases that we work on. We're working on something in the background now. A guy shows up dead, and the wife makes a 911 call. They have it on tape, it's an old guy, he had a heart attack and he died. But there is this huge civil estate suit, and they contend that somehow this guy's voice is in the 911 call in the next room dead, lying on the floor.

Some people got a hold of some basic noise-reduction technology and really attacked this audio so they have all this kind of white noise and processing, and you'll start to hear all kinds of things. Now you can hear the guy whispering he's dying. Well, he was already dead—he's on the floor in the next room, the phone is in the living room. So how is his voice at the same level—also considering the time delay that would occur from the next room? We look at it from the laws of physics. And you're not going to learn that from taking a course in Pro Tools.

One of the most fascinating cases of this type was the Kennedy assassination. I visited the scene there in Dallas; I think it was in the Warren Commission. There was an open channel in a police microphone; they actually picked up the gunshots. They re-created the scene, looked at that tape, and analyzed the time delay of the shots and the echoes. They actually re-created that with a number of different microphones, got out some kind of big tape measure, and measured the distances. That's just an example—you've just got to know this stuff.

Do you have to be in a major metropolitan area? What is the most desirable geography?

Courtesy of the Internet, I think you could do this just about anywhere today. Many of my clients are here in the downtown area—the cops are here, the courts are here. However, I have many fine clients from all over the country—I don't even know what they look like, and it doesn't matter to them where I am physically located.

What are some downsides to a career in forensic audio?

You have to be prepared for a lot of overhead. I have my own building in downtown Toledo, and I have to take care of everything. I'm a loyal member of the NFIB, and I take advantage of certain benefits like a credit card machine. This really helps the ball get rolling with initial retainers and things like that. At Team Audio, we name the price, and if you want to do business with us, you've got to lay some money on the table.

So your fees are project-based as opposed to hourly.

We'll assign an estimate to a project, but it is further broken down by an hourly fee in case there is a change. Anytime I start feeling blue or lonely, I just raise my prices.

What is the potential income in a field like this?

Potential can be half a million before all the overhead. A chunk of that is dispersed to overhead and salaries. You really have to have an extensive set of references and your CV. To start out, it's like anything else. You make yourself useful—make the coffee, deliver the tapes, vacuum. Don't come in, sit down, and read a music catalog. What a turnoff. Show me something. The kid who is cleaning the coffee cups and taking the garbage out, he is the one I'm going to hire right there.

Tell me about the restoration side of your business and how it differs from forensics.

If someone has the right skill set and chops, anyone can do this. Restoration work is a lot like cataloguing. I have one famous client I can mention: Mother Theresa. Through some weird networking, I came across a little old priest, Father Angelo. He is now in his 80s and worked with Mother Theresa for years and just recorded everything that she did. The guy comes in the door and he's got a carton of microcassettes. It was really something—you've got a saint. What are we going to do with it?

These tapes could be hugely significant to millions of people.

We have to document it. We take pictures of the tapes, we catalog everything. We hand-inspect each tape, punch the tabs out, we record it, make a log of it. At that point we made CDs of it. Today, we would probably put it on DVDs.

I hope you had business insurance.

We did—I think God was looking over our shoulders. I really couldn't even charge for anything at the end of it. It took us over a year to do it, and we did it on the side. We had hundreds of hours into this, but in fairness to myself, I only asked for a couple thousand dollars for parts—everything else we threw in. I'll get my reward in Heaven maybe.

Who is a typical client for restoration?

We could have hundreds of hours of a civil trial, and it's always converting to some other format. Then how is it disseminated? We often use a secure FTP site where we can park hundreds of hours of tape, an online archive. They don't teach this stuff at the famous recording schools.

What about handling the source material? How do you accommodate all the incoming formats?

I have professional broadcast turntables and a battery of different stylized cartridges. As soon as you get it to play, you've got to make sure you're recording, though. I have ¼-inch reel-to-reels, some that go down to the really, really slow speeds like 1-7/8 inches per second up to 15 or 30 ips.

So presumably you outsource other funny formats that come in. Clients don't need to know this, as long as you deliver what they're looking for.

That's right. There's no point in our keeping 2-inch tape technology around. When I need to, I'll just get on the phone, get a nice digital transfer done, and put it on a hard drive.

Are there larger companies or government agencies doing what you do?

Sure. The government does; they have Quantico in Virginia. They have a huge lab of every kind of forensic everything. The CIA and NASA also do this—there are all kinds of technicians that process hundreds, thousands of hours of audio and video every day. When working with the government as a client, you have to be very careful how you handle process and documentation, and it can take a long time to get paid.

How about your work/life balance?

The family is very important, and I make time for that. I teach at the university at night and really aspire not to work here on the weekends or at night. I did that when I was young.

Is there a lot of stress?

That's the right word—it kind of spikes. The stress level is generally on the low side and it is typically driven by deadlines or when something breaks—how do we fall back and fix it?

What are the predominant obstacles?

The technology. From the recording perspective, everything is in such a complete state of change, future shock. The Internet and computers have changed everything. If I go out and buy my Waves plug-ins, the heavy-hitters will keep calling me.

A Closer Look: Howard Sherman of Howard Sherman PR

Howard Sherman built his own PR practice in New York City many years ago, principally around pro audio clients. He has since garnered coverage for clients such as Walters-Storyk Design Group, Sony Professional Audio, the Audio Engineering Society, and countless others over the last several years. Speaking with Howard, one realizes he is all about relationships and helping clients grow their businesses. Howard's work has found its way time and time again onto the covers of *Mix*, *EQ*, *Broadcast Engineering*, and many other publications.

Photo by Harrison Wise.

Howard Sherman.

Howard, tell me about your first job in professional audio.

My first real job was for a small public relations company. The guy had a two-pronged business—he had a record promotion company and a fledgling PR company. At that point there were a number of trade publications that now exist and a number that don't exist anymore. Obviously, *Billboard* was always a major publication, but there was *Record World*, *Cash Box*, and a number of others. Anyway, he hired me as a writer—I was always into writing—and one of his first clients was a brand-new recording studio called The Record Plant here in New York City on West 44th Street. I had never been inside of a recording studio before, and the place was like a spaceship—it was amazing. It was very cool, and the people who ran it were very cool. I would go to sessions with my camera. I'd see John Lennon, the Who, many others. It was just an amazing thing. I would write these news releases and get them into the trade publications.

We worked for recording artists, and he also handled small record labels. Sometimes he would do public relations and record promotions. For example, when Nilsson's first record came out, we were doing PR for the record and we would also do record promotion. I had nothing to do with record promotion—never went to a radio station.

Did you ever consider a career outside of audio?

I liked writing and I had a facility for writing press releases—I could knock them out pretty quickly. It was never easy to place press releases, but we had good relationships with editors and writers, so we got in. I worked there for a few years. After a while I realized that I was having a great time, but I wasn't making any money. I took a three-week vacation to Europe. When I came back I gave notice—I must have been in my mid-20s. I started with no clients at all, and a friend of mine told me about a new recording studio that was opening up in the Brill Building—the Rosetta Stone of the pop music industry. It was called Sound Mixers. I called the guy who was doing the studios, Harry Hirsch. He asked me, "How long have you been in business?" I said, "Fifteen minutes." I spoke his language; we had immediate rapport. There was simpatico there. He hired me to do PR, and the studio was being designed by a fellow named John Storyk.

Tell me more about this rapport.

I have never worked for a client that I didn't have a rapport with almost immediately. I have interviewed and been interviewed by clients, and if there was a vibe that wasn't right, we shook our hands and went our separate ways. You don't get every client, you don't sell every story, and you don't always hit a homerun. But I get along pretty well with 99 percent of the people that I meet. Every once in a while, for whatever the reason—chemistry, vibe, call it what you will—not everybody is going to like you, not everyone is going to want to work with you; it's a chemical thing, and either it clicks or it doesn't.

When did you feel like you were in your pocket and you could make a living doing this?

At the same time that I started to work for Harry, I was also working as a journalist for a magazine called *Millimeter*—it was a filmmakers' magazine. The editor of *Millimeter* was familiar with my writing through press releases—he asked me if I wanted to do feature stories for him. My first feature story was about commercial directors who almost die during the course of a shoot. One guy is in Africa and an elephant charges him; another guy almost fell out of an airplane. Interestingly enough, a couple of the people that I interviewed for the story asked me to do public relations for them!

So the first month I was in business, I had hoped to be able to pay my rent and feed myself. I was doing that plus. I saw right away that I had a facility to generate business. I didn't want to work in a huge conglomerate, and I liked the idea of being hands-on and having intimate relationships with my clients. Harry Hirsch to this day is one of my closest friends. That was the way I always envisioned my business.

Your ability to network with people and your relationship-building skills were fundamental, right?

Exactly. I knew the drill. With very rare exceptions, most of the clients I began working with when I first started my business stayed with me throughout the years.

Tell me about the community of audio and how you built your business around this community.

It really is a tight community. One of the best examples of that is the Audio Engineering Society. Exactly 10 years ago, I was recommended to the AES as their public relations counsel. I was recommended through another guy named Ham Brosious—he had a company called Audiotechniques. I met him the same time I met Harry Hirsch, and he had sold him his consoles and outboard gear. Years go by, and Ham Brosious was going to be the chairman of the AES committee for their 50th anniversary, which was in 1998. He recommended me to do PR for the AES. Of course I knew many of the members, but I had never been to an AES meeting or convention. I've been working for them ever since, and when I go to an AES convention, it's like a college reunion.

This is a huge industry, but it is a tiny industry—a microcosm of United Nations, of government. It's a number of people who are bound together by a love for audio—and audio has all of these different aspects, whether it is live sound, audio for broadcast, audio for Broadway, recording, mobile recording. All of the variables are insignificant when you think about the main objective: to capture the best possible sound and to reproduce it in as pristine a manner as possible.

I see my role as kind of like the fiber optic. I'm helping to spread information and open dialogue. It goes back to community. I have to tell you that the people I have met throughout my career have been intelligent, charming, honest, and incredibly helpful to their contemporaries and peers. There is an enormous support system in this industry.

There is a common draw we all have.

I think it's music. Even though I can't play an instrument, music has been part of my life since infancy, whether it be large concerts, Broadway shows, or record collections. Music is a commonality in this industry.

How important was it for you to have a journalistic background before you started your own business?

It was critical. I studied journalism at NYU, I learned how to write, and I was hired as a journalist. I was writing for a couple of magazines at the same time that I started my PR company. I always look at my career as a journalist as much as a publicist. I think the difference is that a publicist is a focused journalist—a journalist for hire. I try to be objective in my news releases—I try to play stuff down. One of the reasons I think I have long-term relationships is because most of my clients, with a few exceptions over the years, are more interested in sharing the credit rather than taking all the credit. It is not a one-man band. Early in my career I did represent artists, and I tend to gravitate toward the guys behind the scenes rather than the guys with the huge egos who are up on stage.

What are some of the stumbling blocks you've had over the years?

I started to get fairly busy early on, and I realized that I needed help—I just couldn't cover all the ground. So I hired another writer on a freelance basis because there wasn't really enough room in my home to have a full-time person. Eventually, I found another space about a block away from my home, where I have been for more than 20 years now. One of the biggest stumbling blocks for me in my career was accepting the fact that I needed help and trying to scale up. At one point I had four people with me, which was tremendous overhead, but we had major clients. I was hired by Sony almost 10 years ago.

After 9/11, things changed dramatically. Business went into a major recession. I had to cut my staff. Interestingly enough, this is around the same time that computer technology became very prevalent in the industry—more and more I came to rely on technology to get information out the same way that I had used outside writers or outside people to do similar work in previous years. Technology has changed my business dramatically—I have not had a permanent person in my office for probably the last four or five years.

What has stayed the same and what has changed over the years in terms of how you deal with your clients?

There are fewer venues; there are fewer magazines. I grew up in a world of print, and coverage is now predominantly online. I am not entirely happy with this, but you can see your coverage almost immediately. It is very, very gratifying. The sad thing about it is that it doesn't have the lasting value of a hard news article or a feature story in a glossy magazine.

I never wanted to have a gigantic company—I always wanted to maintain a small and almost anonymous profile. Once in a blue moon, I take the credit for an article I have written. I will be asked by an editor if I want a byline, and once in a while I will take that for whatever reason, but I've never sought them out. I think a publicist's job is to get stories into publications that benefit their clients, and the stories should never look like puff pieces. They should be based on real, solid news and real information. Most of the people I work with are interested in building their businesses, not their celebrity. I would never want to work for a movie star.

Howard, I don't know of any other publicist in the audio field who has gotten more cover stories than you. What are the building blocks of a cover story?

There has to be a real story and something unique about it. Say we are talking about a new recording studio—there has to be something intrinsically interesting. Either the history of where the studio is coming from, the credentials of the owners, the design aesthetics, and the size. There has to be something valid about the story and equally in the visuals—the artwork has to be outstanding. With very few exceptions, you will never get a cover story if the imagery is less than outstanding. The pictures have to be great. Having access to outstanding imagery has been enormously beneficial in building my career—I get calls from editors who know I have access to great artwork. It's like a chicken-and-egg thing.

One of the things that has contributed to any of the success I have had is genuine enthusiasm and an appreciation for what my clients are able to do. I get enthusiastic about getting the word out about what they have been up to.

What are the three most important traits someone needs to have in order to break into doing PR in the audio world?

Number one, you have to be a communicator. You've got to be able to write. You can't be a publicist if you are not a writer—it is impossible. I have seen press releases that editors have sent me that are virtually unreadable. You've got to be a people-oriented person and not take things personally. You have to take them seriously, but when you get shot down if you pitch a story, you can't agonize over it. You can't complain about losing a story opportunity, because you've got to go back to that person. In terms of stress, I tend to be able to leave stuff at the office. I tend to blow off steam, but then it's gone. I can vent and then move on. There is always another opportunity, and you've got to be able to pick yourself up.

10 Careers in Academia

Opportunities in the post-secondary education market are very good, with more and more colleges, universities, and vocational schools creating audio and technology tracks each year. The fundamental reason for this is the fact that students are being exposed to technology much earlier in their academic lives than ever before. In many high schools around the country, for example, teens are exposed to MIDI technology and recording programs, such as Apple's GarageBand. Education programs all around the country are striving

The Emergence of Cross-Disciplinary Audio Education Programs

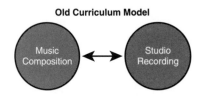

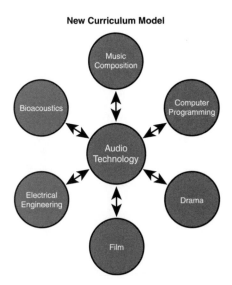

to give their students the best possible chance at success, and quite frankly, many more students are interested in becoming involved with music and recording technology than ever before.

This is further evidenced by the degree to which the post-secondary educational market for music technology has evolved. Just two decades ago, there was only a handful of colleges with reputable recording technology programs, among them Berklee College of Music. Now, audio and recording technology has gone further into the mainstream, with places such as University of Michigan, University of Colorado, New York University, and countless other prominent universities around the country offering full-fledged degrees in audio technology programs.

Market Viability

Needless to say, there is an intense demand for both qualified instructors and curriculums that will attract new students. Facilities are being upgraded and added at an astonishing rate, and both four-year degree and vocational institutions are competing fiercely for tuition dollars—which students are freely willing to spend.

Photo courtesy of Expression Center for New Media.

At audio schools, the control room is very often the classroom.

According to the U.S. Department of Labor, there were 1.6 million teachers in post-secondary institutions in 2004, 78,000 of whom taught art, music, and drama. Another 42,000 taught engineering (all types—not just audio), and 26,000 taught communications. The U.S. government expects employment in the post-secondary market to increase 27 percent or more than other sectors between now and 2016; therefore, employment prospects for skilled candidates are very strong indeed.

A recent education feature in *Mix* magazine identifies 225 dedicated post-secondary audio programs in the U.S.—a number that has grown substantially over the years, since institutions increasingly recognize audio as essential in many disciplines besides the recording arts. When you add places such as online institutions and community college programs, the number of academia programs in post-secondary institutions is likely closer to 500.

Job Profiles and Career Opportunities

Academia has traditionally been an island unto itself over the years. The best institutions not only provide practical knowledge students will be able to apply in the real world, but also teach the theory and rationale behind this knowledge so students can apply their skills in different environments. Typically, the teachers or professors who have a good command of the theory as well as practical application of a given subject matter are able to command a higher salary than those who simply have the practical knowledge.

Whereas a couple of decades ago, a tangential knowledge of audio or recording studios could help a teacher land a job in some capacity, the typical requirements in this day and age are much more rigid. To succeed in academia as an audio professor, you need to be a leader with an entrepreneurial streak, as well as having some demonstrable track record—from the academic world or the private sector. An entrepreneurial element is critical because the industry is undergoing a profound redefinition and is looking for trailblazers with new ideas.

On the whole, if you have a passion for teaching or helping students reach their potential, there has never been a better time to get into an audio-focused track in academia. There are more students and educational institutions than at any other time in history that are looking for talent to drive their audio curricula forward. In fact, some of the best opportunities—especially for leaders and visionaries—may be in those places that *don't* have audio education programs but that have the financial wherewithal to attain them.

Job Descriptions and Compensation

The roles in a four-year post-secondary environment versus a trade or vocational school can be significantly different and will appeal to different personalities. Career tracks in a traditional post-secondary environment are fairly regimented and defined, whereas tracks in vocational or professional schools can be much less defined. Whether you are seeking a position in a post-secondary or a vocational environment, you should not take for granted that there is a specific path cut out for you—in fact, many entry-level jobs are for part-timers or for those not on the tenure track.

In general, people who teach music technology are paid along the same lines as music teachers, who in a college environment have a relatively lower pay scale. The closer a job is to a science such as engineering, the better the chance for higher pay. If you are considering a teaching career at a state university, be aware that salaries and resources can be directly impacted by the health of state economies.

According to the U.S. Department of Labor, the median earnings were $52,000 per year for post-secondary teachers in 2004, with the middle 50 percent earning roughly between $37,000 and $72,000. Entry-level pay is around $25,000, while a fully developed career for the top 10 percent is around $100,000.

The day-to-day duties of a teacher are mostly what you'd imagine—lots of giving lectures, supervising labs, monitoring classroom exercises, and issuing/grading exams and papers. Post-secondary teachers also supervise graduate students' teaching and research. The following sections comprise a summary of some of the prominent positions available.

Career Path in Academia

This illustration represents what a career ladder might look like in academia.

Audio Engineers and Computer Consultants ($25/Hour to $25,000/Year)

Most audio programs require infrastructure staff to keep them running, just as a recording studio relies on techs and engineers to keep it running. To be successful in this role, you need a basic knowledge of engineering or maintenance—enough to keep a session running or to troubleshoot a noisy connection. At most educational facilities, these kinds of positions typically don't pay a lot unless they somehow correlate to a teaching or research role. Because a school's "clients" are most often students, you can expect modest compensation, and talent is relatively easy to come by. Very often students themselves take on these roles, and they can be compensated in credits.

Adjunct Professor ($25/Hour to $2,500 per Class)

Adjunct professors can be part-timers who are moonlighting or industry professionals who aren't able or willing to make a commitment to teaching full-time. Education departments often rely on adjunct professors to build out their staff in areas where they would like to strengthen their offerings, or in areas where the staff is not fully developed. An adjunct position is an excellent "foot in the door" position that can easily lead to full-time employment for the right candidate. Adjunct professors may teach as little as one course per year; they may also be used to fill out summer programs or as substitutes during the regular academic year. An adjunct professor will need to be on his feet, because a different type of course may be required by an institution at any given time. Therefore, this role is an excellent way to test the waters, as well as to home in on which teaching subject is most suitable. Adjunct professors are typically paid by the hour or by the course.

Assistant Professor or Instructor ($27,000 to $38,000)

Assistant professor is the full-time position in which most academic careers start. Most of the assistant professor's time will be spent in the classroom, teaching—the challenge is for the teacher to become completely confident and at home in this environment. After six or seven years in this role, an assistant professor is typically reviewed for tenure, which essentially equals lifetime employment and an almost unequalled degree of job security. It also means more freedom to teach new ideas or controversial subjects.

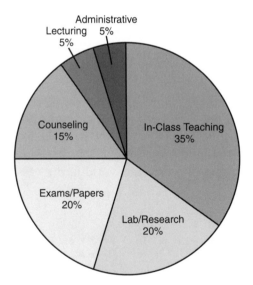

Sample Time Allocation of an
Assistant Professor

Assistant professors are granted tenure after a formal review, when they are recognized as competent and fully effective in their role. Many assistant professors never make tenure, while still others are granted tenure after a period of 15 years or more. Making tenure generally coincides with a promotion to associate professor.

Associate Professor ($45,000 to $75,000)

As your academic rank increases, so does your salary. At major universities, you can expect an increase of around 10 percent. This is considered high in both the academic and the corporate worlds. Achieving the level of associate professor is more than sufficient for many. Colleges and universities expect associate professors to provide strategic input for the curriculum, as well as to have a good pulse on what coursework will drive student enrollment.

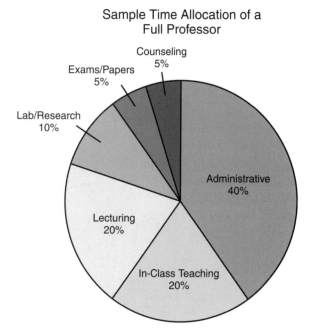

Sample Time Allocation of a Full Professor

Before becoming a full-fledged professor, you may need a broad dossier, along with a host of institutional recommendations and peer approval. This process can be highly political and often painful to undertake. Being reviewed by your peers can put pressure on your professional relationships—and obviously impact your career if your peers don't see the world in the same way you do.

Professor ($75,000 to $125,000+)

Professor is the highest academic rank, and although the role still involves a very significant portion of teaching, a professor can be eligible to become a department chair or gain other board distinctions. These sorts of distinctions mean more responsibility and administrative work, and possibly more classroom hours. Full professors are also expected to do much more research and be able to share and articulate that research in papers and lectures. Professors need to drive the curriculum and be able to anticipate and plan for future trends. A promotion to professor obviously coincides with another salary bump.

Entering and Succeeding in Academia

Entering the traditional four-year post-secondary institution is a completely different ballgame than entering a two-year vocational school. In general, the university-style environment will require a college education and very often a master's or PhD degree. Your academic achievements, including dissertations and research, are very important in the four-year college/university environment—typically, a candidate's accomplishments in the professional world are much less emphasized.

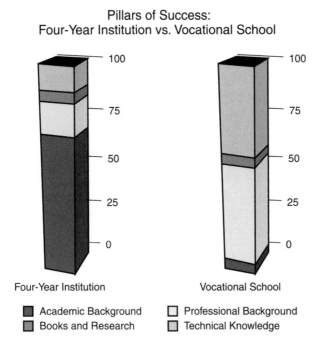

Pillars of Success:
Four-Year Institution vs. Vocational School

Conversely, vocational or post-university colleges that focus solely on the technical aspect have much less stringent academic requirements and a much greater emphasis on professional accomplishments. If you are light on the academics, but you have a few Grammys under your belt as an engineer, for example, you stand a greater chance of entering this kind of educational institution.

Although there is no shortage of jobs available in audio-related education, those who succeed need to have a very strong and entrepreneurial skill set. With the market changing the way that it has been, the new market will be looking for leaders who are capable of reinventing and redefining how the audio market brings value to consumers. Folks who have demonstrated this skill set by starting their own companies or who have successfully pursued their own innovative commercial ideas will have a distinct advantage.

Those considering making a career of teaching at a four-year liberal arts college will definitely want to consider a master's degree and even a PhD—academia is one area where these distinctions and the associated knowledge really pay off, helping a candidate command a much higher salary. Also, as mentioned earlier, teachers at these kinds of institutions are also expected to understand the theory and not just the practical application—good students need to know *why* something works the way it does, and not just *how*—a good teacher will need to have a solid theoretical background to answer these types of questions in the right context. Students will very often pick up the technical aspect later at a vocational or technical college.

It is very important to recognize and understand whether you are on a tenure track at an institution. Many post-secondary colleges and universities offer two- to five-year contracts, which of course can be renewed, but you may find that after your contract is up, you are not eligible for tenure. Tenure-track jobs are much harder to come by and are becoming even more so as time goes by because institutions are seeking greater flexibility in the way they handle curriculum and staff.

Staying current with technology and market developments is very important. Often, teachers will take courses and attend conferences, such as AES or NAMM, to learn about new products and trends. They also need to keep a good rapport with peers and industry professionals on a regular basis. It is also important for teachers in audio to keep up with the latest research from organizations such as AES, as well as keep current with trade magazines and industry literature.

For those considering teaching at one of the many well-known vocational or technical colleges (often one- or two-year types of places), a relatively narrow bandwidth of knowledge is expected. However, since these institutions emphasize application, you had better have a very strong understanding of technology and its real-world applications.

Traits Valued in Academia

Academia is an area that hopefully finds you (versus you finding it). In other words, many successful teachers are naturally inclined to want to help other people and share their knowledge. Teaching is perhaps one of the few verticals covered in this book where personality characteristics can play a determining role in whether pursuit of a career in academia is a good idea. For example, patience and intellectual curiosity are vital to the success of any teacher in any subject.

Patience   Presentation Skills
Curiosity
Communications Skills   Intellectual
Ambition   Entrepreneurial
Open-Mindedness
Discipline

Some of the traits academia values.

Having intellectual curiosity will drive any teacher to stay current on his material. In the case of audio, there are relatively few disciplines that are changing as rapidly; staying ahead of the curve will help anyone in academia stay relevant and ahead of the curriculum. Also, anyone in academia should be open to ideas and be able to value the perspectives of other people—being open-minded helps gain the respect of others, including your peers. It also demonstrates maturity and a willingness to learn.

Good presentation skills and communication skills are very important in effectively conveying your ideas. Being able to organize and present your thoughts on the fly in a classroom setting can come naturally for some, but most people have to work hard to attain good public-speaking skills. Having the dedication to relentlessly improve yourself in areas such as this will help you rise to the top. Because the audio industry is undergoing a period of reinvention, this specific segment of academia definitely values leaders and visionaries who can figure out where the market is going before it gets there.

Benefits and Drawbacks of Working in Academia

The benefits of working in an academic environment are enormous. What could be more valuable than imparting your own knowledge and experience to hundreds of students on a given day? Very few career paths can provide the level of personal gratification that comes from seeing students develop and grow, then pursue careers of their own. Academia provides the opportunity to interact with many minds more brilliant than your own, teachers and students alike. Such interaction has the natural effect of expanding your own mind and better preparing you for the next group of students.

Benefits and Drawbacks of
Working in Academia

Help Others Grow	MA/PhD Often Required*
Tenure = Security	Long Road for Tenure
Good Work-Life Balance	Can Be Political
Nine-Month Work Year	Pay Can Be Relatively Low
Relatively Low Stress	Lots of Administrative Work
Outstanding Benefits	Promotion Can Take Years

*Four-Year Institution

Some of the more material benefits are worth noting, too. For one thing, teachers are usually on a student schedule, which means they get summers and extended holidays off. Take the fact that teachers are on a nine-month schedule into consideration when you compare their salaries to other corporate salaries, which can appear higher at first glance. With extended periods of time off, you can consider getting summer gigs at other institutions, guest lecturing, or consulting, very often with travel allowances.

At most educational facilities, the hours are flexible and enable a balanced work/life arrangement. Although teachers need to be present in class and during office hours to accommodate student visits, most decide for themselves the time and level of preparation a course demands. Classroom time is usually 12 to 16 hours per week, while office hours are usually 3 to 6 hours per week. Teachers are very much in charge of budgeting their own time and getting all their work done outside of the classroom.

Working remotely is becoming more and more common, obviously except for those times when classroom presence is required. Perhaps the biggest benefit is tenure, which provides a level of job security that very few other markets can compete with. Most university environments also provide rich benefits, including health, retirement, and free tuition or the ability to audit classes for free for both employees and dependents. Many educational facilities are based on a rich intellectual and cultural environment, and access to facilities and programs can be complementary for employees.

Is Academia Right for You?

The decision to pursue a career in education—even if it is in audio—must be made very carefully. When you consider the academic commitment that most four-year colleges require for teaching staff, which can equal years of degrees and loads of student loans, you might want to put the money and time into building a world-class home studio. But if you truly want to help other people attain their own career goals and if you have an unquenchable thirst for knowledge, academia could be the perfect environment for you.

It much easier to move in and out of a career at a vocational or professional school, where talent is mostly drawn from diverse parts of the audio industry. This path will require a lesser investment of time and money on the front end, but will also likely result in less compensation overall.

Teaching is something that can be highly rewarding during any part of a career—whether you are just out of high school, seeking to moonlight as an adjunct professor, or even looking to reapply skills you learned earlier in your career.

A Closer Look: Mary Simoni and Working in Academia

Mary Simoni is Department Chair of Music Technology at University of Michigan, which has recently installed a state-of-the-art recording studio designed by Walters-Storyk Design Group. The enrollment in University of Michigan's audio technology program has increased substantially under Simoni's leadership and due to the strengthening of their overall program and the dedication of the staff. Mary is the epitome of a focused, committed professor, ultimately concerned with the welfare of her students. She is also committed to following and understanding developments in audio technology.

Mary Simoni.

How did you get involved in teaching music technology?

I really just stumbled into it, which is a really fortunate thing because I absolutely love what I do. I finished my doctorate in 1983 in music theory, then finished a degree in composition. I thought I was destined for teaching tonal theory in higher ed. Of course, that was the same time that the MIDI specification hit: The DX7 and a number of other things were happening in the commercial marketplace that really intrigued me. From an intellectual perspective, I really wanted to understand what MIDI was about; I really wanted to understand synthesis, mostly for my own music. So I started studying on my own and at the Brooklyn Conservatory. Then I went to Stanford and Mills College. I just kind of zipped around the country to find out what other people were doing in this area and decided that this was the area that I wanted to be in.

At that time, unfortunately, the higher ed hadn't really caught up to the commercial marketplace in terms of kinds of curriculum that were being developed.

Not just at U of M, but throughout the whole country, right?

That's right. Then I found myself at Berklee College in Boston, one of the first places that had embraced what was happening in the commercial music industry. So I went out there and tried to pursue this passion, and for family reasons I needed to move back to Michigan, which is my home. It was interesting: I ran into a faculty member at Michigan whom I consulted with when I was working on my dissertation. He found out that I had returned to Michigan, and he asked me if I would serve as a curriculum consultant to the school. I said, "Sure." This was in the late '80s. So we started developing the first program at Michigan, then it was passed by the faculty and then actually hit the books in a fairly traditional way because it was trying to position itself in a conservatory. It was a first step.

And at some point you must have seen things lining up—that this could ultimately be a program you could spearhead?

Oh, I really wanted it to line up, but I wasn't sure whether the organization dynamics would allow me to take a leadership role in it because at this point I was just serving as a consultant. And then a number of things had happened in terms of the positioning of the program in the school. They needed to have people teach, and there wasn't really a long-term strategy to get classes covered and that sort of thing. Then I started working as an adjunct lecturer. There weren't provisions actually for developing courses, so I started developing courses and teaching.

The person who was my predecessor was engaged in another area that was taking him further and further outside of the school, while I was getting further and further inside the school, developing and delivering the curriculum while I had this other job. Eventually, he decided to leave the university, and then I applied for his job and I got it. Which was great, because then I could do what I really loved starting full-time in 1994—once I was inside, it was easier to effect change.

Did this make you feel more secure in terms of gaining a career for the long haul?

Yes, I felt more secure, but at the same time I was tenure track. So that carries with it that incredible responsibility for research productivity, and I wasn't quite sure how my work would align with the values of the school—because it had to be reviewed by your peers and tallied. So it was interesting—I struck up a lot of alliances with our College of Engineering. Because of that, it lent this kind of academic scholarship to the work that I was doing, which was composition, so I was able to get tenure. Once that happened, that was a liberating moment. By then the field was pretty firmly established in higher ed, and I was getting contacted a lot by other institutions to help them set up their own programs. This was about the year 2000.

We also ended up starting Bachelor of Fine Arts programs and Bachelor of Sciences programs in Music Technology and Sound Engineering. So that liberated the curriculum from what is referred to as the core curriculum, so we could branch out and do things in art and design, and we could do things with video. The programs became tightly integrated across multiple disciplines. That's the amazing thing about Michigan—that it is strong in a number of areas that contribute to the media arts. So when it's possible to draw from other areas through partnerships, it strengthens the curriculum and it strengthens the research.

Obviously, this enhances students' possibilities and their own experiences too, right?

Absolutely. For example, just today I just got a call from a faculty member who is in Screen Arts and Cultures, and he is trying to work with students in Performing Arts Technology to do film scoring for particular classes that they have set up. So it's very typical that we have these cross-campus partnerships. The students might be involved in sound design or sound for games in a gaming class that happens in the College of Engineering. They might also be doing sound design for interactive installations through Art and Design. So they get some really great experience in interdisciplinary collaboration, even at the undergraduate level.

Image courtesy of the University of Michigan.

The main control room in University of Michigan's audio program, recently redesigned by Walters-Storyk Design Group. Pictured here is the new API Legacy console they acquired as part of the upgrade.

Once you had the collaboration aspect in full gear, did it make things easier? It seems like building up that basic capability must have been so much work.

The collaboration really started as early as 1994—people wanted to do it, but it was often difficult to do. In some cases there were disincentives that had to do with the way tuition revenues flowed. It was hard for students of, say, the School of Music, Theater, and Dance to attend classes at, say, Art and Design. We tried to get people to focus on the greater good—what is the long-term benefit? So some of these financial models were altered so they can be more supportive to this type of curriculum.

We are now 21 years after the first Bachelor of Music program was developed, and we're going through internal curriculum review to alter the framework to make sure it's even more flexible. Now we are working toward formalizing those types of relationships.

It seems like the timing of these cross-disciplinary trends at the university couldn't have been better.

That's exactly right. It positioned us for the long term. It's hard to anticipate where the field is going to go, and a lot of what I am challenged with, as far as the people I report to, is like, "We think this is great that this is all happening, but where is it all going and what shape is it going to take in the future?"

I would imagine you need metrics on that stuff, and nobody has those metrics on that stuff!

Absolutely. Nobody has those metrics, so I have to at least identify the influential parameters that are going to shape the way things unfold over time. That is something that I am working on right now because we're trying to leverage a lot of funding for an additional renovation—we'd like to develop the facility to support the curriculum, so there is a lot of work we have to do to justify a substantial investment in the studio and how it will influence what kinds of jobs our students can get. What does it mean for the quality of research, and what other institutions are doing this sort of thing? Part of it is also developing funding models so the facilities are sustainable.

How is higher education set up in terms of the different specialties?

There is an interest in increasing the interdisciplinary grasp across all programs. I think people have organizational challenges in terms of supporting those collaborations. If other programs they want to reach out to aren't developed enough, this can present more of a liability than a benefit. If you want to move into a certain direction and broaden out from a school of music into engineering, you've got to provide all the horses and the substance—this can further tax internal resources. I keep telling people that anybody could have landed in my job and done a good job. At University of Michigan, you have a great support system that can enable you to succeed.

What are some memorable moments when you've felt totally aligned with your profession? When did it feel like you were really in your element?

One of the most notable moments was when we had a guest composer from Earcom, and we had a faculty member do a performance of one of his compositions, which at the time involved control of a computer. We did a master class, and the level of intellectual and artistic engagement by the school was impressive. To have that reinforced by the composer, I felt like, "We're doing something right here. They're getting it and they know how to work through the different issues of technology and art." Another big moment was when we had just finished the audio studio and we had a student meeting and we took everyone over there. We were listening to Pink Floyd's *Dark Side of the Moon* in surround. I'm tripping back two decades and thinking, "Oh my God, this sounds so good." Students started taking pictures of the console and sending them home to their parents. We knew we did something really good.

What is the most important trait you possess as a teacher?

I realize my role as a teacher is to be a facilitator and not necessarily the person who knows everything. Many times a student will know better than you know, and you have to yield to them where appropriate. You have to be comfortable with this. This is something that wasn't necessarily the case years ago. Set your own ego aside—new collaboration has made people able to come in with more knowledge.

How are you able to manage a healthy work/life balance and find time with your family?

Having been in a nine-to-five staff position and worked as a professor, I find life in academia to be much more conducive to family life. Quite often, a faculty member has the freedom to set his or her own work hours. We kept our family together by making sure we scheduled at least one sit-down dinner a week where everyone could be there. It's a small thing, but it communicated the message that family is important. Now that our kids are older, we keep in touch with cell phones, AIM, V-Chat, and even Facebook.

A Closer Look: Rob Lehmann, New England Institute of Art

Rob Lehmann is the Audio Production Department Chair of the New England Institute of Art. He is the chief architect of NEIA's audio program and is very much in tune with market trends. Rob spends a lot of face time with potential employers to gauge the strength of his program and to ensure it is relevant to the needs of the market. One thing that struck me about Rob is that he is acutely aware that he is involved in something greater than himself—he takes great pride in watching his former students excel.

Rob Lehmann.

How did you get into your current role?

I went to Berklee College of Music as an undergrad. A lot of guys back then were into performance, but I was into this new major called production and engineering, which had just started in 1983. I think I started there in 1984. Back then, there weren't too many accredited programs that focused on this—now they are all over the place. When I got out of Berklee, I was mixing nightclubs around the area, I was recording jazz and classical live to two-track stuff, and I had clients in the studio.

After a while, some of the studio clients became curious and asked, "What do all these knobs do? What does all this stuff do?" I would explain it, then I had a couple of clients who said, "You're good at making this accessible. You explain it well." Then I thought, "I'll run a seminar on Saturdays." We were running a lot of rock and pop, so I thought I would run a little morning seminar. I put up some flyers and did a six-week intro to recording class. The studio has since long gone, but I enjoyed teaching. Then, a few months later, I ran into a guy I had gone to Berklee with, and he said, "I'm teaching at this Northeast Broadcasting School." It was one of these emerging unaccredited places. They had radio and television broadcasting but were just adding this audio component. He asked, "Why don't you teach a basic audio class?" So I started teaching that. At the same time there was a community college; I went to them and asked them if they needed a recording studio. They said, "No, but we need a music history teacher. Would you like to do this?"

How did they ask you such a thing?

Well, having a bachelor's degree from a place like Berklee in production and engineering was like gold. Northeast Broadcasting School eventually became accredited around 1994 and got the license from the Board of Education to award degrees. They became a college while I was an adjunct professor. Lo and behold, the chair of the department moved away, so I applied. I got the job as department chair.

What is New England Institute of Art like?

We are a for-profit organization, and there are about 32 Institutes of Art around the country with a model similar to ours. A third of our curriculum is general education—it's traditional English, physics, arithmetic, humanities, social sciences—but then there are these vocationally focused classes like audio theory, practical audio in the studio, live sound, location recording, all that stuff. That is our profile. We saw this need in the post-secondary education market that people want to go to an accredited college, earn a degree, then get a job in their field within six months of graduation, because that is typically when loans mature and banks want their money. For 10 years, consistently, we have placed over 90 percent of our graduates in audio production in that field.

We are vocational but heavy on the academics. The laws of physics aren't going to change as technology evolves, and you've got to start there. You've got to understand the decibel; you have to understand the physiology and the perception of sound and the ear. Many vocational schools don't offer these things.

When did you really feel confident in what you were doing?

I would hate to have been a student in my first class! Like anything, there is a learning curve, and it is a performance in some ways because you are up there. It's you and a class. A studio class may be 10 to 1, and a lecture class may be 25 to 1—they both take a lot of energy. You try to anticipate questions; you master pedagogy, which is the study of the science of teaching. You have different learning styles, and accommodating these different styles comes with experience. The other thing is patience—you have to be ready to say things a hundred times in a hundred different ways, in different angles. Something you've dedicated your life to—you may think it's simple, but it's not. It's easy for you because you've done it every day.

So you have to be empathetic.

You will ask the kids, "Do you get this?" And they will all nod their heads yes. But they don't get it—they don't even understand what you're saying many times, so you have to be patient. Also, an ability to be objective is important—the ability to see yourself the way others see you and know how you are coming across to your students. When you are dealing with 18- to 22-year-olds in general, they are immature. They think they know everything about everything, and they think they are going to graduate and have a successful recording studio and, what the heck, a label on the side! They don't have a realistic idea. You have to be careful not to blast them with reality and remember what it was like to be that age.

How do you determine a relevant curriculum and know what kinds of classes to offer?

When we look at adding a new class or changing our curriculum, we have an advisory committee that we meet with twice per year. These folks will include executives and industry professionals. I might have a couple guys from Bose, a few software companies like Cakewalk, the manager of the Tweeter Center, or the Department of Recreation. You get these guys all in one room and ask them, "What do you want from our graduates?" You get a portrait of what they are looking for in the graduates. Then the faculty sifts through that, and we come up with a course that can reflect what is going on out there in the field. It is very deliberate.

What is the level of stress like in your role? Can you balance everything?

It is cyclical. The fall and spring, there are big demands. Even within that, during advising when the students are signing up for the next semester, the students want to talk about their careers, their grades, and what classes they want to take next semester. Advising week is a killer—you're putting in a lot of hours that week. Finals week is rough. The grades have to be turned around in 48 hours after the last final, so you're grading papers—you're cursing yourself, "Why did I assign all this stuff?" But then it all ends, and you've got three weeks off. So teaching can be intense, but there is lots of downtime. Because of the vocational nature of what we do, in the downtime most of my teachers are doing something involved in their professional careers in audio. On Sunday I am going to be at Boston College recording a bunch of concerts for them.

What is a typical career path at New England Institute of Art?

Usually, in all but one case, any full-time professor that we have hired has been a promotion of an adjunct professor. In our school, full-time teachers teach four classes per semester. Then they have advising and committee work. Sometimes there is marketing work, like an open house. The full-timers are ranked full professor, associate professor, assistant professor, and lecturer, which is what anyone who starts is called. If you want to get into six figures, you're probably going to have to be a dean unless you have other audio gigs. I've got guys that are recording in the Symphony Hall in Boston and things like that, so all the combined income can be pretty good.

How would you characterize the opportunity for teachers in audio?

I would say it is exceptionally strong. Everyone has Bose Surround Sound systems now, so the production value going in has to be a lot higher. There is a need for people who have A-1 backgrounds, who know what they are doing. My program is growing like gangbusters. My program has 541 students in it this fall, and I never would have imagined this when I started out as Chair.

Do you feel like your skills are transferable and that you are secure in your career?

Teaching is a pretty transferable skill. I still teach that music history class at the community college—it's online now, but it's still a lot of fun. The audio skills are transferable, too—they're needed everywhere, right?

Looking back, what is it that you like most about what you do?

The graduates that go on to eclipse me and my career and do great things in audio. That really makes me proud. I've had graduates get hired by Bose, television stations, Diddy, the Tweeter Center…and many graduates have started their own companies. I had one kid who bought the company eight years after he started as an intern. I thought that was just great. Sometimes I run into graduates, and they thank me for their experience here at the program. That has happened several times, and that's magic.

A Closer Look: John Scanlon of Ex'pression College for Digital Arts

John Scanlon is director of sound arts for Ex'pression College for Digital Arts. As founder of the college, one of Scanlon's priorities is to keep the "art" in sound arts. He feels that many students can miss the importance of this, given all the technology they must learn and are expected to understand. Above all, Scanlon hopes students leave Ex'pression with a greater sense of what it takes to create quality content.

How did you get into recording?

I started recording when I was probably 16 with a rinky-dink four-track, then went to Full Sail when I was 18. I moved back to the Bay Area and did a traditional internship for free for about a year. One day the assistant engineer didn't show up, and I got my assistant gig. I started Ex'pression back in January 1999 and have been here ever since.

When I got out of school in 1996, 1997, it was very difficult to get a job in the music industry—it always has been. So I found that the more versatile you are and the more ground you can cover, the better chance you have of making money at it. When we started Ex'pression, the primary focus was music production—now our focus is really multimedia.

Students at work at one of the consoles at Ex'pression College for Digital Arts.

What are your staff positions like?

We have lab instructors up to course directors. The lab instructor's equivalent might be a first engineer at a studio. A course director will run the course here and teaches the lectures. Above and beyond that, we have a studio manager, three maintenance technicians, an associate program director, and myself—the program director—to oversee all courses, all the staff, and all the studios to make sure everything is running on a day-to-day basis.

Is there a common background of folks who work there?

The easiest person to find is someone who knows Pro Tools. The hardest person to find is someone who has had real time in a large recording studio behind a large-format console. Someone who has been on a large desk is a plus for us, and it's a really usable skill to teach the students. Teaching Pro Tools is one thing, but teaching them where that came from and how you can use that in conjunction with the consoles is more complex.

What are some of the valuable skills you are trying to impart now that the market has changed? What basic skills do your instructors need to be able to teach?

The skill set we still value the most here is someone who still looks at this as an art form and not what set of plug-ins they may or may not have. We need people who are creative and know their place in the process. When you are teaching students, you need to be able to communicate the art form to other people—just knowing a certain piece of software or hardware isn't really going to help anyone understand the art behind the production process. That's really what we try to hold onto here—people can get wrapped up in the technical, which is important, but ultimately they need to produce quality content.

What is the profile of a typical professor at Ex'pression?

You've got people here who have chased records all their lives, who want a place to settle in. We have 50 engineers right now who are teachers. About 95 percent of our full-time or part-time instructors are actively working in the business in some way. If a person is here 40 or 50 hours a week, obviously they won't be doing as much production outside, but they always have some record project going on or they are bringing someone into the school to work on a project. One of the requirements of our instructors is that they must be actively involved in some part of the business; otherwise, we will become stagnant. It is a disservice to the students if we are teaching them something that nobody is doing any more.

Someone who wants to come in here and keep their knowledge going by teaching is on the edge—we always have the latest equipment and are updating our curriculum.

How many of your teachers are full-time?

I think we have 15 course directors who are full-time, then about another 6 or 7 people who are full-time, kind of support staff. Then we have another 15 people who are full-time hourly—sometimes they will take off a month or so to work on a project. We have other part-time people who work about 20 hours a week who usually have other gigs.

What kind of background do you require? Are there academic requirements?

We grant a bachelor's degree now, so a teacher needs to have at least a bachelor's degree. This is a requirement by our accrediting body. Then they have to have at least four years of experience in the field and some teaching experience. That can be classroom time or in a studio, teaching interns. We want to know that they have taught some people before. After the interview process, you start as a lab instructor, then as instructor jobs become available, people can move into those roles. We have also had people move from instructor over to our maintenance department as technicians, and part-time instructors have become full-time instructors.

What have you enjoyed about your career track?

The cool thing about being at Ex'pression is that I have been introduced to things I never would have dreamt of trying. We teach a lot of things outside of audio, like video editing, creating a website, marketing yourself. There is something very gratifying about seeing one of your students go on to do the things you've always wanted to do.

11 Bioacoustics and Audiology

Bioacoustics and audiology are among the lesser known audio "tracks"—tangential at best to most of the more typical audio tracks we are familiar with. Indeed, most professionals in this field enter it by way of the medical sciences and biosciences, rather than through more traditional audio routes. However, bioacoustics and audiology can still represent an absorbing and lucrative career for those fascinated by sound and acoustics and how sound characteristics interplay with humans and animals. You can develop an extremely lucrative career in either area, and there are plenty of jobs for those who are willing to invest the time, effort, and money.

Market Viability

There has been great innovation in both fields, and where there is innovation, there is opportunity. In bioacoustics, recent areas of interest include how animals and other creatures vocalize in their environments to mark and seek out their acoustic territory—sometimes referred to as *biophony*. Scientists use underwater acoustic tools to help them understand biomass in large bodies of water. Sonar, a tool used for diverse purposes such as mapping underwater terrain, identifying shipwrecks, and estimating fish populations, determines the physical makeup of objects by comparing them to the acoustic mass of their surroundings.

In an ever-changing world, topics you can study as a bioacoustician are almost limitless—especially when you consider ecological considerations of our day, such as global warming and conservation of natural resources. It should be encouraging to those embarking on a career in this area that more colleges and universities than ever are now offering PhDs in bioacoustics—Cornell University is one such institution that has helped define the field.

As a career field, audiology has enjoyed spectacular growth as scientific breakthroughs continue to improve the conditions of those experiencing hearing loss. Also, audiologists can have a very important role in helping companies measure and reduce the impact of noisy environments that can cause hearing damage.

Bioacoustics and audiology are very much "academic" careers that require an extensive and targeted educational path. Because much of the work is research-based, it is not uncommon for students to work as a professor's apprentice before going out, securing grants, and doing research of their own.

An audiologist at work on an audiometer.

Job Profiles and Career Opportunities

Before actually landing in the working world, bioacousticians and audiologists often spend an enormous amount of money and time on post-secondary education. These career tracks aren't for the fickle—after spending all this time and money, you will have secured a very specific skill that might be difficult to translate to other areas. If you become well-versed in bioacoustics or audiology, there are many opportunities within the U.S. government, medical institutions, colleges and universities, and even zoos.

Photo courtesy of Marc Dantzker, Cornell Lab of Ornithology.

Chris Tremblay, project manager at Cornell Lab of Ornithology, in the cabin of a ship reviewing map locations of where buoys are being deployed.

Bioacousticians can be hired by the U.S. government to do acoustic surveys of U.S. parks, they can be commissioned by companies such as the Smithsonian Institute or National Geographic to capture the songs of whales or birds in remote parts of the world, and they can work for conservation-driven companies to protect marine life in the oceans from the "acoustic smog" of shipping lanes. Essentially, their job is to listen, document, and evaluate. A bioacoustician gets his information from his environment, just as a reporter gets his information from a press conference. He then documents that environment by recording it and taking detailed scientific notes. He also observes changes in conditions and usually makes a conclusion by issuing a report or scientific paper.

Recording nature can be more complicated that it might seem at first. First, there are the elements. Bioacousticians can spend hours waiting for a sound, in less than hospitable environments. (Think bugs, cold, wind, and almost anything else found in nature.) Also, because animals and other creatures have physiological differences from humans, the devices used to capture their sounds can be significantly different than what you might be used to. For example, sounds in the water are captured using a hydrophone, super high frequencies are captured using an ultrasound detector, and substrate-borne vibrational signals are captured using a laser vibrometer. These sounds are then imported to more traditional DAW environments so the audio signals can be controlled and manipulated as required.

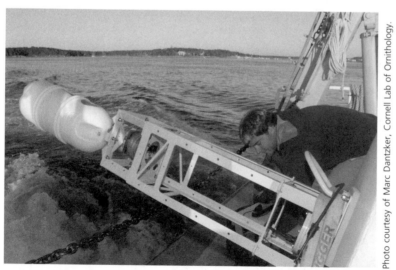

Photo courtesy of Marc Dantzker, Cornell Lab of Ornithology.

Chris Tremblay attaches a recording/transmitter unit to a buoy aboard a research vessel.

Audiologists can work in the private sector with industrial consulting firms who go on location to perform hearing tests on workers, as well as testing their work environments. (You have probably seen the trailers they bring on site to perform these tests.) The Occupational Safety and Health Administration (OSHA) requires companies to meet certain standards so workers aren't exposed to unsafe sound-pressure levels over a specified period of time. Obviously, since a government agency has set minimum standards, there is a market for firms who help companies achieve this. This market can be quite lucrative for both smaller and larger firms (who also often offer contracting services for soundproofing and treatment).

Job Descriptions and Compensation

Although very attractive compensation often accompanies careers in bioacoustics or audiology, most people in this area have a genuine passion for what they do. The money generally comes after they have paid their dues, both in their studies and as apprentices.

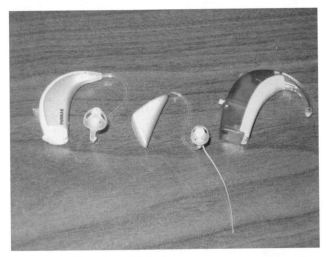

A variety of hearing aid devices.

Compensation varies greatly for bioacousticians and audiologists and very often has to do with geography and the type of company or institution. For example, there tend to be fewer audiologists in the northern United States; therefore, compensation can be higher in these regions. And audiologists who take jobs in VA hospitals tend to receive excellent benefits but are often compensated less. Conversely, audiologists who work in private practices tend to be compensated more but receive fewer benefits. Work for bioacousticians can be almost anywhere—on staff at a museum, at any number of universities around the country, and of course on location anywhere in the world.

Staff Audiologist ($40,000 to $80,000+)

Staff audiologists test patients for hearing. Patients can be almost any profile, but in a retirement community, for example, older patients will be more common. Staff audiologists perform all necessary clinical tests, document the results, use the equipment, and fit hearing aids. Much like doctors, their time is scheduled in advance with patients, usually in half-hour to hour-long intervals. Much of their time might be spent in meetings held by hospital or practice administrators. As much as 30 percent or more of a staff audiologist's pay may come from production-based incentives.

A custom ear mold utilized by audiologists.

An industrial audiologist does much the same thing as a medical audiologist, but he also measures "hotspots" in manufacturing environments using acoustic instruments, such as sound-pressure level meters and dosimeters. After mapping out these hotspots, the audiologist may work alongside an acoustic specialist to reduce employees' exposure to decibel (dB) levels over time.

Senior Audiologist or Head Audiologist ($80,000 to $100,000+)
Senior or head audiologists often handle the role of clinical and apprentice supervisor. Their job is to guide young audiologists and help them make the right choices. They are also responsible for handling operational matters, such as writing proposals for new equipment and setting the overall direction for the department. Senior audiologists also ensure the practice has adequate resources and look after the business side of things.

Bioacoustician ($20,000 to $100,000+)
Bioacousticians study both the physiological and psychological aspects of how living organisms produce and receive sounds, and they study how these sounds interact with their environment. A typical day for a bioacoustician might be recording and documenting the sounds of a bat or a dolphin, ultimately to share this information with a sound library so others can research or share the experience. Bioacousticians can have highly successful commercial careers because museums, films, zoos, and many other products and environments require high-quality nature recordings.

Photo courtesy of Marc Dantzker, Cornell Lab of Ornithology.

Chris Tremblay and Dr. Christopher Clark of Cornell Lab of Ornithology aboard a research vessel, discussing deployment of a buoy transmitter.

Bioacousticians' career tracks most often sprout from academic environments; therefore, it is not unusual to begin a career as a research fellow in a university environment. After the required coursework, which can cover both biology and physics, is complete, students may seek out research grants or become staff members at any number of organizations. Work as a bioacoustician is limited only by the imagination, but typical employers include research firms; government agencies, such as NOAA; colleges and universities; conservation-oriented organizations; and independent consultants.

Entering and Succeeding in Bioacoustics/Audiology

One thing bioacoustics and audiology have in common is the need to listen. For bioacousticians, listening imparts a context and a greater respect for the environment in which they are working. For acousticians, listening gives them empathy for patients who seek to improve their hearing.

Unlike many other audio careers, bioacoustics and audiology are very closely associated with academia, and therefore they require a great deal of post-secondary education, up to and including master's and doctorate degrees. This is the most traditional path to careers in these fields, and although it can be incredibly time-consuming and expensive, it can also be very rewarding.

The best way to learn about jobs and careers in this area is to begin developing your own network in this field. Seek out the advice of professionals who are already successful and begin to associate yourself with accomplished professors who are doing research that is closely aligned

Photo courtesy of Marc Dantzker, Cornell Lab of Ornithology.

Bioacousticians aboard a research vessel deploy a buoy transmitter to track underwater marine life.

with your interests. Another good source of information is academic journals, which capture and disseminate a great deal of information on this kind of research.

Jobs are typically offered after a period of apprenticeship in which the employer has time to evaluate and work alongside a potential employee—this isn't the kind of field where you are likely to find job postings on a web bulletin board. As stated earlier, you should not embark on a career path such as this for strictly monetary reasons. If you have a love for the science behind acoustics as well as an interest in biology, you may find this a rewarding career path.

After you have become established in a field such as this, you can expand your opportunities into more entrepreneurial avenues. Acousticians can open their own practices or work for hearing-aid companies as consultants/salespeople. Bioacousticians can sell their sound libraries to museums or research institutions or have them licensed to film, television, or other media. Opportunities are limited only by your imagination and ingenuity.

Traits Valued in Bioacoustics/Audiology

If you plan on pursuing the bioacoustics or audiology route, you should have a naturally strong aptitude for math and science. Both fields deal with acoustics and the physics of sound, each of which are expressed through mathematics. Although each field can be immensely gratifying and creative, the logical or left-brain oriented individual may become more successful, because each of these fields requires basic problem-solving skills.

Bioacoustics

There is no typical working environment for a bioacoustician. Because most animals and other creatures live out in the wild, bioacousticians find themselves in the wild as well. Therefore, someone who is serious about this career field should be ready to deal with the elements and have a relatively strong constitution. Because travel is an absolutely critical part of the job, you should be enthusiastic about getting on trains, boats, or planes or even donning a pair of snow-shoes if necessary. Recording in the wild can be a very lonely business, so you should be someone who truly loves the outdoors and can spend a lot of time with nobody else around. Another important trait bioacousticians should have is patience—recording creatures in the wild can often mean waiting hours for a single sound.

Audiology

One of the most important traits for an audiologist is empathy. By and large, an audiologist's most important concern is his patients—other human beings. Audiologists not only deal with the fascinating science of sound on a day-to day-basis, they also deal with many people who are not always in an ideal state of health. Common patients for audiologists can be the elderly, who face varying degrees of hearing loss. Audiologists also deal with folks such as cancer patients, who have experienced loss of hearing due to intense chemotherapy drugs.

Inquisitiveness   Love of Science
          Patience
Academic Interest Communication
    Empathy
      Dedication   Problem Solving
          Independent Thinker

Some traits valued in the fields of audiology/bioacoustics.

As an audiologist, you must have an innate desire to help people, as well as the ability to communicate with people clearly. Audiologists routinely need to communicate to patients that they have irreversible hearing loss. Part of an audiologist's job is to provide counseling to help patients come to terms with this. They also need to be problem-solvers. As in many roles in medical science, an audiologist's role involves diagnosing a wide array of possible medical conditions.

Benefits and Drawbacks of Working in Bioacoustics/Audiology

Although they are related fields, the sciences of bioacoustics and audiology provide very different benefits—just as they will appeal to different personality types. Let's look at bioacoustics first.

Bioacoustics

Bioacoustics provides a vivid window into the natural world from the unique perspective of audio. For those who love the outdoors and want to feel closer to nature, few career paths can offer the serenity and intrinsic satisfaction of capturing sounds in the wild. Most bioacousticians consider this the greatest benefit, whether this involves capturing a whale's mating calls or a hawk's call across the mountaintops. Whereas most people likely spend their day-to-day working lives in structures made of brick and mortar, a bioacoustician's work environment is the great outdoors. Many people believe this can have a positive effect on both physical and mental health.

Other very positive aspects of bioacoustics include the prospect of traveling to remote and interesting places around the world. Capturing the sounds of rare species can translate to more money and greater recognition in scientific journals. Published research and sound recordings of elusive creatures can lead to lucrative grants and greater financial security. For the more entrepreneurial-minded, commercial opportunities are nearly endless if you think about the possibilities of producing and marketing sound libraries or commercial recordings.

With bioacoustics, the downsides are easy to identify, too. As mentioned earlier, it can be a very lonely business. Being a bioacoustician can mean being away from your family for weeks at a time. It can mean 16-hour days in less than hospitable environments that are home to things such as malaria, poisonous snakes, and other naturally hazardous conditions. Also, the path forward in bioacoustics can be less certain than in other fields—it really requires more confidence, determination, and self-sufficiency than most other audio fields.

Audiology

Just as bioacoustics is rewarding for those who love nature and the wild, audiology is rewarding for those who love the science of sound and being around people. Whether you work in a private practice or at a VA hospital, you will generally have fantastic benefits and good to above-average compensation. Perhaps the greatest benefit in audiology is the knowledge that you are helping others gain increased auditory perception through devices such as hearing aids and, less commonly, through medical procedures. Audiologists, like most doctors, tend to keep office hours, so this career path is highly conducive to those with families or other outside interests.

As far as compensation is concerned, the ceiling can be extraordinarily high in audiology, especially for seasoned professionals with private practices. A good audiology practice in the right location can draw many patients, and as technology advances and hearing solutions become more complex, good practices can command substantial amounts of money.

Benefits and Drawbacks of
Working in Bioacoustics/Audiology

+	−
Close Proximity to Nature#	Limited Transferability of Skills
Improve Patient Hearing*	Arduous Education Track
Relatively High Pay*	Challenging Recording Environments#
Great Health Benefits	Difficult Work/Life Balance#
Secure Career Path*	On-Call All Day*
Interesting Research and Travel#	Volatile Career Path#

*Audiologist
#Bioacoustician

Some possible drawbacks in this career field include the fact that your skills are fairly pigeon-holed into this particular area of medical science. That said, as indicated earlier, there are varying options within this field, such as industrial audiology, hearing-aid consulting, and other areas that can present interesting options for growth. Another possible drawback alluded to earlier is the fact that audiologists tend to see people who are more challenged than others. They deal with the elderly, the mentally ill, children with ADD, people with severe disabilities, and accident victims. This aspect can be very gratifying for those who like to help people in need.

Is Bioacoustics/Audiology Right for You?

Bioacoustics and audiology are for people who are naturally inquisitive and interested in the science of sound. These are very tangential fields that don't deal with music or other traditional areas of audio. However, they very much deal with acoustics and listening.

The best way to learn whether this might be a fit for you is to speak to someone working in this field. Bioacoustics and audiology are two areas in which there is much less published career information or guidance available, so personal interviews with those in the field would be the most advantageous route toward making an informed decision. However, the most fundamental aspects to have in place would be a love of nature (for bioacoustics) and a love of being around people (for audiology). Although both careers deal with sound, they are built on these foundations.

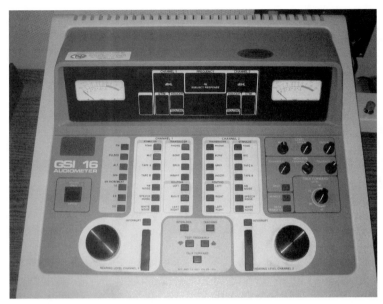

Grason-Stadler audiometer, used in audiology.

Before you embark on a career in bioacoustics or audiology, consider the intense academic commitment. Opportunities in these fields require much more work and investment than careers in other areas, and it might take years before you are able to actually begin working in the field.

A Closer Look: Christopher Clark and Bioacoustics

Christopher Clark is I.P. Johnson Director, Bioacoustics Research Program, Cornell Laboratory of Ornithology and Senior Scientist, Department of Neurobiology and Behavior at Cornell University. Cornell has one of the world's most highly regarded programs in bioacoustics and has completed innovative research on creatures of land, sea, and air, particularly birds and whales. Of all the people I spoke with, Chris's passion came through the most clearly—he seems wildly enamored of his profession, and it was clear in our interview that one of the key reasons he succeeded was because he wasn't afraid to take risks. This trait, combined with his vast intelligence, confidence, and love of bioacoustics, was a key aspect in propelling his career forward.

Was it science or audio that attracted you initially?

I grew up in a very musical family, and my three uncles, when they were young boys, all went to the Cathedral of St. John the Divine choir school, and I followed in their footsteps. So when I was between 9 and 13 years old, I lived in New York and was in the cathedral choir school. I sang twice a day in that cathedral for four years. I had a lot of voice training as a boy soprano. I sang evensong, morning song, and all that kind of stuff. Religion passed me by at an early age, but I loved music. The resonance in that cathedral is incredible—it is not surprising that I was attracted to whales, and particularly the low-frequency whales. I attribute that ambiance of my

Photo by Susan Spear, courtesy of Cornell Lab of Ornithology.

Christopher Clark.

early life of being around music and singing to the success of what I'm doing now. In high school, I was in the chorus, dance, jazz band—everything I could get my hands on that involved music.

When does the interest in sciences and animals come into play?

That was another part of my upbringing. I was raised on Cape Cod in the town of Wellfleet, and I was basically running wild all over the outer Cape as a kid. My grandmother always had bird books around and bird feeders—those kinds of things were embedded into my upbringing.

In high school, I always had a dual left/right hemisphere kind of convergence. I loved AP writing and poetry, but then I was very taken with mathematics and science. I come from a family that has a lot of engineering folks in it—a few doctors here and there, but more in the engineering/mathematics kind of thing. When I left high school, I didn't know what I was going to be doing. I knew I wanted to go to college, because everybody goes to college. The next thing I knew, I was at Stonybrook University on Long Island as a freshman out of Massachusetts, like a fish out of water, but I started out in the school of engineering.

Eventually, I became very interested in auditory prosthetics, which were pretty primitive back then—how are you going to restore someone's hearing, and things like that.

Audiology-related things?

Yes. In those days, they hadn't done any implants, but I was really fascinated by the base of the membrane, auditory processes, neurophysiology, and the mechanics. I was on my way to biomedical school at University of Cincinnati, and through a professor I had taken a class with, I met a friend of his who was about to go off to South America on a National Geographic expedition. By late summer, he had asked me if I would take a leave of absence from biomedical school for three months to come to South America on this expedition.

For some odd reason, he thought that because I had an engineering degree and a biology degree, I knew how to fix radios and stuff like that. It was like, "No, I don't think so!" I was willing to try, and it wasn't alien to me because I'm always willing to rip things apart and put them back together. Anyway, suddenly I found myself living in a tent on a beach in South America, on a bay that was a lot like Cape Cod bay, except we were living in tents and eating out under the stars every night. I'm looking around going, "Holy shit! This is what this guy does for a living?" His whole family was there, he had all this great camera equipment, and we were listening to the ocean. I said to myself, "Someone is paying this guy to do this? This is not so bad!"

Then I went back, and I decided that after I left medical school, I was going to go into graduate school in electrical engineering because there were things that I wanted to learn about gizmos. What could I build that would apply to this fascinating world of underwater acoustics? That was the turning point—I basically said, "Geez, this is a totally different avenue than I ever thought of!"

What were some of the things you were exposed to on that trip to South America?

The whales. The person on the expedition was named Roger Payne, who went with his wife, Katie. He and Katie were to me the people who converted the raw, crude early discoveries and understandings of whales and song to what we know now. They are both fabulous musicians themselves. As soon as Roger and Katie heard humpback-whale recordings that some guy in Bermuda had made, they could recognize the stanzas and could hear the repeated phrases.

They managed to find a machine with which they could render 2-1/2 seconds of a song into a visual image. Of course, a song lasts like 15 or 20 minutes. They tediously made a whole series of these pieces of paper that are about 11 inches long by 5 inches wide. They scotch-taped them all together and put them on the side of their barn, and they created a visual matrix where they could see the patterns—the themes, the phrases, and the notes. They translated what they were hearing into the visual rendition. They did this in the '70s, a couple years after they put out a record of sounds of the humpback whales.

When I was down there on that expedition, Roger literally put a Sony tape recording on my lap and a bunch of 7-inch reels, and said, "Here. Why don't you record the whales?" We had some old NADY hydrophones that I had resurrected and modified. At very low tide, I would go out and mount these things in the bottom of the bay, which had about a 30-foot tide. We would wade out there, up to our waists in very low tide, and we would stake these things in the bottom, then run the cable all the way back up the cliff so we could listen to them.

You'd stand on the cliff, and the whales would come in. The environment was absolutely gorgeous, like the Serengeti of the marine habitat. You'd look out and you could see the whales, and then you could hear them.

How did you feel when you first heard the whales?

I think the very first time I heard the whales was in air. I arrived in Buenos Aires, and after a long ordeal of getting cables and all my equipment through customs, I flew down to Tierra Del Fuego, then drove for hours over these dirt roads. Suddenly, I came to the cliff. They took down this gate—there was this whole thing I went through to get there. I got there in time for the sun going down.

Everyone was sitting outside; we have our bottle of wine, we have a side of a roast we are cooking out on the grill. The stars are out, and suddenly you just hear the whales breathing. They are 100 meters away from you, and you just hear this pronounced, deep roar from their breath because they are cavorting—this is their playtime. So it was like, "What was that?! It just sounded like a monster!" Then everyone is saying, "The whales are here!" and you hear them slapping the water. These are the sounds you go to sleep to. Then the next day you get up, and there is this spectacular scene of rugged cliffs and sage brush, and the wind is blowing. We didn't have any hydrophones in the water at that point, so Roger threw this equipment in my lap and said, "Let's start listening."

Eventually, we got the hydrophones in place and had a cable coming up the cliff so we could stand there 150 to 200 feet above the water. You could look out, and there below you were all these giant animals moving about the surface. Then you listen, and you hear a call. It's a contact call, which is very simple—these sounds travel spectacularly well through the ocean. Then you hear these screams from a big orgy that's going on a couple miles away. Your mind starts linking what you are seeing to what you are hearing, and you become more curious. Which whale made the sound, and what are they doing?

So this experience was really moving for you and really set the course for your career?

Absolutely. Suddenly, you find yourself just rushing down a mountain—you can't wait to go faster, find out more, then try it out again. I did that for about three years, and then I came back and got the master's in engineering.

At what point did you feel your career was secure financially?

That part never crossed my mind. That is part of my personality—heck, life is life. I am not in life to make money. I come from a broken family—my father left when I was four and a half, and I was sent off to choir school. Then after that, all of us—my two sisters and I—were pretty much all on our own. So I learned how to take care of myself at a very early age. In my family if I asked for money, it was so emotionally loaded that I just decided to take care of myself. I was never worried about the money part, and people would say later that I took so many risks. I would say, "I don't think that's really risky." If you know what you are doing, you can climb a cliff with bare hands. I can go out on ice that is only two inches thick, and if I know what I am doing, I'm fine.

So you've always had this confidence and self-assurance. You didn't second-guess yourself, and you knew you would figure things out.

Pretty much. The first time I ever ran across somebody challenging my career was when I was in a post-doc position at a place called the Rockefeller University in New York, a very prestigious arena to be in. My mentor and advisor essentially challenged me, asking me why on Earth I was going to go to the Arctic and work on a whale that lives in the ice. I was told, "This is not good for your career." The person was mad at me—and I couldn't understand why someone was mad at me for a decision I was making about myself. It was really because I was not doing what he wanted me to do. And the notion of a career was so foreign to me. When I got down and was exposed to this world, which to me was like heaven, I wrote songs, I wrote poetry, I could build preamplifiers and listen to whales all at the same time. I thought, "What else do I want?" My PhD advisor did eventually walk in one day and say, "Chris, your chapters are almost all done, you've got your defense statement all lined up, so what are you going to do next?" I thought, "Huh?" I was 30 years old and was always able to make ends meet. I wasn't worried about it.

What was entailed in all the coursework you were undertaking?

I was fascinated by the mechanism and the science of how animals produce sound and the ways they have evolved to produce sound. For example, I worked with someone who worked with crickets, and you learn there is a whole group of organisms that rely on rhythm as opposed to melodic overtones that you hear in a humpback whale. Animals will use every single thing they can: They'll rub bones, they will rub teeth together, they will drum on a bladder. It is just crazy out there—everyone is making sound.

The notion that evolved in my thinking is that the whole world is singing. If you can imagine standing back and watching the earth rotate, and there is that cusp between night and day, just imagine following the transition from dawn. When the world goes from light to dark and dark to light, all along that border, from the highest latitudes to the lowest latitudes, the world is singing. It is singing underwater, it is singing in trees, it is singing in the ground, it is singing in the highest canopies and even in the sky. The more exposed I get to this, the more I realize that this is the resonance of the earth.

What did you do after your PhD?

I got in touch with this person who was very well known in animal communications at Rockefeller University. He asked me if I would give a seminar, and I did. The seminar was on playbacks, a subject where I had done some of the very first successful work. I would play the sound of the whale's own voice back to them, and then watch how they would react. The notion was to see whether I could emulate a situation that they would then interpret as being real. Then I could get an idea of, "What does this sound mean to you?"

I had become pretty good at imitating their various sounds, and one of the first times I did one of these experiments, I was out with Janie, who is now my wife. We were out in this little Zodiac floating offshore; all we had were a couple of paddles. I lowered one of these el-cheapo, synchronized-swimming pretty blue loudspeakers that I bought. I lowered it over the side of the boat, took the microphone up to my mouth, and I just imitated their calls. Out of nowhere, this whale showed up and came right back to the boat! The whale is big enough to lift us up on its back. I'm going, "Holy shit, it worked, it worked!" The whale, she then went away. I did it again and she came back—she then wouldn't leave us alone.

That was not scary, but inspiringly hair-raising. I couldn't believe it. My professor said, "Now I think you have to be a little more scientific about it, because you can't just go around calling animals!" [laughs].

From the PhD, I went up to work in a field site along the Hudson River, which was part of the Rockefeller. It was where people worked on all kinds of animals. Some people were working on monkeys or chimpanzees, some people were working on birds, and I was working on chickens, which was very distressing because chickens weren't quite what I had in mind.

Not as inspiring as whales, anyway.

Anyway, I did a lot of work on birds that learn their songs, and looking at the ontogeny of vocal learning in these sparrows. They have to hear their parents, then they babble, then they practice like crazy, and suddenly their song crystallizes. I did a lot of that for a while.

There are a whole series of instances in your life that you can say are sort of serendipitous, but then they aren't so serendipitous because they keep happening! I was just finishing my transition from PhD to post-doc, and a friend of a friend called me up and said, "We understand that you have some equipment and that you know how to record whales. Would you like to come up to Alaska, because we have a problem with these whales that are being hunted by Eskimos," et cetera, et cetera.

At that point, someone says, "I'll buy you a ticket to the northernmost point in Alaska, and you can go out on the ice in a tent." I thought, "Yahoo! That's great." So the next thing I knew, I was out on the ice recording a whale that is basically a close cousin of the whale I was studying in South America. It's called a *bowhead whale* because its head is bowed very strongly for breaking ice. I was walking around in –20 degrees, and this was an amazing experience—you are out there on the ice, total sensory deprivation, you're bundled up to stay warm, you can't smell or feel anything. You put a hydrophone in the water, and it's an absolute jungle. It was an absolutely crazy place underneath the ice.

The seals are out of their mind—it sounds like a *Martian Chronicles* thing. You're going, "What the hell is that?" Then the whales are coming by, and they can scream, sing, and click with three voices simultaneously. You are listening to this stuff, thinking, "This is absolutely phenomenal." Topside you are barely able to see, and then in the water, that's where life is happening. That is another thing I learned early on from Roger and Katie: Roger was the person who proposed 37 years ago that prior to ocean shipping—just a short 100 years or so ago—blue and fin whales could once have communicated with each other across an ocean basin. Their voices are so low and so loud that the sound travels through the ocean like it's on a fiber-optic network.

In the early '90s, I was invited by the Navy to participate in using the anti-submarine warfare listening system in the Pacific and the Atlantic Oceans to monitor whales. So suddenly I was allowed to walk into a universe of sound in which I had access to the best underwater telescopes humans had ever invented, and I could actually listen throughout an ocean basin wherever I wanted to listen. That is another experience where the hair literally went up on the back of my neck as I realized Roger was right. I was actually listening to a whale that was 1,600 miles away. This is an animal that was singing off of the Grand Banks of Newfoundland. I was off of Puerto Rico, listening to it. When I listened to that stuff, it brought me right back to the cathedral. That voice was magnificently coupled into the resonances of the ocean.

Photo courtesy of Marc Dantzker, Cornell Lab of Ornithology.

Chris Tremblay works on a buoy aboard a research vessel off the coast of Maine.

I just came back two weeks ago from a place where I've got real-time access to where the whales are. I am acoustically tracking singing whales and watching them. I follow them for days and days and days. I watch them as they slalom through the ocean from one geographic feature to the other. I am tracking them acoustically, and when you put the track together, they are using their voices like a lighthouse. They are illuminating the large structures in the ocean because how else can an animal come around the corner of the Grand Banks and head on a line directly for the New England Seamounts, 300 or 400 miles away, on a straight course? It gets to the Seamounts, comes around, then changes direction and heads directly for Bermuda. We can now detect the echoes of their voices off the Seamounts, the mid-Atlantic ridge, the continental shelf. They are now illuminating the ocean on that scale.

Then you say, "I thought I knew a little bit." But what you don't know is almost incomprehensible to imagine.

It changed the whole context of everything, right?

Exactly. In our world, acoustic communication is instantaneous—in fact, I get irritated if I make a call or send an email and I don't hear something back pretty quickly. Now imagine that I am a whale on Bermuda and having a conversation with you off of Newfoundland. That's a thousand miles. For every 50 miles, it takes a minute for the sound to travel. It takes 20 minutes for the first note of your song to reach me from Newfoundland. Now I've got to think about it—my heart beats four times per minute, and a single note in my song takes 20 seconds to sing. The notes in my song are separated anywhere from 70 to 120 seconds. So everything—the time, the cadence—is just incredibly slow compared to what you and I are used to working with, and the space in which we work is immense. Trying to project my mind into that kind of world has been an incredible challenge. From that, you move into the world of an echo locator, which works at 40 kilohertz, and everything is happening incredibly fast. You realize this whole space of acoustics that is occupied by all these different things—whether it's a 4mm fly versus a 90-ton blue whale. Everybody is singing, and they've all figured out their own little niche.

One of things I say when I teach is to try to put yourself in the universe of sound. Recognize that the universe that we think of as the human sound universe is really just a constellation in the universe. The scale at which whales are working is so big that it is almost beyond comprehension.

What advice would you give someone who wanted to get in this field?

First of all, I'm not interested in clichés for professionalism. The exciting part of life for me is pushing the limits. Let's just pretend that we're raw observers with the raw material in front of us. What do you hear and what is your experience? That's where the revelations come.

I have students who have been in engineering, in natural resources and conservation. Engineering students typically go off and have jobs in industry—whether it's AOL, Qualcomm, or starting their own companies. Many times they are in the business of writing software or building gizmos. There is a former student who worked in Congress for a year because she wanted to be involved in that nexus between science, policy, and regulations. She is now working in a national sanctuary using her experience with sound and her experience with the critical role of sound in whales to implement a phenomenal new policy that will force the shipping industry to reduce the acoustic smog that they are injecting into the ocean habitat. She is a scientific activist. I have other students in academics who have started not-for-profits, and others who become faculty members at small colleges or universities.

In the more recent generations, there seems to have been more concern and awareness for a career or a flow of money into your life so you can have things and make plans. One of my roles is to find a mold that fits to the student rather than fitting a student to a mold. Some kids can do anything with numbers, and math is easy, yet then they can't communicate at all. One's a philosopher but can never finish a sentence. Another can stand up and mesmerize an audience, but when you ask him how he tests for this statistically, his eyes cross, and then there's a puddle on the floor. You just say, "Let's go to your strengths," rather than force them to face a broken mirror all the time.

Coming to an institution is a phenomenal opportunity—all you are being asked to do is think for four or six years, whatever it is. That is a luxury that will never come again.

What are some raw skill sets or personality traits that would help someone be successful in this field?

The skill set that I was able to acquire and had a predisposition for was numbers, equations—the mathematics and the physics side of things. That kind of discipline and facility of solving problems is the reason I've been able to gather this phenomenal group of people who are computer scientists, applied mathematicians, and engineers. You get this collection of people where there is that synergy—they resonate—and then it is like a laser: Everyone gets into a coherence where you do things that none of us could ever do alone.

Someone who has a really good background in the hard sciences can learn evolutionary biology and behavioral ecology in their 30s. But I've found that you can't take someone who has had these disciplines and then teach them math in their 30s. There is a window when you are a teenager and in your young 20s when a lot of that stuff clicks, and then you can't even explain how you do it anymore.

It is because I've had those assets that I have been able to do things almost unconsciously that might otherwise appear risky, in saying, "We can build something like that," or "We can put something at 1,000 meters in the ocean and have it do the following things," or "We can write software for that." That opens up doors that otherwise would have never been available to you.

Get as broad an education as you possibly can. If you can afford it, take five years. Take advantage of the literary capabilities and expertise in your college years. Learning how to communicate is very important—this opens so many opportunities. Above all, don't be afraid. If you have an intuition, trust it. Because if you are afraid of your intuition, than someone else is going to lead you by the nose.

Where is bioacoustics going as a career field?

I go back to that image I was trying to paint before. We are now Major Tom floating in space, halfway between the moon and the earth, and we're just looking at the earth rotating now and we're listening to it—that constant radiance of music of the earth. Notice how everybody loves music. If there's one thing I can do when I go into a foreign country—even I can't speak the language—if I can pick up a guitar and sing, it creates a bond. I see an opportunity for more and more people to hear the voices of the earth, and there are opportunities for more and more people to participate. When we write software, we are trying to give people opportunities to listen to and understand that the world is alive. The world is musically alive, and it is not just the grinding of trucks and the roaring of planes. Music is everywhere—whether it is an insect or a fish, a bird or a whale. That, to me, is part of the majesty of life and the opportunities to explore that now are better than they ever have been in the history of the world.

A Closer Look: Jocelyn Fillian and Audiology

Jocelyn Fillian is a clinical audiologist. In her role, she uncovers patient hearing problems and helps to resolve them. To succeed in her role, she spent several years studying human hearing and sound characteristics, both in college and as an apprentice. On speaking with Jocelyn, her deeply rooted empathy for patients was immediately apparent. I also picked up on her love of the science of sound and hearing.

Jocelyn Fillian.

What led you down this road, and how did you get involved with it?

If you ask most audiologists, they would give you the same answer. We were speech language pathologists, or speech therapists. My undergraduate degree was in communication disorders. You take all your undergrad courses in phoneme production, anatomy of the mouth and of the lungs. Phoneme is the most basic unit of speech, like the P, T, or SH sound.

What attracted you to this major?

I had a lisp; I still do. I had a speech therapist when I was in grade school and I became very interested in it back then. I also became interested in sign language, so I thought it would be nice to learn sign language or be involved in deaf education in some way. So I took those two things together and decided I wanted to become a speech pathologist. I wanted to learn how speech works, deafness, the whole combination of these things. I was also really interested in languages and human communication.

As an undergraduate, you are taking a cross section of both: speech and hearing. For me, the speech stuff was either very interesting or impossibly nebulous. In speech, there is a range, a pattern of development, but it is not concrete. Audiologists tend to be more concrete people, and that's what draws away from speech and toward audiology. You get a graph; you're getting numbers. It's very quantifiable—you either heard it or you didn't.

What were you really learning in college when you started to pursue this?

In the undergraduate program there is heavy biology; you are learning anatomical structure. I didn't have to take organic chemistry or courses a medical student would. But we did have to take speech science, which gives you the background in both anatomy and phonation, which is how you maintain air through your vocal folds. What is really neat about that is there is a whole area of speech science where you are looking at spectrograms of different speech sounds. I worked with a professor whose expertise was fluency—fluency is a nice way to say stuttering. So he did recordings of people who were stuttering, then we went through with the spectrogram and tried to figure out the length of their utterances in milliseconds. It had all the compressions and rarefactions of the sound from the vocal folds.

What other things did you learn in your coursework that were interesting or attractive?

There was a course called Audition. It was about the act of hearing and was this great combination of physics, hearing, anatomy, and just how the ear and the brain work together. It was by far one of the hardest courses I ever took. You learn about decibels, sine waves, frequencies, and the logarithmic nature of sound.

Was there a moment when you knew you could make a career out of audiology?

The *aha!* moment was when we were learning about the anatomy of the ear, specifically the cochlea. We learned about standing wave theory. The root of this is that the cochlea is a shell-shaped hearing organ—if you were to unroll it, which you cannot because it is bone, you would find that it is linear. It is tonotopically organized—when you enter the cochlea, you find the high frequencies, then, as you work your way down, lower and lower pitches.

If you think about the function of hearing, it is basically that compressions of air hit the eardrum, which vibrates the eardrum, which cause the bones in your ear to move. The smallest bone is the stapes, which is up against the round window of your cochlea. As the stapes sort of moves and pumps up against the round window of your cochlea, it forces fluid called endolymph through your cochlea. Those waves of fluids just "know" which nerve cells are sensitive to that frequency.

There are computer models online of the basilar membrane, which is the membrane that the hair cells are attached to. These models show basilar membrane motion, and it is wild. It is one of the enigmas of the human body. To some degree some of these surrounding hair cells do respond, because it is kind of like wind on a wheat field. But for the most part, it just goes to the frequency, or hair cell, that it is meant to stimulate. That just blew me away. Also the fact that it is organized like a piano. It is tonotopic. Not only that, but the auditory nerve coming off the cochlea is also tonotopically organized. So if you have a tumor growing on your auditory nerve, depending on where it is, it will only affect the relevant frequency—6k, 8k, 4k, wherever that may be.

If you think about it, when you consider how many people are fascinated with microphones and other "vintage technology," it really doesn't hold a candle to the human ear.

It just happens—it is so mechanical in nature. You also get an enormous amount of amplification in your middle ear just in the transformation of power. The eardrum is only moving a little bit. So the electronic mimics all of this at an infinitely more simple level. What is really fascinating to me about it is that it turns it into electricity. We've all seen the matrix: human nerve impulses. It goes from compressions of air to electricity, which I measure on a daily basis.

When did you get your first gig out of college?

There are some governing bodies in audiology: There is the American Speech Language and Hearing Association and the American Academy of Audiology. All I need to practice audiology is my state license, technically. When I graduated, you also needed a master's degree, which you no longer need. Your certificate of clinical competence comes from the American Speech Language and Hearing Association. There are letters that are put after your name—everyone has them because they are afraid not to have them.

In audiology, you also have to have a clinical fellowship year. This is nine months if you are full-time and a year if you are part-time. You work under another audiologist.

So once you go down this path, it is very hard to change tracks if you change your mind.

It would be an enormous waste of time. When you come out the other end with a master's in audiology, you have to know what you are getting into. Most people don't even know what an audiologist is until they are exposed to it through their bachelor's degree program. So the sense of calling isn't as strong as another profession. I believe that audiologists have their sense of calling come when they realize how profound of an effect they can have on someone's life. Perception precedes production. If you aren't hearing it, you are not going to produce it.

It's kind of like when I identify an infant as having permanent sensory neural hearing loss. It's like, "This is terrible," but on the other hand, I get to be instrumental in making a positive impact for this child. I can do everything I can to help this child develop normal speech and language.

Was it hard to break into the industry?

No. I came out of grad school with my master's degree at the perfect time. With most clinical fellowship years, it is sort of like, "Let's see what happens after nine months." Many audiologists take the opportunity to work no strings attached wherever they want. I interviewed for positions in Ohio, Florida, and others.

How confident did you feel in your employability?

I knew, and I always know, that I can get a job. But what's hard for us is that our colleagues on the other side—speech pathologists—are in much greater demand. It used to be that hearing and speech were joined together, but now I don't feel that camaraderie with speech pathologists. We are more focused on hearing. Speech language pathologists can basically write their own ticket. They can work anywhere they want, in any town—and they know it.

When were you really able to apply your knowledge for the benefit of a patient?

All programs have on-campus clinics or very close associations with local hospitals. So I had experience working with patients during my first year of grad school. It is highly supervised, then you become more and more independent as you go on.

What are some of the issues you face in your industry?

It depends on the program, but I think there is an internal conflict between evidence-based practice in audiology and clinical lore. This is something that gets written about a lot: "Why do we do these things?" "Has anybody proven that they are effective?" The graduate programs used to have more than one class in instrumentation. For example, looking at the audiometer. Being able to open up the audiometer and understanding how it works—not just pressing buttons. When you are measuring auto-acoustic emissions, what is the machine doing?

You have to validate what the measurement system is, right?

Exactly. You should be able to calibrate the machines. For example, today, all of our frequencies were half an octave off.

What was the most profound moment you've had in your professional capacity?

I had one patient who was a year and a half old—she was adopted. She had mild to severe permanent hearing loss. Going through the identification process with her and then aiding her. We went though two or three pairs of hearing aids, and then gradually trained her to respond—the behavioral stuff—it was just like pulling out everything I knew. Now she is rather intelligible within speech. It has been really rewarding and a really great experience.

How complicated is your day-to-day job? Is most of it interpersonal?

A lot of audiology is nodding and smiling. A lot of our instrumentation has made things so easy and automatic for us. Programming hearing aids has become such a science even though there are so many features nowadays. Being a good counselor for the patients coming to terms with their hearing loss is a very important part of the job, and helping the patient develop realistic expectations. As advanced as the technology is, with noise reduction, directional microphones and the like, with any amount of neural sensory hearing loss, you're looking at neural cells that have died. The signal is never going to be correctly coded. No matter how clear I get it into the ear, the signal will be degraded.

Physicians schedule patients on 10- to 20-minute intervals. We see our patients from a half an hour to an hour at a time, so it is really very time-intensive. Many times you are dealing with an elderly population who may need repeated orientation to features of their hearing aids.

What are the natural attributes someone needs to be successful in this area? What capacities and abilities are required?

You really have to like to be around people, and people who are not at their best. You have to be a compassionate, tolerant person. You have to be comfortable being around people who are failing physically and mentally. We work closely with social support groups for people with mental and physical disabilities—some can't speak for themselves; others have very little physical control of themselves. Others have had traumatic brain injury or are stroke victims. You can play the beep, and it might take them several seconds to respond—you have to be very patient and tolerant of people.

A lot of audiology is just troubleshooting or problem solving. What's wrong? If this, then this. If not this, then this. We also rely heavily on our equipment—we really wear out our stuff, and things break down. You have to be able to deduce what is wrong technically because we see patients on a tight schedule. You've got to be able to manage repairs, oftentimes on the fly.

What do you think people would like most about this field?

It's rewarding working with different-aged people. For children, it's nice because you are catching them at the beginning. You are helping sounds get into their ears so they can learn to produce them. It's funny, because one way babies interact with their world is through their suck. Their suck increases when they are stimulated by their environment—be it a visual or sound stimulant. Once I put a hearing aid on a little guy who had very, very poor hearing. Then his mom leaned down to him and said his name and he started sucking like crazy! To help people maintain connections between each other is very important.

A Closer Look: Bernie Krause and Bioacoustics

Bernie Krause is a renowned innovator in bioacoustics. As a young man, he had a musical ear but wasn't able to find an educational program that would support his instrument of choice, guitar. After some interesting turns in his career that involved synthesis and engineering, he finally came upon his vocation: listening to and recording the sounds of nature.

Bernie, what was your entrée into the world of audio? I am assuming it wasn't immediately in bioacoustics....

I've always been involved in sound at some level. First with music, and then with natural sound. The reason, I think, is because I don't see very well, so my world is informed from the acoustic perspective. For the first 30 years or so I was pretty actively involved in music, and then in 1968 I made the transition from music to natural sound because it was more interesting to me.

Bernie Krause.

At what point did you realize that you could actually have a career in audio and support your living?

I kind of had a hunch that I was going to end up somewhere in audio. We gravitate to things that inform us best, and to me it was the acoustic perspective that was informing me. I tried to get into music school in 1955—I applied to Juilliard, Eastman, and other music schools around the country. But every one that I applied to, because my major instrument was guitar, informed me that the guitar was not a musical instrument—that was the case in America at that time, so I was kind of running up against a dead end. I didn't have the money to study abroad, so I ended up at University of Michigan and my major was Latin American History.

I would imagine that your liberal arts background came in very handy in your career. I also assume that when you were pursuing a degree, there were very few audio programs in existence, if any.

Don't forget that when I started college in 1956, the tape recorder had just been around for eight years. So recording and acoustics of that type were just in a very early state.

What did you do after graduation? Was it difficult finding work?

When I got out of college I went to New York and worked there as a musician for awhile, playing backup for several groups. Then I went to Boston and entered into a special graduate program at MIT. I wasn't at MIT for very long before the Weavers held auditions for the Pete Seeger chair. The Weavers were a folk group of the 1940s, '50s, and '60s. I won the audition and got the Pete Seeger chair for their last year together.

It seems like this love of music was an important thread in your audio career. How important was having a liberal arts degree at the end of the day?

I certainly think it was important. I look around today and talk to young students who are in highly specialized fields, and I get the sense that something is really missing from their lives that I was lucky enough to have from where I went to school. When I went to school, in the '50s and '60s, it was kind of a golden age of education in the United States—it was a time when one could ask questions. It was a time when the idea of reading and literature and the arts was considered important and embraced certainly in higher education. It really does give you a foundation from which to make important decisions in your life, and I think the people who don't have this higher-education liberal arts experience are missing a wonderful opportunity.

Can someone get the required background for an audio career through trade schools alone?

There are certainly trade degrees. The other dimension of education is being outside and being connected to the natural world. We have become more pathological—as a culture, we become distracted from the natural world. People need to be connected to nature again.

When in your career did your interest move from music into audio and electronics?

After my experience with the Weavers, I came out to California and studied electronic music at Mills College for a short time and met up with a fellow named Paul Beaver. The synthesizer sounded interesting to me, and they were offering courses there by people like Karlheinz Stockhausen from Germany. It gave me a real opportunity to expand my thinking in the field of sound. Paul Beaver and I went off on our own, bought one of the first Moog synthesizers off the line. and introduced it to pop music and film. Paul was a good mentor for me. He was extremely patient and he actually showed me what was going on electronically. I took notes and developed *The Nonesuch Guide to Electronic Music*. That was our first album for Nonesuch, and it is still a standard reference in schools today.

How were you supporting yourself financially at this point? When did this become an important consideration in your career?

The thing that led me into it was certainly the money factor. I was playing guitar as a studio instrumentalist, but I found I was making very little money doing that. I read about this guy in *Time* magazine—about this guy back east who had a prototype of the Moog synthesizer. He had done a commercial for American Express—he made $35,000 for seven seconds of sound. I thought, "Well, that makes a lot of sense." If someone is going to sell their craft and their art, why not sell it for some serious money? So I got on a plane and flew out to meet him.

Wow, that's motivation for you.

His name was Eric Satie. I wanted to see for myself whether this instrument was viable. Sure enough it was, and Paul and I bought one. We couldn't get any work with the synthesizer because it hadn't proven itself. But we went to the Monterey Pop Festival in 1967, and a lot of the producers and record companies were there with contracts in hand, with very liberal advances for a lot of these artists. I think we sold something like a dozen or 15 synthesizers at $15,000 each. Paul and I had a lot of business all of a sudden.

In 1968 we got a contract with Warner Brothers, and we were having lunch with Van Dyke Parks one day. Paul and I were talking about what kind of album we were going to make, and

Van Dyke said, "Why don't we do an album on ecology?" It was the first time I'd heard that word. I thought the idea was really intriguing because nobody had ever done anything like that before.

It was like a confluence of events because at that moment in time, the technology had just come out. The Nagra recorders and the microphones came out in the field. These were devices that just wouldn't fail. I was very intrigued with the idea of using a Nagra in the field. I went out and did some natural recordings not very far north of San Francisco and in and around the beaches in the Bay Area and put together this album called *In a Wild Sanctuary*. It was the first album ever to use natural sound as a component of orchestration.

It sounds like there was a lot of serendipity involved in how you got into bioacoustics. Did you have any formal training in this area?

I have a PhD in the field of bioacoustics. I knew right away that this was a viable career field, and I also knew that this was what I wanted to do. I soon began to go into the field more and more to record natural sound and began to collect a whole archive of material. Paul and I did three albums for Warner Brothers, then I did another album for Mobile Fidelity.

This entire time you were also doing films, correct?

Yes, in fact I worked on *Apocalypse Now* and got fired eight times by Francis Ford Coppola, which worked out really well for me, by the way. Each time I got fired, I got hired back again for double the salary, and I'm now living in a house that was funded by this. All in all, I worked on about 135 feature films—*Apocalypse Now* wasn't the last film I did, but it was the last *major* film that I did.

What exactly did you do on that film?

I did one-third of the score and a lot of the helicopter sounds. These were physical sounds, not sound effects. Most of the films we did, we did music and effects with a synthesizer. I've subsequently done a lot of film work with natural sound, such as *The Shipping News*, *Castaway*, and *The Perfect Storm*.

How much does film work represent for you in terms of income?

Films are a very small component of my natural sound work. By far the larger components are our album downloads off of our website. Our CDs are very large sellers—we've sold over 1-1/2 million CDs online through The Nature Company. We also do a lot of soundscape installations at museums, aquariums, and zoos.

What is a typical day for you like?

I like to spend as much time as I can out in the field. When I'm doing that, the days are often 20 hours long and about as far from human habitation as one can get. I go to places like Latin America, Africa, any of the more remote places on the planet. I found that travel was important in this job the minute I realized I couldn't record nature in the United States because it is too noisy. Also, fully 40 percent of my archive from North America, mostly the United States, comes from now-extinct habitats.

What is it inside you that drives your interest in recording nature sounds?

It makes me feel good to be out in the wild. It makes me feel good to hear those sounds because they are part of our DNA and part of our Pleistocene past. They are the things that we used to turn to for healing. It's a very spiritual experience. I'm not a religious person in the traditional sense, but these are the sounds of the divine for me. There is nothing that resonates with my spiritual and emotional side more than this.

What kind of personal traits do you need to succeed in this field? I imagine patience, because the sounds you are trying to record likely do not come on command.

Yes. Sometimes, you're out there waiting for 32 hours for a sound. You need to be patient and persevering to do what I do, but I don't consider it work. I consider it a delight and a blessing to be able to do this. I'm still able to do it at 70 years old.

Would you consider this a viable career for persons just entering the audio field?

Absolutely. When I started in 1979, there were about six PhDs. Now there are close to 600, and it is exploding exponentially every year. What's neat about bioacoustics and the recording of natural sounds is that it involves so many disciplines. For instance, the kinds of disciplines that are involved are biology and computational mathematics—because you need to have an analytical framework to interpret what you are getting. It also involves physics, anthropology, music, natural history, environmental study, resource management, sociology, medicine, philosophy, and architecture. These are all related disciplines to the soundscape. It is fabulously resonant, far-reaching. It is important for people to learn to listen. If people really know how to listen, they become involved in all these disciplines.

What coursework would one seek out in higher education to gain expertise in this?

There are now specific, up-to-date programs in bioacoustics. Interestingly, the older academic collections at various schools and museums are based on the abstraction and deconstruction of sounds of the natural world. In other words, science from the 19th century had focused on taking the individual critters out of context. As a result, nothing was really learned because they shouldn't be examined out of their environment. You need to listen to them in relation to everything else that is making noise, which is the reason that they are making the vocalizations in the first place. They are looking for acoustic territory. This is what I call the *biophony*, a word that I invented.

Even though this sounds very interesting, it sounds like a very niche field. Are there lots of employers out there for folks with this kind of background?

There are a lot of companies that are beginning to employ people with a background like this—there is so much work to be done in the field. For example, we are doing a lot of acoustic mapping for the National Park Service and the U.S. Fish and Wildlife. We are mapping different territories to get baseline information to see what the effect from global warming or climate change is going to be. There are a lot of grants to be had for those who are really interested in doing this, who want to be outside and have a love of sound.

We recently did a study through the National Park Conservation Association, or NPCA, out of Washington. We went to Yellowstone in 2002 to record the sound of the snowmobiles, which are terribly intrusive and continue to be so. We went up there to record for several days, then I was invited to make a presentation to Congress.

The vote was 100 against snow mobiles to 320 for before I went in. I said to them, "All I want is five minutes of your time, and you'll be able to make an intelligent choice." I came in with 2-1/2 minutes of sound with the snowmobiles, and 2-1/2 minutes with the natural sound as it was without the snowmobiles. I played it at the real levels, which really pissed a lot of them off.

After my presentation, the vote changed around to 210 to 210 and was turned around by the administration. My presentation simply consisted of an introduction, "My name is Bernie Krause, and I am a bioacoustician." I then showed a slide of a wolf eating a bison carcass and said, "I'm going to play you two sounds. You decide which goes sound goes with which picture. This is what you're voting on." So the vote changed substantially in five minutes— sound is a very powerful source.

Bernie, what kind of work/life balance have you been able to maintain over the years? Has your career been "all-in," or have you had a relatively normal outside existence?

When I was younger I had more time because I had more energy. Recently, I've been pretty much focused and driven on just this and getting my archive in place—much to the chagrin of my wife and friends. People could put as much time into this career as they want, which is neat. It is always springtime somewhere around the globe, in either the northern or the southern hemisphere—one just needs to figure out what they want to do and how much time they are willing to invest in doing it.

How much money can you really make in this field? Don't academia-type jobs generally pay a lot less than what you can make in other careers?

It depends on your business acumen. If business is really important to you, then you can develop a source of income on any of these things as a resource that can be several million dollars a year. If you're not hell-bent on making money and framing these things as a product, you have the choice of going into academia and being supported through grants and other programs. Either way, I can't imagine a better life.

Are your chances of success increased by living in one part of the world or another?

You want to be near an airport, and you're going to have to get out and travel.

Overall, how would you characterize your cumulative experience in bioacoustics?

It's a wonderful career and it touches so many other disciplines. You might want to go into bioacoustics and medicine, for example. For me, the healing part of this is very much a reason I am in it, because it relaxes me and makes me feel good.

As it turns out, I am on the board of Harvard's Institute for Music and Brain Science. The studies that are being done now show clearly that natural soundscapes have much more of a healing effect than any musical thing that one could introduce. If you could show a correlation between the effect of natural soundscapes and healing to an insurance company or a medicinal drug company, and you could do that through large-sample studies, you could get a patent. You're talking about how you'd use this as a resource to make a living. This probably has more potential in what it can give back to the individuals who are really inventive than any other aspect of sound that I can think of.

12 A Career in Freelancing

The *American Heritage Dictionary* defines a freelancer as "a person who sells services to employers without a long-term commitment to any of them." The U.S. Bureau of Labor Statistics reported that in 2005, there were 10.3 million independent contractors in the U.S., representing around 7.5 percent of the entire workforce. Freelance workers are an increasingly viable option for companies who can't afford to hire full-time talent, given the increasing costs of healthcare and other benefits. Also, skilled freelancers can often deliver services at a lower cost because they don't have the overhead associated with a large company.

Market Viability

The freelance market is an extremely valuable component of the audio market—not just for individual freelancers, but also for the hundreds of companies in the industry they serve. In the audio industry, freelance talent comes in a variety of roles, such as writing, teaching, engineering, producing, maintenance, marketing, and any number of other conceivable roles. But although the benefits of freelancing can be enormous, the risk and uncertainty can be equally as daunting.

Freelancers obviously rely on their own ambition, skill, and ingenuity to deliver any number of services to their clients. Because they don't benefit from the resources of a large company to back up their efforts, they have to be extremely resourceful to ensure consistent income. They also need to stay ahead of the latest trends in their field so they can make a relevant contribution to the task at hand—be it a feature article, a song remix, a studio wiring project, or a product launch.

Although freelancers enjoy a substantial amount of freedom, success is never guaranteed. They must always be chasing the next story, the next integration, or the next recording project, because time spent idly can equal a cash-flow imbalance. Therefore, freelancers should strive to build up a cache of retainers or predictable monthly income where possible. Unfortunately, the "feast or famine" lifestyle is often all too familiar to even the most experienced freelancers.

Freelance competition is often fierce, and as social media evolves, freelance networks are becoming more and more organized each day. As an example, networking sites such as MediaBistro.com provide writers with an arsenal of resources, such as story-pitching tactics, online courses, and industry news resources. People who put these kinds of resources into play most effectively will usually win the work and the opportunity to work again.

A Freelancer's Life is Often One of Feast or Famine

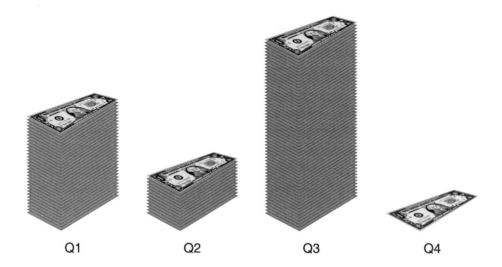

Q1   Q2   Q3   Q4

Breaking into Freelancing and Going It Alone

There are many ways to begin freelancing, but it is safe to say that each of these ways begins with good relationships. The most successful freelance careers begin when an individual can successfully retain the loyalty of an already established client base before going out on his own. In other words, if you do a good job at a company and clients appreciate your attitude, skills, and knowledge on a personal level, chances are they will be more than happy to give you a shot at doing business with them on your own if you choose to go solo. Having an established base of a known clientele can make the transition to working for yourself much more appealing and less frightening to a beginner.

Why Companies Hire Freelancers

- It's cheaper than hiring their own talent.

- They can leverage the vast knowledge/talent base of individuals.

- This practice can reduce a company's liability and red tape.

- Freelancers are perfect for projects of limited duration.

- Companies can quickly scale their workforce by hiring more or fewer freelancers.

- Freelancers enable company staff to stay focused on specific tasks.

- Freelancers can bring about new opportunities.

Another way to break into freelancing is to make a gradual transition from your day job by moonlighting. For many, this is a favorable option because it allows you to test the waters and gradually gain expertise while maintaining the security of a day job. It also equates to "found money," which can support expensive hobbies that many of us have, such as acquiring the latest and greatest audio gear or taking an occasional weekend vacation that otherwise might not be in the budget.

Fortunately, developments in the networking world have enabled most audio-oriented freelancers to work remotely, where their physical presence is not required. This has always been true for freelance writers, but is now true even for people such as adjunct professors, who can often teach online courses from the comfort of their own home. ISDN; smart plug-ins, such as Source Connect; and collaboration tools described in Chapter 9 dramatically improve the chances for a producer/engineer to "virtually" handle a project from start to finish.

The Internet and developments in social media have enabled freelance workers to truly enjoy a global clientele. All kinds of work can be found for most skill levels, regardless of geography. Additionally, portals such as Elance.com, iFreelance.com, and MediaBistro.com have created centralized marketplaces for freelancers, where potential clients and freelancers can seek a match based on project and compatibility.

Getting Your House in Order

As mentioned earlier, your ability to be successful in freelancing depends on your ambition, skill, and ingenuity. Your success is also dependent on your ability to be efficient and remain focused on a few key areas, discussed in the following sections.

Scheduling

Keeping a calendar might seem like one of the more rudimentary skills one acquires without much effort during the course of a career, but efficient planning is absolutely essential—especially if you have more than one client. You need to allocate sufficient time for tasks such as pitching new business, invoicing and accounting, attending trade shows (when appropriate), and most importantly, completing the work itself. For a freelancer, double-booking or even being late for a meeting can result in lost business. You need to plan major activities months in advance and learn to correlate time and potential income to avoid extended periods of little pay.

Learn to spend your time efficiently and compartmentalize your efforts. This means staying focused on the task at hand and seeing it through to completion. For example, you should not be doing accounting one minute and trying to mix a track in the studio the next. Making a checklist of tasks for yourself and remaining focused on completing those tasks—no matter how small—is an invaluable discipline that will ultimately reap great rewards.

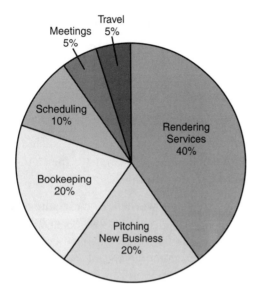

Sample Time Allocation of a Freelancer

Travel 5%

Meetings 5%

Scheduling 10%

Bookkeeping 20%

Rendering Services 40%

Pitching New Business 20%

Social Networking and Communication

Networking is where opportunity begins and ends—after all, business doesn't create opportunities, people do. Take great care in how you communicate with people and be careful not to burn bridges along the way. Successful freelancers learn to see opportunity in all their interactions with people—even negative interactions, which will invariably occur. Successful networking for freelancers means communicating frequently and being proactive rather than reactive. It means anticipating the needs of a client before they realize they need something.

It can't be stressed enough: Personal and professional networks are the lifeblood of a freelancer. Take advantage of all the powerful social media tools that are now available, including Facebook, Technorati, Digg, and similar portals. Make the effort to reach out beyond your own circle of contacts—you will be surprised by who your friends know and how eager they will be to help you once they learn about your specialty or interest as a freelancer.

Invoicing and Bookkeeping

Most people cannot get work unless they create a proposal, and most don't get paid unless they generate an invoice. This is a simple business process that, if not followed, has the potential to crush any freelance business. All your work won't make a bit of difference if you do not have the discipline to send invoices on time. You also need to be able to identify slow-paying clients and follow up; otherwise, this can have a direct negative impact on your cash flow.

It should go without saying that freelance workers need to keep accurate financial records as well as copies of their work. This is important not only for legal and tax purposes, but also to document interaction with clients should a job go beyond the original proposed scope. Also, freelancers need to make sure they comply with all tax laws, doing things such as requiring that their own suppliers submit an I9 form. By having a freelance business, you are eligible for deductions on business expenses, which can have a positive effect on your personal tax return. You should meet with your accountant on a regular basis because he or she can help you understand tax law as well as plan for big-picture implications.

When you are freelancing, keeping receipts of all your business activities becomes very important, since you are eligible for write-offs and deductions, which can positively impact your cash flow in a big way come April, when it is time to file. Keep a journal and track any business-related expenses, such as travel, meals, and entertainment, and any other legitimate expenses required to run your business.

Discipline on the bookkeeping side isn't just limited to your own business. You must ensure that your clients agree to your financial terms and that they pay you accurately and on time. This can mean sending out statements on a regular basis or occasionally interacting with relevant accounts payable departments.

Traits Valued in a Successful Freelancer

By far the most important trait of a successful freelancer is his or her reputation. You develop a good reputation by having integrity and completing jobs on time and with high quality. A freelancer's reputation is vastly important because it directly correlates to his ability to bid on and win new projects. If you let a client down, it can take years to regain trust and rebuild your reputation. Businesses are a lot easier to build on a good reputation than on a poor one. As an independent freelancer, you have no one to blame but yourself if you develop a poor reputation.

Reputation   Organizational Skills
Persistence
Risk Tolerance   Discipline
Perseverance   Resourcefulness
Confidence
Networking Abilities

These are just some of the traits that are considered valuable in the freelance market.

You don't need an enormous amount of intelligence to be successful in freelancing, but you do need to be resourceful, organized, and competent in your chosen discipline. If you are a freelance engineer, for example, you better be able to set up and execute a session confidently—there is no learning on the job when you are a professional. Having a good attitude and being able to network effectively are both important skills in attaining success, but raw talent is essential. If you can't deliver on your promises once you have the job, it's very likely you won't be asked to work again.

You should also be willing to live with a certain amount of risk—freelancing is by no means a secure path, and disaster (or at least a setback) can lurk around almost any corner. That said, if you are someone who is not willing to let go of your dream and you feel that attaining freedom is a true measure of success, chances are you also have what it takes to build a career in freelancing. If you *do* experience a setback, consider it a character-building challenge—if you make a mistake and decide to crawl into a little hole instead of picking up the pieces and learning from your past, chances are you might not make it as a freelancer.

Desirable Qualities of a Freelancer

- Integrity and a good reputation

- Organizational skills and resourcefulness

- Ability to deliver value that differentiates the freelancer from the competition

- Ability to deliver measurable results on time

- Ability to network and effectively utilize social media

- Ability to effectively manage schedules and budgets

- Ability to identify new business opportunities

A good freelancer will be able to set concrete goals and measure his or her own progress. Each year, establish a reasonable benchmark of what you need to achieve financially and try to build on that. Break down how you intend to achieve your financial goals by itemizing potential income sources. Spend the most effort in developing those that have the greatest income potential. If you give it your best effort, chances are you will be able to increase your annual income by 10 percent or more, which is much higher than the typical raises that many corporations offer to their top employees.

Increasing your income means not only doing more work and bringing greater value to your jobs, but also asking for more money when the time is right. Unlike a corporation that may be looking after an employee with fairly predictable raises and bonuses, freelancers need to look after themselves when it comes to compensation. This requires having knowledge of what other suppliers are charging for a given service, as well as doing a periodic examination of how your services have increased or become more valuable and correlating that to appropriate compensation.

In terms of performance, it is very important to be able to set client expectations and provide measurements of your success at defined moments of your relationship. Establish a very clear scope early on and agree upon the metrics on which you will be measured. This is very important because when a job goes out of scope, "project creep" can end up costing you profit, which can be painful for a freelancer. If work beyond the initial scope is required, it should be outlined and priced accordingly, with very specific and measurable milestones so both you and your client know when the job is complete.

Benefits and Drawbacks of Freelancing

There is a saying that "the devil you know is better than the devil you don't know." Put simply, although working for a company or reporting to a normal day job may be monotonous or might not be your idea of creative nirvana, most companies offer benefits that are often taken for granted. Retirement plans, disability, insurance, health coverage, and other benefits matter if you get sick, become disabled, or die—assuming you have dependents or loved ones you want to look after financially. Benefits are expensive, and the sad truth is that many full-time freelancers don't have them (though they will rarely admit to this). Although the cost of medical and disability insurance can be expensive, if you become very ill or physically impaired, the cost of not having insurance can be nothing short of devastating.

Benefits and Drawbacks of
Working as a Freelancer

You Are the Boss	Feast or Famine
Choose Your Own Clients	Loss of Client = High Risk
Control Your Own Schedule	Expensive Benefits
Tax Write-Off Benefits	Accounting a Hassle
Not Location-Dependent	No Promotion Path
Set Your Own Terms	No Support Staff

Perhaps the biggest disincentive of freelancing is the "feast or famine" rule. There can be huge windfalls of cash, but once again, since you are responsible for all your overhead and expenses, more often than not these amounts are just enough to cover your expenses when the jobs aren't coming in. One way to minimize this phenomenon is to diversify your work portfolio just as you would a financial portfolio. Incorporate a mix of clients and different types of work in your freelance activities so if one client goes sour, you have another to fall back on.

The concept of "vacation" is relative for freelancers. Indeed, many freelancers turn into work-aholics because they know they always have to keep filling the pipeline with work to stay finan-cially secure. Many freelancers find it hard to take a break for fear of jeopardizing their income stream. As a result, they can burn themselves out by not recharging—a concept good companies consider very important to keep workers productive.

The best (or worst, depending on who you are and how you look at it) aspect of freelancing is the fact that you are responsible for your own destiny. You build up your own skills, contacts, and talent. You choose your own clientele and work approach. You decide how much to bill and who you want to continue working with. This can be very liberating, but also intimidating for someone not acclimated to this sort of enormous flexibility.

Is Freelancing Right for You?

Take some time and explore how you would establish your initial freelancing base. Make a list of prospective clients or people you know who could help you get off the ground. Do the math and set reasonable goals for year one, year two, and year three. Identify other markets where your skills may be valued outside of your own comfort zone or ecosystem. Many people need your services but don't even realize it yet. If you can find these people and help them become more successful, the rest will come naturally. The best measure of success a freelancer can pos-sibly have is a happy client. As Peter Fish observed earlier in this book, focus on making clients happy, one at a time.

It helps to literally create a visual or graphic map of where you want your freelance career to go. Much of successful freelancing isn't in reaching a destination per se, but reaching the next step. After you've reached a few steps and you look back on your cumulative progress, you might realize that you went further than you had originally planned. It must be said, though—if you have no vision to begin with, at the end of the day you won't know whether you are going forward or backward.

A Closer Look: Dan Daley and Freelance Journalism

Dan Daley is an accomplished freelance journalist who specializes in entertainment technology and business. In the audio world, he is regarded as an innovator who is able to articulate and even predict trends in several of the industry's leading magazines. Always a keen journalist look-ing for the why behind the what, Daley began writing freelance for audio-related publications such as *Mix*, *Billboard*, and *Sound on Sound* and eventually branched out to major consumer magazines and newspapers. Daley is the consummate professional: He has never missed a

Dan Daley.

deadline and is always thinking of the angle. As a published songwriter, musician, and engineer, Daley's background is diverse and gave him the knowledge he needed to launch a successful six-figure freelance career.

How did you begin your career in freelancing and when did it start to gain traction professionally?

When I was eight years old, my first poem was published—obviously I had the bug for it early on. My career as a musician and songwriter began when I was about 14 years old, playing clubs down at Bleecker Street, in the East Village, and at colleges. My high school band, called Revival, was signed by Neil Bogart on Buddah Records about a year after I graduated from high school. The record wasn't very good, but it did enable me to continue touring for two or three years.

All the while, I had been developing myself as a songwriter with the group Revival—I wrote most of the songs. I began to get covers, hooked up with United Artists publishing, and had a top-10 R&B hit in 1977. There were a couple more like that. A big one was "Still in Saigon" with Charlie Daniels, then another with Johnny Winter. I was pursuing a career in music, but was writing my way through it.

Where do things take a turn to journalistic writing versus songwriting?

I was also touring a lot during in the late '70s, and I remember being in Texas. There was a broad, studio news–type magazine that said, "If you're down there, we'd love an article on

Dallas Onyx Studio." So I did a story in maybe 1978 or '79—it was where Doc Severinsen recorded. I said, "Whoa—there's this whole infrastructure of magazines that want to serve this sector." I was working in recording studios, but it just never occurred to me that there were a whole bunch of magazines about them. In the mid-'80s, I did two things: I went back to college and finished my degree.

What did you focus on?

The program was really writing for multiple media, but it focused on journalism. At the same time, I also became a partner in a recording studio based in Manhattan, called Pyramid Recording, which is when I got a better look at the business of recording studios. I'd been working at them as a client, but now here I was operating one. I got a better idea of the business and at the same time began working toward being a journalist. The path of least resistance for me into the world of journalism was the magazines that catered to recording studios and musicians, and the first ones I wrote for were for *International Recording World* and *Mix* magazine.

So you were really aligned with your original interests and passions.

The advice to aspiring novelists is, "Write what you know." And that works really well for aspiring journalists. Begin in an area where you have a lot of expertise. You'll know what's going on before other people do, and you've got some understanding of the machinery inside that niche.

Did you ever have a full-time career in writing outside of freelancing?

I'd never gotten a W2 in my entire life—I've always been freelance.

It appears that you adopted a multi-source income model very early on with your journalism, songwriting, and studio work.

In those days, you had two types of writers—someone who was in the music business who would occasionally contribute an article, or someone who was on staff at a magazine, who was the editor or the associate editor, who would be writing the stories. Those people may or may not have had recording engineering experience, and they were not in the middle of the business.

Where I changed it was I said, "I know how to make music, I know how to record it, I know the dynamics and the business of it. I want to go out and see how other people are doing it." That's when I started doing spotlights on different studios, on different engineers. I actually convinced *Mix* magazine to start a business section, which lasted for two years. They then cancelled it because they said they couldn't sell advertising into it. That was a shame, since 10 years later, everyone was focused on the business of recording—now, many of those studios are out of business.

The problem for me was always that the studios were not paying enough attention to business; they were living in an older business environment paradigm. So one of the things I did was to branch out myself—now I write regularly or semi-regularly for the *History Channel* magazine, the *London Daily Telegraph*, and others.

When did you feel comfortable that you could really do this as a career and support yourself?

Truly, when I broke $100,000, which was back in 1991. There's probably a good analogy in this story for someone: I got an assignment from the *Daily News* to go interview the Weinstein brothers, the film moguls. Their first movie had just come out, and they still just had offices in Manhattan. I'm thinking to myself, "I don't know anything about making movies, and these guys are supposed to be the next hot thing." I was really worried about pulling this off. I was also nervous because I was doing it for a flagship newspaper, the *New York Daily News*. But when I got to that office I realized something: They were more nervous about having a reporter in a room with them than I was about being in a room with them. As soon as I got that sense of, "Wait a minute, I'm driving the boat here," it got so much easier.

But the reality is you took a risk and put yourself in a vulnerable position.

Absolutely, and I did that for two reasons. Number one, I knew I needed to move my career forward, and number two, I knew I needed to move *me* forward. At that point, I wasn't saying to myself, "Recording studios are going to go away," because in 1991, everyone thought the world would continue to be as it was. What tipped me off about studios going away was the whole HARP controversy back in the early '90s, when the Hollywood Association of Recording Professionals got together to try to stop project studios. That's when I realized that project studios are going to wind up eliminating the big guys. And that's pretty much what happened.

All these kinds of things contributed to my desire to expand the realms in which I wrote, but at the same time, I wanted to chronicle the end of the Roman Empire, which I did. I was able to chronicle how studios were beginning to close up, how they were not able to adapt to business changing.

After your first dozen articles, you get into a rhythm and begin to adopt a methodology. How do you choose where to expand and what other avenues you want to pursue as a freelancer beyond just music technology?

My strategy for that was to take what I knew and bring it to places where I hadn't done it before. So if I was writing about recording studios, for instance, the first question I would ask was, "Who's building recording studios these days?" Billionaires. Okay, let me find three billionaires who put together unbelievable, amazing studios. Who would want to read about that? People in *Wired*. So I put the pitch together, sent it to *Wired*, and that was my first piece for *Wired*. It was about how Paul Allen had the place in London. Luczo, who started Seagate, had this unbelievable place in San Francisco, so I did that story. That readership didn't care whether they had an SSL or a Neve in there. What they cared about was, "Huh, this guy is my competitor, and he's building a recording studio."

How difficult was it for you to adapt to writing for a completely different audience?

I was getting better as a writer, and my abilities as a writer were outstripping the environment of trade magazines, which I still love very much. Once you break out of the trade magazines, now you're looking at a bigger landscape. You say to yourself, "I'm pretty good, but I'm not good enough to do the *New Yorker* yet." What you do is find the magazines that appreciate some style. That's why I jumped to the London papers—the London papers really let you write. I did a lot of great stuff for the *London Daily Telegraph*, including a story on Virginia Beach, which became Ground Zero for hip-hop in this country. They like that stuff. Find stuff you know and find places that might be interested in it. That's the perfect paradigm—I knew about Virginia Beach turning into hip-hop central for a while.

You not only broke out of your genre, but you turned things international, too. How did you know what magazines to go after in the U.K.?

Over the course of doing it over the years, you go to the trade shows and you meet the people. I knew the editor of *Studio Sound*, and he said, "I've been reading your stuff. Would you like to write for me?" I said "Absolutely." I had to learn to write in British English, of course, where the spellings are different and where the nouns and verbs agree in a different way. It was a good learning experience, just like writing for the web.

Obviously, connections are important in getting your sources, but connecting professionally and keeping those bridges open are just as important.

Woody Allen said 50 percent of life is "just showing up." That has been one of my mantras. Maybe they'll read you, but when they meet you, that puts it all together for them.

Let's talk a little bit about keeping up productivity and maintaining output. Can you describe your daily routine?

Being afflicted with obsessive-compulsive disorder works in your favor. I just have a routine where I wake up in the morning; I come down to the computer and get to work. I also take frequent breaks. I like doing this stuff most of the time; sometimes you get assignments for articles that are really boring, but that's just part of life. Most of the time I enjoy wondering, "What am I going to learn today?" I also look forward to the fact that I get close to a lot of people I really admire. I'm now good friends with people like Al Cooper and Linda Ronstadt because they were heroes to me. Had I stayed as a musician or a recording engineer, chances are I would never have met them, let alone become friendly with them. As a journalist, however, I've gotten to know and even become friendly with a lot of people I admired in my younger days.

How important is discipline in making it as a freelancer?

You need the same amount of discipline as you would need to be successful in any other field. You're writing for magazines most of the time, and magazines have a monthly deadline. If you're writing for newspapers, they have a daily deadline. So rule number one is you can never be late. You can't miss the deadline. In my 22 years of doing this, I've never missed a deadline. The other thing is, find out what the magazine is really about, what the magazine really wants. I write for the editor. I don't sit there and try to figure out *EQ*'s readership—I try to figure out *EQ*'s editor. It's *EQ*'s editor's job to know his readership. So write for the editor, and you'll be fine.

What kinds of stumbling blocks have you encountered over the years, and have you ever taken a wrong turn? Where have you had to course-correct yourself?

I may have gone out on limbs here and there into areas where I may not have had any true expertise. I've just had to pull back. For instance, I took a look at a new algae-growing farm down in El Paso, Texas. I have a science background as an engineer, but I realized something in pitching this over to *Popular Science*. I realized that I don't know enough at a granular level about algae growing. I won't be able to bring the extra bit of insight to this story that someone else would have, the same way that I can bring a bit of extra insight to a story about Muscle Shoals or studio economics.

However, it made me an in where I never had an in before, at *Popular Science*. So I said, "While I've got you on the phone, let me pitch you another story about going green: Thomas Dolby is about to make his next record completely off the grid, using solar and wind power in a hut on his property and aboard a sailboat." Then she said, "That's interesting." So that's how I got my first piece in *Popular Science*. It started out as algae growing, and I realized I didn't have the expertise, but it opened the door and gave me the opportunity to pitch another type of story.

So someone else might have given up and walked away with their tail between their legs.

I'm always working the angle. Anytime a door opens, I'm looking in my briefcase and asking, "What kind of shoe should I stick in to keep it open?" All I need is the elevator pitch—all I need is 3 minutes or 100 words to give you a story idea, and 8 times out of 10, I get a yes.

Have your pitches had to become more complex? How have your pitching methods changed over the years?

They just get better—I pitch the way I write. You have to convey a sense of knowledge, a sense of insidership, and a sense of humor.

How do you pitch?

I pitch by query emails. There are publications out there that will help you with this. Becoming a member of MediaBistro is a really good idea because they will tell you who to pitch and they'll tell you what the etiquette of pitching is. There are magazines out there that still demand you send letters in the mail through snail mail.

What is the market like right now? Is it overly competitive?

My situation is not unlike what independent recording artists are facing: There are fewer and fewer record labels out there, but there is more and more music being made. The same situation is happening on the writing side. The economics of magazines is in a reverse situation right now. There is more consolidation—however, there is no shortage of people out there who want to write. Many of these folks are going through blogs and alternative distribution channels. That being said, there's still plenty of opportunities to write in magazines. You just have to think about it like you have something to sell, and there are people out there who want to buy.

Make sure that what you are selling is what they want to buy. Find out what the editor wants—this can be a number of things. It could be a good writer—somebody who really knows their subject or knows how to learn that subject.

Freelance writing, not unlike music, is often filled with a lot of people who have a lot of ambition, but not a lot of follow-through. Sometimes the drummer doesn't show up for the gig, and sometimes the writer just doesn't turn it in. If you can be the guy who they know will always turn in the copy clean, edited, and on time, you're gold.

It comes down to integrity and holding up your end of the relationship, right?

It's about not f- - -ing up. So many people in the "creative arts" do f- -k up. That's why they are in the creative arts. I don't want my music written by an accountant; I want it written by a really f- - -ed-up person because it comes out better. But that's writing the music. Writing about the music, you want someone who is really going to turn it in on time.

Are there any specific memories you have of things lining up for you when you felt you had chosen the right career?

I was doing a story for *Mix* magazine, an interview with Linda Ronstadt as a producer. I had done the interview with her in Nashville; she was staying at a bed and breakfast with her kids. I'm getting on a plane to fly from Nashville to Los Angeles, and I'm sitting in the second or third row of the plane, and I hear people talking behind me trying to arrange themselves. So one guy says, "There's a seat empty in the row in front of me; let me take that." It was the seat next to me. He sits down, and it turns out to be Peter Asher. I ended up doing an interview with him on the flight from Nashville to Los Angeles. And that came out in *Mix* magazine. It was one of those serendipitous moments—I knew I must have been doing something right if I'm working on a story on Linda Ronstadt and sage sticks Peter Asher next to me. I'm doing the right thing!

Where are things going for you now? What's next?

It's funny you ask. I've been trying to figure out what the third act of my life is going to be. The first act was as a musician/songwriter; the second act has been as a journalist. They've both been successful. I'm thinking about going and getting a master's degree and teaching journalism—the third act might be as a teacher. I'm not going to stop writing, though—I'm just not going to continue writing this hard.

How much do you have to write to break $100,000? Do you ever worry that you're not going to hit that mark?

I'm probably always going to hit that mark, but I'm always going to worry about it because I'm just a worrier. The worry is part of what prompts you to get up and get cracking. But I know it can't go on forever, which is why when it's going good, you figure out what the next move is going to be. I'm pitching constantly—in fact I'm pitching a story today to a magazine called *Drinks* that I've written for before.

A Closer Look: Matthew Cullen and Freelance Engineering

Matthew Cullen is an engineer based in upstate New York. He made the jump to freelance while working at Allaire Studios, the world-renowned destination studio. While at Allaire, he worked with diverse acts including the Holmes Brothers, the Lemonheads, My Morning Jacket, and Martha Wainwright. Matt wears his passion for recording on his sleeve, and it is abundantly clear that he is doing what he loves—and getting paid for it.

Matthew Cullen.

How did you get involved in freelancing?

My hand was slightly forced. I kind of worked myself into a corner where I ended up in the hospital being exhausted. My workload had been so heavy—for me, going freelance meant a greater choice of what I wanted to do. I had built up a decent client base and I was getting enough calls to do stuff from people who couldn't afford working at the high-end studios. Having worked as an in-house engineer definitely helped me develop my client base to some degree.

Does it help your reputation as a freelancer to come from a studio with a very good pedigree?

Yes, it helps having come from a place like Allaire. People expect a higher level at the outset, and you sort of carry that reputation or stamp of approval with you. But you're only as good as the gigs that you do. It's not that big of an industry, and word gets around.

How do you get your gigs?

Everything I do is by word of mouth—I haven't hustled anything too much. People call me and say, "I got your name through someone else who you worked with." I've gotten a bunch of gigs through Craig Street and people he knows, for example. I don't really cold call anybody; at least I haven't had to yet. There's always been some sort of introduction through another industry professional.

So it seems like most of your work comes from developing existing relationships.

Yeah. I've never really been one to go out to shows and drum up work because I'm a little shy and self-conscious. Fortunately, somebody I know who does that successfully is a producer and has a studio, so I get work off the back of his efforts. That's probably something I should work on a little bit—it would probably help me out. I've been spoiled in that I haven't had to do that with most of my work coming through existing channels.

How much time is consumed managing the business and maintaining your networks?

I'm still trying to work it out, really. I wish I had someone who could handle the administrative side of things, especially when I get busy. I just try to stay in touch with people to see what's going on without appearing to be desperate. It's difficult to stay disciplined because you suddenly go from having a fairly regular income, like a paycheck, to suddenly moving to more like a feast-or-famine scenario. I've been fortunate in that I've been able to work fairly steadily, but I certainly think that putting money aside to cover the quiet periods is important. This is not anything I've ever had to think about before.

Do you ever work on spec to gain future work?

A little bit. I have some friends that I work with—we are doing an instrumental record, and nobody is getting paid for it right now, but we're recording music for a company who does library music for films. Most of my friends are musicians, so we often record these instrumentals and try to pursue things like this because you never know when something will break. Depending on the opportunity, I can make myself expensive or less expensive—a less expensive project with a small budget might actually open up more doors. I've worked on records that have been self-released that have turned out great and have done really well.

How do you feel now that you have essentially traded security for freedom?

I feel a lot happier. I loved working at a big studio, but like anything else, you have to go to work every day, and you have to please a boss. Now I get to choose the projects that I do, I can turn down stuff that I'm not interested in, and I'm a lot happier. I can schedule myself around the things I like to do. When you choose a project, you choose it because you really want to do it. You're going to devote a large chunk of time. It's hard work, and you're really going to get into it.

Working on projects you like probably means you are doing a better job, too.

If I choose to work on something, I'm really going to give my all to it. Not that I didn't do this before, but you really feel like you have a personal investment in it.

What kind of financial hit have you taken since you've moved to freelancing?

It's been pretty good. I've been fortunate in that I've done some big projects that have paid pretty well. I kind of use this to offset the fact that budgets are a little bit smaller than a large studio project would require. The income comes in chunks and it is a little less predictable.

How do you network with other freelancers? Is having a social network with other freelancers important, or are they now your competitors?

These are people who are my friends anyway. When you work in-house you meet so many people that come through. We sort of look out for each other, especially in my community, where there aren't so many freelancers.

Since you've been freelancing, what have your gear requirements been? Do you find yourself not needing your own rig since you are still working in professional studios?

I have a portable rig, like a little Pro Tools rig that folds up into a case. I basically wanted to have something so I could show up somewhere and record a band. It's got 16 inputs and works fine for me. Probably 90 percent of the stuff I do is done in the pro studios, and the stuff I do at home is mostly editing.

How important is it to align yourself with producers and other people who can introduce work?

Very important. A producer in the strictest sense is someone who doesn't have any desire to get involved in the technical side. They are looking for work, and if they get it, you'll get a call eventually. If you work with the same people, the expectations are pretty straightforward in terms of pay.

Since you started freelancing, has there been a vindicating or justifying moment when you really felt you were in your element and had made the right decision?

Pretty much every day I go to work. I love what I do and I love making great records. I get to work with so many interesting people—I get paid for this, and I can't believe it myself sometimes. I have no aspirations to ever work for anybody else again.

A Closer Look: Internships

One of the best ways to get a taste of a career without fully immersing yourself is through an internship. Although internships typically do not pay much, they can be very rewarding in experience and can provide insight that just can't be offered in a formal educational environment. When choosing an internship program, you should be just as thorough as you would be in choosing a college—there are good programs, but there are also programs that are not worth your time. John Storyk, architect and founder of Walters-Storyk Design Group, shares an intimate view of how WSDG's internship program developed to become well respected in the industry.

John Storyk, Principal and Designer for Walters-Storyk Design Group.

When did you start your internship program?

Around 15 years ago—it goes back almost to the beginning of WSDG. I actually started as an intern in the beginning of my career, so the internship program isn't new to me. I got hired by Jimi Hendrix—the next day I quit the only job I ever had as an architect and went to work for an acoustician for free. Period, end of conversation. I walked into Bob Hanson's office and said, "I'll do all your drafting if you let me."

What was your reasoning?

I felt it was the only way I could learn—textbooks alone wouldn't do it, and I didn't want to go back to school. And even school never would have taught me the hands-on nitty gritty of how to do my job. Interning is not a new idea. If you just change the word "intern" to "apprentice," it's been going on for 5,000 years. Plato, Socrates, Michelangelo had interns; everybody had interns. Frank Lloyd Wright was an intern for Sullivan, the famous Chicago architect. So there is a long history of artists and architects starting as interns, sometimes getting good money, sometimes getting no money, working their way up, and more than likely leaving their master mentor to do whatever their life is supposed to do.

It is particularly applicable to architecture because there is a lot of mentoring going on. There is that kind of hands-on application that just can't be taught in any type of institution.

How has your intern program evolved?

At first, the internship program was pretty simple. I've always lectured, mostly at professional audio schools because those kinds of lectures were in demand. The internship program more or less started by people raising their hands, saying, "How do I get into this world?" I would say, "Well, I'm not a guidance counselor, but I suppose you could come and hang out at our office for a while." Plus, in my early days with Full Sail, they always required interning. I don't know if they require this anymore, but you had to intern for three months to get your final degree. Since I started my lecturing there, I said, "I'll become a Full Sail intern accredited mentor," and we started the three-month cycle.

Three months is more or less standard. It's not a bad time window, and we've kept it. Every now and then we break out of it, but this time period unpaid has a few advantages. It is enough time that somebody can get their hands full. Much longer than three months, and many people just can't afford to do it; much less than three months, and you aren't able to give anything to them but terrible slave labor. So the way I look at it is, the intern is costing us money, the second month we hope that you break even, and the third month we hope that we can make a little money from you. Every now and then, somebody breaks that mold, and one of two things happens: We dismiss them instantly, which doesn't happen too often anymore, or we end up hiring them before the end of the three months.

We try to always have at least one and sometimes two—we never have more than two at any one time since there isn't enough room, and it takes too much supervision.

If you were a student looking for an internship program, what things would you look for?

Sometimes certain internships appear to be sexy and very meaningful from the outside, but when you look at the inside, they're not. For instance, for many years, everyone wanted to be an intern at one of the top-10 recording studios. Oh, wouldn't that be exciting. But what it really meant was that you were doing the lunchroom, bringing in the food, menial copy backups—you weren't doing very exciting work. In exchange for hanging around "famous studios" and every once in a while seeing a star walking in the lobby, you were more or less wasting your time. Whereas in my opinion, it would have been better to get an internship at a slightly less prestigious studio that really needed you and you would be doing more work! Let's use an operating engineer as an example—instead of being the number 7 intern at XYZ Famous Studio, try to go into a different environment and become the number 2 or the number 3 guy, where you actually have a chance, where somebody might get sick, and you may have to run a session one night! Now you're really getting your hands dirty and you're really getting some experience.

But you're doing it in a safe environment where you can make mistakes.

And you're going to make mistakes. Our internship program is a little bit different. We obviously get interns who are interested, or they think they are interested, in the very specific line of work that we do. For instance, we just finished a three-month internship with a young lady from Germany who wants to be an interior designer, and she wanted to come to the United States—it couldn't be any better.

Think about where you are going to be for those three months—some people have gone to a small school, or a school in a second- or third-rate city, and they want to be in New York City because that's where they want to spend three months. That's good. On the other hand, another person may have just finished four years in a big city and would like to be in the country for three months. Maybe they want to be in an internship in a country environment that is 45 miles from a ski slope in the winter. We had an intern apply from Texas who had never been in the snow. When I asked if he had ever seen snow, he said no. Part of your internship decision-making should be thinking about where you are going to be for those three months. Maybe you want to be close to where you will meet some people or be near a music scene. We are 45 minutes on the train from New York City, and our interns take advantage of that all the time.

We've had many interns who are not necessarily interested in becoming world-class studio designers, but since they want to be involved in the studio world, maybe they want to build their own studio, they want to get on the other side of the table and see how the process works. Also, many people coming into an internship program have never been in an office environment—they went right from high school to college and they've never answered a phone. But they know that in the next portion of their life, they will have to be in that world or manage people in that world. So they see the internship program as a crash course in managing office life—the not-so-sexy nitty gritty of how things really get done.

I can't tell you how many interns we have that in the first 24 hours can't take a message. But when they're done with that three months, they've got that done and they know how to communicate.

What are some things an intern will walk away with from your program that will help them in the real world?

They will see how a small-office environment really works that is regularly in high stress, high crisis, dealing with high-profile clients. They will really see what that looks like—what problems look like, how they get solved, and how they don't get solved. They will also see a new-age company. We have 50 people, but we are in six offices. They will see how that whole thing works—we are relatively small, but we are nevertheless an international company. There is a certain charm and posturing to that. Also, since they are the free labor, the bad news is that the intern has to get up at 6:00 a.m. sometimes and drive me to a meeting at Sony. The good news is that nine times out of ten, they end up sitting in on the meeting at Sony. We've had many interns who all of a sudden, just because they were taking some test equipment in, are in a meeting that they would otherwise never get a chance to sit in on. That word has gotten back to some of the colleges and has given us a favorable reputation.

We try to make sure that every intern gets a few high-profile experiences. For example, we have an intern right now from Webster who will be experiencing a final install for a very high-profile client, the Goo Goo Dolls. We just made a decision to have her go up there with one of our senior employees. Sometimes they can be a nice additional set of eyes.

We had one student who came in; he had gone to an audio school and worked summers at a P.A. company. He was seriously interested in increasing his acoustic skills either to continue in live sound or continue as a consultant. He came in, did a really good job, and by the time he got toward the end of the three months, he realized he wanted to go back to school to study acoustics. You need serious grades to get into the heavyweight programs—these are graduate-level programs. This guy didn't have the board scores to get into these schools—he just wasn't a book guy. As it turns out, we know the dean at one of the schools because I've lectured there, and I basically called him up and said they should look at this guy. I explained that the scores were not that good, but I said, "I am telling you, he will get As or Bs, and he will kill to make his course requirements. I promise you." They accepted him. There's no way he would have gotten in if he hadn't interned here. Needless to say, we've had interns that have become employees. I've had interns that have even become partners.

We've had interns that think this is what they want to do, but after 48 hours, they realize it's much harder than they thought, and they implode. We try to draw interns from four-year programs because they come in and they are more mature. I love the vocational audios schools—I think they have a place and a purpose—but in my heart, I believe studying liberal arts at a young point in your life brings you an education and a skill set you can use the rest of your life. You need to learn how to work DAWs, but you also need to learn how to cry. Where do you learn how to cry? Maybe I should have read that Shakespeare or that Wolfe. You can see the movie, but it would also be fun to read the words. The best students I've ever seen are the ones who go through the liberal arts education first, then the vocational school. I employ two of them now!

Audio Education Programs

The following list contains just a few of the many institutions throughout the U.S. that provide dedicated coursework in audio. There are education facilities in almost every part of the country, as well as Canada. For more information, take the time to contact each institution and ask to speak to a representative.

Image courtesy of Full Sail Real World Education.

Art Institute of Seattle
Seattle, WA
www.aii.edu
206-269-0274

Audio Engineering Institute
San Antonio, TX
www.audio-eng.com
210-698-9666

Audio Institute of America
San Francisco, CA
www.audioinstitute.com
415-752-0701

Ball State University
Muncie, IN
www.bsu.edu
765-285-5537

Barton College
Wilson, NC
www.barton.edu
252-399-6487

Belmont University
Nashville, TN
www.belmont.edu
615-460-6000

Berklee College of Music
Boston, MA
www.berklee.edu
617-747-1400

California Polytechnic State University
San Luis Obispo, CA
www.calpoly.edu
805-756-2406

Central Michigan University
Mount Pleasant, MI
www.bca.cmich.edu
989-774-7284

The City College of New York
New York, NY
www.ccny.cuny.edu
212-650-8217

Cogswell Polytechnical College
Sunnyvale, CA
www.cogswell.edu
408-541-0100

The College of St. Rose
Albany, NY
www.strose.edu
518-454-5278

Conservatory of Arts & Sciences
Tempe, AZ
www.audiorecordingschool.com
480-858-9400

Del Mar College
Corpus Christi, TX
www.delmar.edu
361-698-1508

DMX-Digital Media Arts at Touro College
New York, NY
www.dmx.touro.edu
212-463-0400

Emerson College
Boston, MA
www.emerson.edu
617-824-8500

Ex'pression College for Digital Arts
Emeryville, CA
www.expression.edu
877-833-8800

Fullerton College
Fullerton, CA
www.fullcoll.edu
714-992-7302

Full Sail Real World Education
Winter Park, FL
www.fullsail.com
407-679-6383

Georgia State University
Atlanta, GA
www.gsu.edu
404-651-1583

Harris Institute
Toronto, ON
www.harrisinstitute.com
416-367-0178

The Hartt School
University of Hartford
Hartford, CT
www.hartford.edu
860-768-4465

Houston Community College
Houston, TX
www.hccs.edu
713-718-5602

Institute of Audio Research
New York, NY
www.audioschool.com
212-777-8550

The Los Angeles Recording School
Hollywood, CA
www.larecordingschool.com
323-469-4160

Los Medanos College Recording Arts
Pittsburg, CA
www.losmedanos.edu
925-439-0200

McNally Smith College of Music
St. Paul, MN
www.mcnallysmith.edu
651-291-0177

MediaTech Institute
Irving, Houston, Austin, TX
www.mediatechinstitute.com
866-498-1122

Mesa Community College
Mesa, AZ
www.mc.maricopa.edu
480-461-7273

University of Miami
Miami, FL
www.miami.edu
305-284-2211

Michigan Recording Arts Institute
& Technologies
Southfield, MI
www.mrait.com
248-569-9650

Mid-Ocean School of Media Arts
Winnipeg, MB
www.midoceanschool.ca
204-775-9231

Middle Tennessee State University
Murfreesboro, TN
www.mtsu.edu
615-898-2578

Milliken University
Decatur, IL
www.millikin.edu
217-424-6300

MiraCosta College
Oceanside, CA
www.miracosta.edu
760-795-6679

Musicians Institute
Hollywood, CA
www.mi.edu
323-462-1384

Minnesota State University Moorhead
Moorhead, MN
www.mnstate.edu
218-477-2001

The New England Institute of Art
Brookline, MA
www.artinstitutes.edu/boston
800-903-4425

Northeast Community College
Norfolk, NE
www.northeastaudio.org
402-844-7365

Ocean County Vocational Technical School
Lakehurst, NJ
www.ocvts.org
732-657-4000 x 4133

Ohio University
Zanesville, OH
www.ohiou.edu
740-588-1455

Onondaga Community College (SUNY)
Syracuse, NY
www.sunyocc.edu
315-498-2112

Ontario Institute of Audio
Recording Technology
London, ON
www.oiart.org
519-686-5010

Owens Community College
Perrysburg, OH
www.owens.edu
567-661-2594

The Peabody Institute of the Johns Hopkins
University
Baltimore, MD
www.peabody.jhu.edu
410-659-8100

R.A.C. Digital Arts College - Toronto
Toronto, ON
www.recordingarts.com
416-977-5074

Recording Engineers Institute
Islandia, NY
www.audiotraining.com
631-582-8999

Recording Workshop
Chillicothe, OH
www.recordingworkshop.com
740-663-1000

Sacramento City College
Sacramento, CA
www.scc.losrios.edu
916-558-2243

SAE Institute
Atlanta, GA
www.sae-atl.com
404-526-9366

SAE Institute
Nashville, TN
www.sae-nashville.com
615-244-5848

SAE Institute
New York, NY
www.sae.edu
212-944-9121

Savannah College of Art and Design
Savannah, GA
www.scad.edu
912-525-5100

St. Mary's University of Minnesota
Winona, MN
www.smumn.edu
507-457-1596

Trebas Institute
Montreal, QC and Toronto, ON
www.trebas.com
514-845-4141

University of North Carolina, Asheville
Asheville, NC
www.unca.edu/music
828-251-6432

University of Arizona
Tucson, AZ
www.arts.arizona.edu
520-621-1341

University of Colorado at Denver
Denver, CO
www.cudenver.edu
303-556-3480

University of Hartford
West Hartford, CT
www.hartford.edu
860-768-4792

University of Massachusetts
Lowell, MA
www.uml.edu
978-934-3850

University of Memphis
Memphis, TN
www.memphis.edu
901-678-2559

University of Michigan
Ann Arbor, MI
www.umich.edu
734-764-2119

University of South Carolina
Columbia, SC
www.sc.edu
803-777-4280

University of Wisconsin
Oshkosh, WI
www.uwosh.edu
920-424-8034

Webster University
St. Louis, MO
www.webster.edu
314-968-6924

William Paterson University
Wayne, NJ
www.wpunj.edu
973-720-3198

Industry Organizations

Alberta Music Industry Association
Edmonton, Alberta
www.aria.ab.ca
780-428-3372

American Electronics Association
Santa Clara, CA
www.aeanet.org
408-987-4200

American Women in Radio & Television, Inc.
McLean, VA
www.awrt.org
703-506-3290

Audio Engineering Society (AES)
New York, NY
www.aes.org
212-661-8528

Canadian Recording Industry Association
Toronto, ON
www.cria.ca
416-967-7272

Electronic Industries Alliance (EIA)
Arlington, VA
www.eia.org
703-907-7500

InfoComm International
Fairfax, VA
www.infocomm.org
703-273-7200

International Radio & Television Society
Foundation, Inc.
New York, NY
www.irts.org
212-867-6650

MIDI Manufacturers Association
La Habra, CA
www.midi.org

NAMM
Carlsbad, CA
www.namm.org
760-438-8001

NAB (National Association of Broadcasters)
Washington, D.C.
www.nab.org
202-429-5300

National Systems Contractors
Association (NCSA)
Cedar Rapids, IA
www.nsca.org
800-446-NSCA

Radio and Television News Directors
Association and Foundation
Washington, D.C.
www.rtnda.org
202-659-6510

Society of Motion Picture and Television
Engineers
White Plains, NY
www.smpte.org
914-761-1100

SPARS (The Society of Professional Audio
Recording Services)
Nashville, TN
www.spars.com
800-771-7727

Index

DISCARDED from New Hanover County Public Library